T0319947

Time, Space and Capital

NEW HORIZONS IN INSTITUTIONAL AND EVOLUTIONARY
ECONOMICS

Series Editor: Geoffrey M. Hodgson, *Research Professor, University of Hertfordshire Business School, UK*

Economics today is at a crossroads. New ideas and approaches are challenging the largely static and equilibrium-oriented models that used to dominate mainstream economics. The study of economic institutions – long neglected in the economics textbooks – has returned to the forefront of theoretical and empirical investigation.

This challenging and interdisciplinary series publishes leading works at the forefront of institutional and evolutionary theory and focuses on cutting-edge analyses of modern socio-economic systems. The aim is to understand both the institutional structures of modern economies and the processes of economic evolution and development. Contributions will be from all forms of evolutionary and institutional economics, as well as from Post-Keynesian, Austrian and other schools. The overriding aim is to understand the processes of institutional transformation and economic change.

Titles in the series include:

Property Rights, Consumption and the Market Process
David Emanuel Andersson

The Evolution of Path Dependence
Edited by Lars Magnusson and Jan Ottosson

Economics, Culture and Social Theory
William A. Jackson

Deep Complexity and the Social Sciences
Experience, Modelling and Operationality
Robert Delorme

Creative Industries and Economic Evolution
Jason Potts

Institutional Variety in East Asia
Formal and Informal Patterns of Coordination
Edited by Werner Pascha, Cornelia Storz and Markus Taube

Capitalism and Democracy
A Fragile Alliance
Theo van de Klundert

Foundations of Economic Evolution
A Treatise on the Natural Philosophy of Economics
Carsten Herrmann-Pillath

How Markets Work and Fail, and What to Make of Them
Bart Nooteboom

Law and Economics from an Evolutionary Perspective
Glen Atkinson and Stephen P. Paschall

An Autecological Theory of the Firm and its Environment
Colin Jones and Gimme Walter

Time, Space and Capital
Åke E. Andersson and David Emanuel Andersson

Time, Space and Capital

Åke E. Andersson

*Emeritus Professor of Economics, Department of Economics,
Finance and Statistics, Jönköping International Business
School, Jönköping, Sweden and Emeritus Professor of
Infrastructural Economics, Royal Institute of Technology,
Stockholm, Sweden*

David Emanuel Andersson

*Senior Lecturer in Economics, Centre of Commerce and
Management, RMIT University, Hanoi, Vietnam*

NEW HORIZONS IN INSTITUTIONAL AND EVOLUTIONARY
ECONOMICS

Edward Elgar
PUBLISHING

Cheltenham, UK • Northampton, MA, USA

© Åke E. Andersson and David Emanuel Andersson 2017

All rights reserved. No part of this publication may be reproduced, stored
in a retrieval system or transmitted in any form or by any means, electronic,
mechanical or photocopying, recording, or otherwise without the prior
permission of the publisher.

Every effort has been made to trace all the copyright holders but if any have been
inadvertently overlooked we will be pleased to make the necessary arrangement at
the first opportunity.

Published by
Edward Elgar Publishing Limited
The Lypiatts
15 Lansdown Road
Cheltenham
Glos GL50 2JA
UK

Edward Elgar Publishing, Inc.
William Pratt House
9 Dewey Court
Northampton
Massachusetts 01060
USA

A catalogue record for this book
is available from the British Library

Library of Congress Control Number: 2017931751

This book is available electronically in the **Elgar**online
Economics subject collection
DOI 10.4337/9781783470884

ISBN 978 1 78347 087 7 (cased)
ISBN 978 1 78347 088 4 (eBook)

Typeset by Servis Filmsetting Ltd, Stockport, Cheshire
Printed and bound in Great Britain by TJ International Ltd, Padstow

Contents

Preface

In this book, we have connected insights from several theoretical traditions in economics—primarily from within the fields of urban and financial economics within mainstream thought as well as more disruptive theories from Austrian and institutional economics—with concepts and theories from applied mathematics, biology, chemistry, economic history, philosophy, physics, political science, psychology and sociology.

The most important among these heterogeneous and multidisciplinary inputs is the subdivision of time into *multiple timescales* as has been proposed in synergetics, with many notable scientific applications such as autocatalytic processes in chemistry. A second key idea is to see all goods and resources as more or less *durable* and thus as *capital* as first proposed by Frank Knight. An implication of our framework is that fundamental (or structural) uncertainty becomes something that we must address. A further implication is that we cannot assume that capital can be easily aggregated, as in standard bookkeeping practice. The value of any aggregation of capital then becomes an emergent property of the activities of uncertainty-bearing entrepreneurs. The firms that entrepreneurs create and organize are to be valued in various markets—notably equity and real estate markets—according to investors' assessments of their expected and uncertain returns. Following Knight, we also regard this type of assessment as an instance of entrepreneurial judgment, even though of a type that expands rather than initiates profit-seeking firms.

We have been able to unite and bring to fruition the variegated ideas and concepts that we draw upon by making extensive use of the theory of synergetics, which was developed originally in the context of natural science by Hermann Haken of the University of Stuttgart. This theory makes it possible to reformulate economic processes as consisting of variables that fall into (at least) four possible categories. We achieve this by simultaneously considering the timescale (speed of change) and the domain of a variable. We term those variables that are relatively stable—that is, change at a slow pace—and affect an inclusive and collective domain the *infrastructure* of a spatially delimited region. With this approach it is possible to construct a theory of economic development that is of general applicability. In short, conventional market interactions are akin to games that people play on an infrastructural "arena." This arena comprises scientific and other widely shared knowledge; transport, communication and utility networks; and the set of formal and informal institutions that constrain individual behavior and individual expectations.

This book is the end result of a long-term collaborative effort between the two of us and with colleagues from several academic disciplines. We have been inspired by discussions that one or both of us have had over the past decades with—in alphabetical order—Nurit Alfasi, Martin Andersson, Brian Arthur, Roland Artle, Jean-Pierre Aubin, Chris Barrett, David Batten, Martin Beckmann, Bruce Benson, Paolo Bianchi, David Boyce, Bill Butos, Gene Callahan, Troy Camplin, John Casti, Lata Chatterjee, Paul Cheshire, Chor-yung Cheung, Benoit Desmarchelier, Pierre Desrochers, Gus diZerega, Laurent Dobuzinskis, Lenore Ealy, Finn Førsund, Masahisa Fujita, Peter Gärdenfors, Kenneth Gibb, Michael Goldberg, Peter Gordon, Saileshingh Gunessee, Trygve Haavelmo, Hermann Haken, Joshua Hall, Lauren Hall, David Hardwick, Björn Hårsman, Randall Holcombe, Rogers Hollingsworth, Chiang-i Hua, Marek Hudik, Leo Hurwicz, Sanford Ikeda, Walter Isard, Börje Johansson, Rune Jungen, Anders Karlkvist, Charlie Karlsson, Wolfgang Kasper, Nathan Keyfitz, Kiyoshi Kobayashi, Bob Kuenne, Lawrence Wai-Chung Lai, T.R. Lakshmanan, Leonard Liggio, Heikki Loikkanen, Johan Lönnroth, Qing-Ping Ma, Benoit Mandelbrot, Leslie Marsh, Christian Wichmann Matthiessen, Stefano Moroni, Anna Nagurney, Peter Nijkamp, Lars Göran Nilsson, Åke Nygren, Tomas Ohlin, Olle Persson, Jason Potts, Tönu Puu, John Quigley, Donald Saari, Nils-Eric Sahlin, Oliver F. Shyr, Dean Simonton, Gudmund Smith, Tony E. Smith, Folke Snickars, Jack Sommer, Ulf Strömquist, Daniel Sutter, Peter Sylwan, Gunnar Törnqvist, Frederick Turner, Pravin Varayia, Aidan Walsh, Wolfgang Weidlich, Weibin Zhang and Gloria Zúñiga y Postigo. The usual caveats apply.

We are grateful for the support from Bo Wijkmark of the Stockholm Regional Planning Authority, to Stephan Müchler and Per Tryding of the Chamber of Commerce and Industry of Southern Sweden, to the Wehtje Foundation, to Johan Eklund and Pontus Braunerhjelm of the Swedish Entrepreneurship Forum and to R. May Lee of ShanghaiTech University for their generous support of our research. We would also like to thank Marek Hudik of XJTLU for drawing several of the figures in this book.

Most of all, we would like to thank our wives, Ethel and Lahu, for their patience and encouragement of our research endeavors.

Shanghai and Falkenberg, 5 November 2016

1. Time and space—an introduction

The theory of capital—including the value of capital and its accumulation—depends on a number of fundamental concepts. The *durability* of a good is the time during which the good contributes capital to production. All goods are to some extent durable and thus all goods have capital values. The durability of a good is the inverse of the depreciation rate of the good (in a deterministic world; for the stochastic case see Lev and Theil, 1978). All material goods are physical and thus deteriorate according to the laws of entropy; all such goods will eventually break down, even with high spending on maintenance. The choice of how durable a good should be therefore has an upper limit, and laws of nature set this limit. Buyers and sellers of goods can however choose a shorter than maximum durability for economic reasons. These economic reasons include the discount rate as well as the valuation of durability, with the latter being associated with various attributes of the good. We discuss these matters in more detail in Chapter 5.

The choice of how *durable* a production process should be is a key economic problem. Among other things, the duration of the production process includes the time spent preparing for the later stages of the process such as research and development, prototype production, marketing and sales promotion. A classic type of problem is the choice of how long to store cheese or wine. Another well-known problem concerns the decision when to harvest trees, grapes or fish. Among practitioners, it is quite common to aim for the point in time that corresponds to the maximum sustainable yield. In Chapter 2 we show that this decision rule is suboptimal, if the alternative real interest rate on capital is positive. The choice of the duration of a production process is more general than the cases associated with storage or harvesting. In complex processes, such as those that are typical of the pharmaceutical, automotive and film industries, there are unavoidable additional stages of production including numerous research, development and other intermediate sub-processes that producers must complete before a good reaches the market. At each stage, there is an optional decision of whether to proceed further or to abort the production process (cf. Dixit and Pindyck, 1995). Both the durability of a good and the duration of its production process have considerable impacts on the growth rates of production and capital as well as on the location of economic activities. We focus on this topic in Chapter 6.

Expectations and *uncertainty* connect the past to the future, and reflect the level and heterogeneity of knowledge among the relevant decision makers. The valuation of capital and the decision to invest in new capital reflect investors' uncertain expectations. It has been shown that even mild increases in uncertainty as approximated by estimated risk levels of capital portfolios can cause substantial decreases in capital values as determined in the stock markets as well as cause less willingness to invest in new capital, leading to reduced economic growth.

Profits, dividends and expected returns are the entities that determine the market valuation of capital. The classical theory of growth assumes that savings out of profits is the main driver of the growth of both capital and income. The value of capital is then proportional to the ratio of the profit and discount rates.

Dynamic interactions between scientists, inventors and entrepreneurs affect the growth of capital. New technological or design ideas spread most easily among spatially proximate firms and can lead to clustering phenomena such as those associated with computer software in Silicon Valley, fashion design in Milan and feature films in Los Angeles and Mumbai.

Surprisingly, mainstream economic theory not only lacks these dynamic concepts; it also even avoids the use of any explicit account of processes of change in time and space. General equilibrium theory—as elaborated upon by Gérard Debreu and other mathematical economists in the 1950s and 1960s—includes time and location in a superficial way as variable subscripts, but there are no *mechanisms* that represent processes of change that involve temporal or spatial factors. General equilibrium theory only addresses the dynamic aspects of an economic system in studies of the stability of equilibrium solutions to static models.

It is however possible to represent time as an explicit dimension of economic processes in many different ways in economic theories and models. The first and most obvious way is to represent changes over time, such as the accumulation of capital and other dynamic economic processes, as *continuous*, mostly real-valued, variables. This implies the use of differential equations in the modeling of economic processes. One early example is Walrasian *tatônnement* (Walras, 1874/1896), in which the process of changing prices at a point in time is a function of the excess demands for the goods at the *same* point in time, with the added assumption that no exchanges will take place before the attainment of equilibrium. The price changes will cease when all excess demands approach zero, which assumes asymptotically stable dynamic bidding processes.

Other neoclassical economists discussed and modeled growing populations, capital and income, using more or less sophisticated differential equations. Cassel (1918/1932) proposes a linear model, which Domar (1946) develops as a simplified ordinary differential equation. In this type of linear differential equation model, the product of the savings rate and the productivity of capital determine the unbounded rate of growth. Leontief (1953) presents a dynamic multi-good model of economic growth that generalizes the results from Domar's linear growth model.

Neoclassical growth theory—as exposed by Tinbergen (1942), Swan (1956) and Solow (1957)—is an example of a dynamic process that would put an upper limit to the growth rate given an exogenously determined savings rate. In these models, the per-capita aggregate product is a concave function of the (somehow) aggregated per-capita capital. These theorists in fact never discussed or motivated their aggregation of capital. In these models, the accumulation of capital per unit of labor equals the product of the savings rate and net aggregate production per person. The implication is that equilibrium with no further per-capita income growth corresponds to the point of equality between the savings rate and the rate of depreciation of capital per person, as Figure 1.1 illustrates.

If the depreciation rate goes down—that is, if capital durability goes up—the capital intensity, k* and output per worker, y*, will both increase. If durability approaches infinity, then capital intensity and output per worker will also go toward infinity—a most surprising and quite incredible idea.

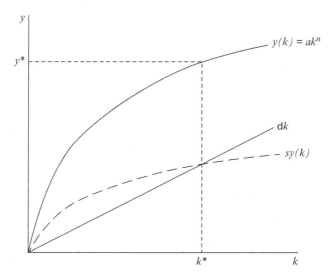

Figure 1.1 Equilibrium in a neoclassical growth model with a Cobb-Douglas production function

According to this model, a growth policy based on an increased savings rate is futile. It is only growing knowledge that can result in per-capita income gains. This conclusion makes no economic sense. Knowledge is a form of capital and its accumulation requires savings, in the same way that investments in physical capital requires savings. This fact implies that a realistic growth theory must include endogenously accumulated knowledge as a type of capital.

EXPLICIT DISCRETE TIME IN ECONOMIC MODELS

The second way to represent dynamic economic processes is as a discrete set of periods (for example as weeks, quarters or years). In this case, difference equations are useful. Such equations are quite popular in economics for two reasons. First, most statistical measurements use an accumulated flow over a period such as a year or quarter. Second, economists often formulate their hypothesized causal structures using sentences of the "if-then" type, which they interpret as "if some economic event happens in this period, then economic effects occur one, two or more periods later." The econometrician Herman Wold first formally stated and defended this type of period-based causality; it was later renamed "Granger causality."

In an article in *Econometrica*, Wold (1954) puts forward his causality beliefs and preference for difference equations. He starts out with a model in which the current price determines the demand for some good, while the price one period earlier determines the supply. Consequently, the price in the current period equals the price in the previous period plus a constant times the excess demand one period earlier. Hanau (1928) is the first instance of this type of recursive relation between the supply and demand for a good. Hanau's article analyzes the price fluctuations of *Schweinefleisch* (pork)—the "Hog Cycle"— as illustrated by Figure 1.2.

Wold modeled the Hog Cycle as difference equations, where demand in this period depends on the current price, while the price observed one period earlier determines the supply. This leads to a difference equation for the evolution of the market price. The price would converge toward equilibrium if the slope of the supply function were smaller than the slope of the demand function. From this example of a recursive process, Wold proceeded to his arguments for a causal analysis that would later form the basis of an econometric school:

The general characteristics of models of this kind are as follows:
(a)   The model refers to a sequence of years, months, or other time units.

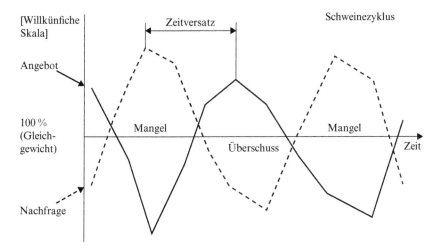

*Figure 1.2   The Hog Cycle as seen by Hanau with a reproductive time
delay between demand and supply. A positive difference
between demand (Nachfrage) and supply (Angebot) leads to
an increase in the price of pork*

(b) All relations of the model are causal, with two types of variables, endog-
    enous, which it is the purpose of the model to explain, and exogenous,
    which are auxiliary. In every relation of the model the effect variable is thus
    endogenous, while the cause variables are either endogenous or exogenous.
(c) The model has one, and only one, causal relation for each endogenous
    variable.
(d) Given the development of the exogenous variables and a set of initial values
    for the endogenous variables, the model allows us to calculate, recursively,
    the development of the endogenous variables (Wold, 1954, pp. 172–3).

But Wold's strongest reason for recursive difference equation models was
probably that the parameters of such models allow the use of ordinary
least squares estimation method without complications such as lack of
identification.

A couple of decades later Granger (1969) offers a similar view of causality in econometrics. Granger defines the causality relationship with the
help of two principles:

1   The cause happens prior to its effect.
2   The cause has *unique* information about the future values of its effect.

Granger (ibid.) claims that the ability of a model to predict the future
values of one time series using past values of another demonstrates

causality in econometrics. The terms *predictive causality* or *Granger causality* refer to this type of ability. Most philosophers would object to this type of causality concept, based as it is on time-recursive relations between variables as represented by discrete difference equations (we discuss this further in Chapter 3). Causal analysis of the Wold-Granger type is of course applicable to situations where interdependencies are very limited, as is the case in the experimental sciences, engineering and other fields where it is easy to avoid interference from unanalyzed variables. This kind of separation is almost never possible in economics. The complexity of an economic system with a multitude of sellers, buyers, goods and resources is the generic case, implying irregular fluctuations and even chaos. Paradoxically, most statistical economic indicators maintain a stability of their quantities over time that may seem to contradict the complexity of the economy. Why are these magnitudes, for example gross domestic products or exchange rates, as stable as they are in statistical terms?

A NEW WAY TOWARD PREDICTABILITY IN A SEEMINGLY CHAOTIC WORLD

A quite novel way to model dynamic processes in many of the sciences and more recently also in economics is to allow for many *different continuous and interactive timescales* of dynamic economic processes. We can use a macro model of the labor market as an example of how these processes play themselves out.

Most macroeconomic models, whether classical, monetary or Keynesian, make use of comparative static time assumptions within an implicitly delimited spatial area. For example, there is no role for explicit time in the Keynesian multiplier analysis, which reflects a recursive sequence of dependence reactions. Even in the latest versions of common macroeconomic models, there are "short-term" or "medium-term" solutions that depend on a hypothesized approach toward "natural levels" of unemployment or inflation, among other factors.

In neo-Keynesian analyses of the labor market the natural level of unemployment depends on the difference of inflation and production from their respective natural rates, as observed from the perspective of a nation state, be it the United States, Britain, Belgium or even Iceland. The assumption is that the same processes are operating, irrespective of differences in spatial and temporal dimensions.

The focus of neo-Keynesian macroeconomic analysis is usually on the equilibrium of unemployment, inflation and real wage rates. In monetarist and new classical analyses, the treatment of time and space is similar, and thus implicit, but such models assume that nominal wage rates and the prices of goods are flexible enough to ensure an equilibrium level of employment, at least in the (undefined) medium term. A natural rate of unemployment is then a consequence of movements in and out of the labor force and of the short time spans needed when workers search for better job opportunities. Unemployment thus only occurs because of necessary market frictions.

In contrast, a Keynesian analysis assumes rigid wages and prices with the consequence that unemployment becomes an equilibrating variable. A high level of unemployment is then possible as a permanent equilibrium condition.

It is against this theoretical backdrop that the political left-right conflict on suitable labor market policies developed, first in the 1930s and then again after the financial crisis that affected Europe and North America for several years after 2008.

Both dominant approaches lack an understanding of economic change processes. A more dynamic theoretical approach to the unemployment problem is possible and necessary in order to explain contemporary unemployment in many different regions around the world. This more realistic approach to the analysis of national labor markets focuses on *parallel processes of change* that both occur on different timescales and affect *spatially separated* labor markets in different ways.

Relative wages, prices of goods and the hiring and firing of non-specialists are quite flexible during the different phases of the business cycle. They are examples of *fast process variables*. Capital of various types is however quite rigid during the timescale of a business cycle and are examples of *slow process variables*. Contemporary science and especially the rapidly expanding field of synergetics show that an understanding of the dynamics of most interactive systems requires a division of timescales into fast and slow processes of change. It further requires a distinction of system variables between private (individual) and public (collective) ones. Variables that are both slow and public jointly make up the infrastructure of the system. Haken (1983; 1993) and Mikhailov and Calenbuhr (2002) provide important and informative examples of synergetic theory as applied to processes of change in physics, chemistry, the life sciences and social theory.

The basic idea of synergetics is that a variable that is slowly changing and public—implying that it influences many of the private and/or fast variables—in a generic sense shapes the structural outcome for the system as a whole. In our context, this implies that the set of slowly changing public economic variables determine the underlying equilibrium structure of all regional labor markets (see Table 1.1).

Table 1.1   Fast and slow processes with private and public effects in the
*   labor market*

Effects/speed	Fast	Slow
Private	Market prices and wages; Market supply of and demand for labor; Unemployment rate; Marginal return to capital	Market supply of and demand for human and physical capital; long-run returns to capital
Public	Labor market information; General economic and political information; Exchange rates	**Accessibility to markets and to knowledge; Formal and informal institutions**

The upper left corner of the table contains the short-term equilibrating processes of each regional labor market. Given a specific set of slow private and public variable values, the regional labor market process will move toward a short-term equilibrium that reflects whether—and to what extent—the slow and public institutional variables make wage and price flexibility possible. If the labor market institutions make it difficult to adjust wages there is a strong case for understanding the underlying equilibrium as a high-unemployment Keynesian one. On the other hand, if these institutions promote quick price adjustments in all markets, the corresponding employment equilibrium would resemble the one typically associated with monetarist and new classical theories (see Appendix 7.1 for a more formal exposition of these ideas).

Accessibility within various spatial networks that convey people, goods and information change at a very slow rate in most places, most of the time. The total yearly increment to the transport infrastructure is in most countries well below .001 in relation to the total network length; the impact on accessibility is even smaller because of natural geographical conditions. Massive infrastructure investment programs, such as the new network of highways and railways that is being put in place in China at the time of writing, may for a short period of time increase this fraction somewhat, but this is—and always has been—a transitional phenomenon. On the other hand, many regions have remained relatively inaccessible for thousands of years and are therefore disadvantaged in their relative access to national and international markets for goods and services.

Spatial differences in accessibility to scientific, artistic and other public knowledge have consequences for the diffusion of ideas, for innovative activities and for firms' productivity. There are good infrastructural economic reasons that explain why highly accessible European regions such as London, Paris, Amsterdam and Stuttgart have persistently higher levels of human capital productivity than more peripheral regions.

When discussing the flexibility or rigidity on wages it is important not to lose sight of the institutions that govern relations among employers and workers in the labor market. Nevertheless, these institutions are only one aspect of a subset of a much wider array of institutions that jointly make up the institutional structure of a group, region or nation. Such institutions may be formal or informal. Sometimes they are both, as when theft of property is both illegal and deemed unethical by most people, regardless of the minutiae of various legal sanctions. Formal institutions refer to codified legal and political systems as well as various laws and regulations. Informal institutions reflect cultural norms, habits and values, and entail various types of informal sanctions that constrain human behavior (North, 1990). Shared public values shape the evolution of both formal and informal institutions, but they only *become* institutions when they prescribe or proscribe specific actions among a group of people.

Political scientists and sociologists (see, for example, Inglehart, 1997; Inglehart and Welzel, 2005) have shown that there is a great deal of interregional variability in the public values that affect institutions, and that these values change at a slow pace because of the dominance of cohort rather than life cycle effects. Thus, shared values are arguably also part of the set of slowly changing and public variables that jointly make up the infrastructure. We should therefore be unsurprised about the attempts to make culture accountable for differences in economic outcomes between nations or cultures. Prominent examples include Max Weber's celebration of Protestant or Calvinist culture and his derision of the Confucian mindset (Weber, 1920/1958) and more recent attempts to view Confucianism as being supportive of—rather than inimical to—economic development (for example Morishima, 1982). As the example of Confucianism demonstrates, there is often a danger of oversimplification, especially since the "grand cultural theorists" often disregard endogenous processes of change occurring within each cultural tradition in response to changing incentives and threats. To take but one example, a supposedly Confucian Chinese culture has at various times and places combined with both decades of rapid economic development and centuries of stagnation within economic frameworks running the gamut from a free-market economy to centrally planned isolationism.

Our analysis in this book views economies as consisting of both slowly and rapidly changing variables with either individual or public effects, and considers an economic actor's location in time *and* in space as key factors we should always keep in mind when discussing economic processes or outcomes. We think that one of the greatest pitfalls in the history of ambitious theorizing has been the elevation of one factor at the expense of others. Wages can be flexible or rigid, but other things matter, too. Institutions are important, but they will not help much if someone is too far from the action. There may be cultural challenges, but cultures sometimes change and sometimes people even adopt a different culture.

Consider the following examples as alluding to the multi-causal reasoning that is often necessary. Britain has more flexible labor markets than France, but France has more flexible land markets. New Zealand has relatively well-functioning institutions with low levels of corruption, but it is in a rather remote location. Since 2010 Beijing has hosted the production of more peer-reviewed articles in science and engineering than any other city, but the mean number of citations per paper is much smaller than in London. The list goes on, and we think it is important to remember that we live in a multifaceted world with a complex structure of different types of capital. Capital includes not only material capital goods but also human and social capital, all of which give rise to different spatial accessibility effects. These accessibility effects in turn affect local, regional and national development trajectories.

SPACE AS AN EXPLICIT DIMENSION IN THEORIZING AND MODELING

Space was mostly absent from the work of the main economic theorists before 1940, with the notable exception of a handful of European economists such as von Thünen (1826/1930), Launhardt (1885), Weber (1909/1922), Palander (1935) and Lösch (1955). Most of these early contributors used German as their preferred language; those economists who did not read German tended to ignore them. Their theories conceived of space as the size of the land area and they modeled interactions as continuous flows in one- or two-dimensional space as seen on a map.

Most economists regarded land use, location choice, and the roles of transport and logistics as peripheral problems. The only exception was international trade theory, but that theory treated space in a rather peculiar way: trade theorists focused on the political entities of nation states. The trade of the United States (with a population of more than 320 million in a land area of 9,183,517 square kilometers in 2016) and that of a small country such as Luxembourg (563,000 residents in 2,586 square kilometers) were treated as if these size differences would be of no consequence from a theoretical or empirical point of view.

The classical economist David Ricardo was the first economist to theorize about economic phenomena with such a rudimentary conception of space. Ricardo's theory of comparative advantage is a prominent example of the discrete division of space into countries. His approach foreshadowed the development of the space-less theory of trade—with two production factors, two goods and two countries—that features in the textbook treatment of international trade to this day. Meanwhile temporal considerations have remained implicit in most of this theory, emerging only as comparative statics; there is no theory of the process that transforms initial conditions into final solutions.

In the first half of the twentieth century, Heckscher and Ohlin (Ohlin, 1933/1967) reformulated international trade and location theory so that it would also encompass the comparative supply of nationally trapped resources. Ohlin had realized that he could generalize the theory of international trade, thereby extending it to interregional trade and location choice among nations and regions. These theories and models use a discrete representation of space, which means that one can denote each of N exogenously given spatial units in the following manner: x_A for the production volume in region A, x_B for the production volume in region B and x_{AB} for the trade or other interaction between region A and region B. The main result is that equilibrium trade flows between two regions imply uniform relative prices of all goods in both regions (assuming zero transaction and transport costs). Subsequent contributions often referred to this result as the law of one price.

In the following example, we assume two regions (A and B) with identical preference structures but with different initial factor endowments and thus with different production possibility sets. The two regions are initially isolated from each other and have to rely on their own possibility sets to produce goods for their own consumption. We can then compare the consumption possibilities without and with trade between the two regions (see Figure 1.3):

1. Autarky equilibrium A^B *and* A^A (no trade implies different relative prices and that production equals consumption).
2. Trade equilibrium with $C^B = C^A$ (both countries consume the same amounts at the same relative prices). Total consumption and welfare exceeds the levels that are attainable at the production possibility frontiers without trade.

In Chapter 3, we show that the Heckscher-Ohlin and Ricardo models of trade are special cases of theories by Johann Heinrich von Thünen and Martin Beckmann. The latter theories explicitly include space and

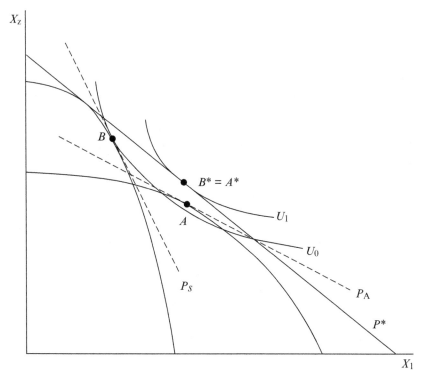

*Figure 1.3   The advantages of trade for two regions (A and B) with
                different trapped resources*

transport costs as well as production possibilities. One consequence of
this more general approach is that it shows that trade is advantageous
even in the case where production possibilities and consumer preferences
are identical in both regions. This is a good illustration of how the explicit
consideration of realistic spatial representations improves the explanatory
power of a theory, and yet another instance of how theories improve when
they incorporate more key variables. It is also an illustration of how there
are three big blind spots in most economic theory: spatial accessibility,
institutions and time-dependent processes of change. Adding one or more
of these factors almost always results in an improved theory.

2. Time and capital in economic doctrines

Most of the classical economists, including Adam Smith, David Ricardo and John Stuart Mill took the labor theory of value for granted. The basic assumption of that theory is that the relative price of a good equals the relative labor input that goes into the production of the good. Karl Marx (1867) contends that this is *the* fundamental proposition in economics, having repercussions not only for most economic theorizing but also for the political implications of economic and social theory. Marx (ibid.) assumes that capital is reducible to a measure of total labor input that is accumulated during its creation.

This assumption was essential to Marx's theory, since his main aim was political and not scientific. The claim that capitalists exploit workers is only defensible if direct and indirect labor inputs determine the value of a good and thus also the value of capital.

Carl Menger (1871/1981) offers the opposite view—central to later Austrians—that the marginal value to the user is the only factor determining the price of a good. Goods must have been produced *before* being marketed. The decisions to produce are based on *expectations* of future demand. Production costs are then sunk costs at the time of supply. The only consideration *at that time* would be the willingness to pay, corresponding to consumers' marginal valuation of the supplied good. The marginal utility of the marginal consumer would determine the marginal utility of ubiquitous goods such as drinking water, which would make it a "free good" with a zero price. Another example is the pricing of old paintings. One of Rembrandt's paintings would, when sold at an auction, command a price that corresponds to the expected benefits to the highest bidder; the historical cost of production would have no effect at all on the price.

Eugen von Böhm-Bawerk (1891) takes Menger's economics as his starting point in order to show the dynamic errors of the labor theory of value in its application to the theory of capital. Böhm-Bawerk (ibid.) introduces the idea of roundabout production and comes to the provisional conclusion that the *time structure* of inputs is essential to the determination of capital value. Formulating a numerical example (see Table 2.1), he

Table 2.1   Böhm-Bawerk's example of the effects of prolonged time on capital value

Without capital	£15.0	
With capital		Increase
1 year	£35.0	£20.0
2 years	45.0	10.0
3	53.0	8.0
4	58.0	5.0
5	62.0	4.0
6	65.0	3.0
7	67.0	2.0
8	68.1	1.1
9	69.1	1.0
10	70.0	0.9

Source: Böhm-Bawerk (1891).

concludes that the time structure and the prevailing rate of interest on loans are essential for determining the optimal value of capital:

> In an earlier chapter I called attention to the well-attested fact that the lengthening of the capitalist process always leads to extra returns, but that, beyond a certain point, these extra returns are of decreasing amount. Take again the case of fishing. If what we might call the one month's production process of making of a boat and net leads to the return of the day's labour being increased from 3 to 30, —i.e. by 27 fish, —it is scarcely likely that the lengthening of the process to two or three months will double or treble the return: Certainly, the lengthening it to 100 months will not increase the surplus by a hundredfold. The surplus return—for there will always be a surplus return—will increase by a slower progression than the production period. We may, therefore, with approximate correctness represent the increasing productivity of extending production periods by the following typical scheme [Table 2.1]. (Böhm-Bawerk, 1891, Book VIII section VII.1.9)

Böhm-Bawerk's conclusion is that:

> [t]he rate of interest under the foregoing assumptions is limited and determined by the productivity of the last prolongation of the production period which is still economically permissible and that of the next prolongation which is not so permissible. (Böhm-Bawerk, 1891, book VIII, section VII.I.9)

In his analysis of roundabout production, Böhm-Bawerk anticipated the much later development of the economics of industrial research and development, which is an obvious case of substantial prolongation of production periods in order to increase the productivity and profitability of a firm. His analysis of capital and time also exerted a lasting influence on the younger Swedish economist Knut Wicksell. Wicksell (1914) writes that:

> I remember it as if it had happened yesterday, a day 25 years ago, when I in a bookstore window in Berlin—where I was living on a Gustaf Lorén scholarship—for the first time read the book title Positive Theorie des Kapitales by Eugen von Böhm-Bawerk . . . this work was to me a revelation. (Wicksell, 1914, p.322, translated from Swedish).

Wicksell was a mathematician and understood that Böhm-Bawerk's tables could be generalized into a mathematical optimization problem. This became the famous wine maturation problem, in which he set out to determine the economically optimal duration of storing wine. He assumed that the value of the wine would be increasing with increasing time in storage. During storage, there are only negligible inputs of labor, but a biological process ("land") occurs in which solar energy and the aging processes of yeast and other chemical components in wine contribute to the increase in value. However, as in Menger (1871/1981) and Böhm-Bawerk (1891), it is the consumer's marginal utility as expressed in her willingness to pay for the wine that determines the value of the matured wine. The constraining factor is the opportunity cost of storage, which reflects the cost of labor (for safeguarding the wine), the rent of wine cellar space and the market interest rate. Wicksell (1914) introduces the following model:

$$K = V(T)e^{-rT}; \tag{2.1}$$

where
K = the present value of the wine;
$V(T)$ = the expected value (price) at time T;
r = the discount rate, which equals the real rate of interest.

The necessary condition for the optimal storage time is that *the growth rate of the value equals the real rate of interest*, which happens at V* in Figure 2.1—illustrating this condition for the case of logistic growth of value over time. The relative rate of growth is then a linear function of the achieved level of value. The wine then attains its maximum value when the growth rate has fallen to zero (MV).

MV is the maximum value, which implies a longer time in storage than the economically optimal duration if the discount rate is positive. A zero real rate of interest would thus imply that attainment of MV yields the optimal storage time. Although this is a suboptimal duration in the real

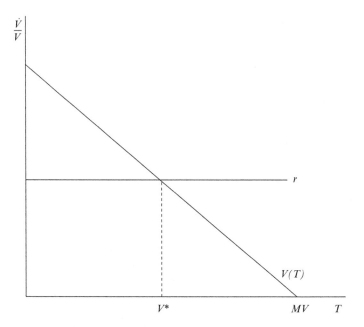

Figure 2.1   Optimal storage time for wine

world of positive interest rates, it is common that managers of forests or
fish farms aim for a duration that corresponds to the maximum gross value
of their output (MV).

Several economists have claimed that this wine storage model is a special
dynamic case that only is applicable to point-input, point-output decision
problems. This claim is incorrect. It is easy to show that the condition also
holds for continuous harvesting of a growing biological resource over time,
for example trees in a natural forest or ocean fish.

> The rule of equality between the discount rate and the growth rate is a general
> rather than special principle for when to harvest a resource: We have shown
> that there is a consistent stopping algorithm, an r% rule, that can be shown to
> apply both to problems under certainty and uncertainty in a consistent manner.
> In each case investment takes place once the value of the underlying asset is
> expected to rise at the instantaneous rate of discount. (Cairns and Davis, 2005,
> p. 22)

With Wicksell's wine maturation model, the debate about the validity of
Marx and his classical predecessors' labor theory of value had been put to
rest, at least among economists who accepted the conclusions of Menger—
as well as of Jevons and Walras—about the importance of marginal utility

as the basis for all economic reasoning. Marx was wrong, according to the mainline of economics. Economists had shown that land—including natural resources—is an original production factor besides labor, as Johann Heinrich von Thünen (1826/1930) had demonstrated 40 years before the publication of *Capital* (Marx thereby demonstrated that an ability to read German does not imply knowledge of German economics). In addition to Marx's disregard of land as a factor of production, he also did not understand that capital could not be reduced to labor by any valid procedure. This was the great contribution of Böhm-Bawerk and Wicksell: with the help of logical reasoning, realistic examples and mathematical formulas they showed that time is a key variable in the determination of capital value.

Despite the conclusive arguments against Marxian economic theory, it still muddies the water among a great number of left-wing politicians, human geographers, sociologists and urban planners (including influential ones such as Manuel Castells, Richard Florida, John Friedmann, David Harvey, Henri Lefebvre and Allen Scott) as well as among a handful of more peripheral "radical" economists. Politically, the labor theory of value coupled with the concept of "capitalist exploitation" remains the explicit or (more often) implicit justification for the redistributive state (the arguments of the quasi-Marxian French economist Thomas Piketty (2014) are typical of such reasoning).

EXPECTATIONS AND THE VALUE OF TIME

Any dynamic economic theory must include not only capital but also *expectations* at its core. A common error among many early economic theorists was the assumption that there had to be a material input (for example a natural resource) that would be accumulated and thereby cause an increase in the capital value of the good in question. In contrast, a simple example in line with the Menger-Wicksell theory shows that an *expectation* of future preferences or prices as revealed in the market is sufficient for determining the *expected* optimal selling time and thus also the capital value of a good.

As an example, let us assume that a museum curator (with some economics training) has formulated a dynamic plan for buying and selling works of art. The board has made a preliminary decision that the museum should auction off some of its items immediately, but the curator opposes this decision. He claims that the timing of sales (T) ought to be a central decision variable for each affected work of art. Thus, a painting with an estimated current value of $C(0)$ should not be auctioned off immediately but sold at the time T with the highest *expected future price*. Based on historical observations, the curator has formed an expectation that the price will be increasing over time:

$$\ln C(T) = \ln C(0) + T^\alpha \ln \beta; \qquad (2.2)$$

where $C(T)$ = capital value at time T and $0 < \alpha < 1$.

The capital value must be discounted by the internal rate of interest, r, which is the sum of the opportunity interest of financial capital plus compensation for the expected risk associated with the expected growth rate of the capital value.

Maximization of the present capital value requires the derivative of (2.2) to be set equal to 0, so that $\alpha (\ln \beta) T^{\alpha-1} - r = 0$.

As an illustration, let us assume that:

$$C(0) = \$200,000, \alpha = .67, \beta = 1.25 \text{ and } r = .06.$$

With these assumptions, the optimal time of sale would be after 15 years, at which time the total expected capital value would have increased to approximately \$785,000. The growth rate of capital is approximately equal to the internal rate of discounting after these 15 years.

DISCOUNTING AND THE VALUE OF CAPITAL

A consumer can save a dollar in a risk-free account with an opportunity rate of return (a real rate of interest) of r. This means that $(1+r) S(\text{now})$ equals the sum of money in the savings account one year later or $(1+r) S(t) = S(t+1)$. Consequently, $S(t) = (1/(1+r)) S(t+1)$, where $1/(1+r)$ is called the rate of discounting. A risk-free dollar that is received in the next period $(t+1)$ is thus worth less than one that is received instantaneously, assuming unchanged opportunities in the money market.

A *consol* or *perpetuity bond* provides another example of a risk-free savings or investment vehicle. It is a binding promise—a bond—to pay a given sum (C) yearly for an *infinite* number of years to the owner of the consol. The capital value of the consol, $K = C/r$, where r is the risk-free real rate of interest when the annual returns are discounted with an infinite time horizon. This condition is also a reasonable equilibrium condition if rewritten as the requirement that $rK = C = \Delta K$, that is, $\Delta K/K = r$. In other words, the real rate of capital growth *equals* the real interest rate in equilibrium. Here we assume the real interest rate to be an exogenous variable. This assumption points to a natural follow-up question: how does the economic system give rise to a rate of interest?

THE DETERMINATION OF REAL AND MONETARY INTEREST RATES

There have been a lot of disputes about the "nature and necessity of interest," using Gustav Cassel's phrase. Cassel (1903) states that the essential cause of a positive rate of interest is the demand for and supply of a time of "waiting" for returns:

> We have seen that the use of durable goods requires, in all cases, a certain amount of waiting, the different uses being necessarily consecutive. From this necessity arises the larger part of the demand for waiting. . ..Thus the demand for the use of durable goods whether for production or for immediate enjoyment is always, indirectly, a demand for waiting. Supposing, then, the supply of waiting to be given, its price will be determined by the fluctuations of this indirect demand. And, vice versa, the demand for the use of durable goods will be regulated by the price which must be paid for waiting, this price acting always as a check on demand, cutting off demands of less urgent necessity. How far the demand can be satisfied, and what price must be reached in order to restrain the demand within this limit depends on the one side, on the intensity of the demand, on the other side on the scarcity of the supply. In this statement which is wholly on the lines of the Principle of Scarcity lies the fundamental explanation of the phenomenon of interest. (Cassel, 1903, pp. 97–8)

Here Cassel views the demand for waiting time as emerging from the production side of the economy, while the willingness of the consumers to delay their consumption determines the supply of waiting time. He concludes that scarcity implies a positive interest rate (Cassel, 1903).

Hence Cassel was opposed to the Böhm-Bawerk's approach in which the "roundaboutness" in production was the most important factor that determines the duration of production, where this duration coincides with the point in time where the rate of return equals the interest rate. Clearly, something else must then determine the interest rate.

However, in an early contribution, Böhm-Bawerk (1891) offers two reasons (besides "roundaboutness") why the interest rate must be positive. First, the marginal utility of an individual's future income is lower than that of the same income at present, provided that she expects positive economic growth. Second, most people are impatient—a psychological factor—and prefer to receive purchasing power now rather than later. Each of these two reasons implies that a normal individual is willing to pay a positive interest rate in order to get access to loans in the present and also that she will demand interest income when she lends money to others. Third, more roundabout production processes offer technological advantages, as described earlier.

In his theory of interest, Irving Fisher (1930) offers slightly different justifications of positive interest rates that reflect individuals' time preferences. He distinguishes between the influence of general economic factors such as income and "personal factors." Regarding income, Fisher (1930, p. 72) states that in "general, it may be said that, other things being equal, the smaller the income, the higher the preference for present over future income, that is the greater the time preference." Fisher then proceeds by listing six personal factors that he believes determine the individual's time preference for consumption. The six factors are foresight, self-control, habit, life expectancy, concern for others (the bequest motive) and fashion (ibid.).

The determination of the interest rate on loanable funds presumes the existence of two categories of agents: lenders and borrowers. Many of the classical economists thought that the lenders were savers whereas the borrowers were investors. From this emerged the quite common assumption—not shared by Fisher and Cassel—that the point of equality between firms' planned investments and households' planned savings determines equilibrium. This is grossly at variance with what we can observe in real life. Much of what is borrowed is not for investment purposes but for consumption, while much lending aims at safeguarding future consumption opportunities. Examples of lending for future consumption include lending that increases consumption opportunities after the lender's retirement and lending that increases the expected value of bequests that beneficiaries consume in the future. Fisher was in fact the first economist to analyze savings from a household life cycle perspective.

Fisher (1906; 1907; 1930) also attempts to find solutions to problems associated with endogenous interest determination as well as consumption loans. He commenced his inquiries by assuming a one-person Robinson Crusoe economy; Crusoe would be willing to give up consuming his capital during the current time period so as to be able to consume it in the future. Abstinence from current capital consumption—that is, preservation of capital—yields future consumption opportunities of a magnitude that is not fixed, but rather depends on the marginal returns to investing (=saving). Faced with a convex transformation set ($T(C_{now}, C_{Future})$) at a given initial level of wealth and a concave utility function $U(C_{now}, C_{Future})$, Crusoe should choose the combination of present and future consumption that corresponds to the point of tangency between the maximum utility level and the transformation set. The slope of the line separating the maximum utility level and the transformation set is the endogenously determined rate of interest (G^*) for a one-person Crusoe economy. In a monetary economy, it is instead the supply and demand for money that determines the interest rate, r.

Figure 2.2 shows how the concave transformation set gives the possible

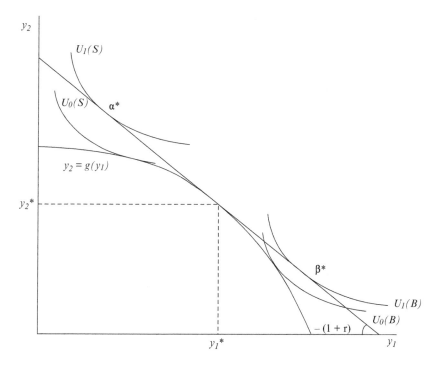

Figure 2.2   Endogenous determination of the interest rate

combinations of consumed income (y) in two periods. $u_1(S)$ and $u_1(B)$ are indifference curves with attainable utility maxima at α^* and β^*, assuming the existence of a credit market with an interest rate of r. Without such a credit market, β^* would become unattainable.

As Jack Hirshleifer (1958) points out, investors have the possibility of using a two-stage decision process:

1. Maximize present value.
2. Enter the credit market to reach the optimal solution of becoming a borrower at point β^* or a lender at point α^* in Figure 2.2.

The points y_1^* and y_2^* are thus suboptimal if a credit market exists. A credit market is therefore a welfare-improving institution. In addition, the discount rate will converge at $1/(1 + r)$ for all borrowers and lenders.

Both Fisher and Wicksell contend that there is no room for personal rates of discounting if the monetary economy is in equilibrium. All these personal discount rates will become equalized at $1/(1 + r)$ as a by-product of the search for optimal savings and borrowing rates.

If the borrower is an entrepreneur, the optimal decision might be a corner solution. She may be best off if she borrows an amount that corresponds to the maximum interest charges that she expects to be able to service in future time periods, so as to exploit an opportunity curve lying outside of $f(I_1)$. She could then use the borrowed money to fund projects up to the point of equality between the marginal rate of return and the real rate of interest. The credit market is thus a precondition for the survival of entrepreneurial activity.

THE NATURAL OR NORMAL RATE OF INTEREST

Wicksell and other early neoclassical economists assumed the existence of a *natural rate of interest*. The existence of a natural rate of interest requires the existence of *social* utility and transformation functions that are tangential at point Y^*. In addition, Wicksell (and Fisher) assumed the existence of *two* rates of interest. First, there is the natural rate of interest. But then there is also the *loanable-fund interest rate* as set by central or commercial banks. According to Wicksell, deviations between the loanable-fund rate and the natural rate cause cumulative inflation or deflation:

> At any moment and in every economic situation there is a certain level of the average rate of interest which is such that the general level of prices has no tendency to move either upwards or downwards. This we call the normal rate of interest. Its magnitude is determined by the current level of the natural capital rate, and rises and falls with it. If, for any reason whatever, the average rate of interest is set and maintained below this normal level, no matter how small the gap, prices will rise and will go on rising; or if they were already in process of falling, they will fall more slowly and eventually begin to rise. (Wicksell, 1898/1936, p.120)

If, for instance, the loanable-fund rate is set below the natural rate, both consumption and investments will exceed the capacity of the economy, leading to a general increase in prices and wages. Using a dynamic period analysis, Wicksell showed that there would be no convergence of this process but a cumulative process of inflation. Interestingly, several central bankers have revived the Wicksell-Fisher view in recent decades. This revival has resulted in monetary policies where the interest rate is set in accordance with the perceived deviation of the inflation rate from its natural rate, which alludes to the view that the interest rate of the central bank should equal the natural interest rate. However, Trygve Haavelmo (see Anundsen et al., 2012) has generalized Wicksell's analysis in a dynamic framework and has shown that the monetary interest-rate policies rest on the erroneous assumption that central banks can use monetary policy to influence the rates of inflation and unemployment without undesirable side effects in terms of general economic fluctuations. During a speech at the Bank of Norway in 1987 he made the following statement:

> My preliminary analysis suggests that the interest rate should have as a target an average r_K [=net marginal productivity of capital] and that delegating the responsibility of short-run stabilization to the monetary authorities seems to be a difficult task. (our translation)

Judged by this statement, it seems that Haavelmo thought that the model he had formulated 20 years earlier finally had gained practical relevance for the conduct of Norway's monetary policy. However, Haavelmo's analysis had no perceptible impact. In 2001, Norway adopted inflation targeting based on blueprints from the Swedish Riksbank and the Bank of England (Anundsen et al., 2012).

RISK AND THE REQUIRED RETURN ON INVESTMENT

Much of the early discussion of required rates of return on investments and savings was based on the assumption of a known future with predetermined rates of return from different assets. If uncertainty of the future was discussed it was mainly implicit. The main exceptions were the *Treatise on Probability* (1921) by John Maynard Keynes and *Risk, Uncertainty, and Profit* by Frank Knight (1921).

Keynes (1921) accepts that a probability is measurable if it has a numeric value. He also accepts that probabilities are measurable in cases such as urns containing different numbers of white and black balls. However, for most cases of decision making Keynes claims that probabilities are not measurable, meaning that they do not have a numeric value. He thus offers an epistemic view of probability in decision making, which implies that a probability is subjective and reflects a degree of knowledge or a degree of rational belief. According to this view an investor in some security would base a decision to invest on a subjective evaluation of the future rate of return based on her knowledge of the firm, earlier failures of the leadership and other such factors. Keynes formulates the position of the epistemic view on risk in the following way:

> The terms certain and probable describe the various degrees of rational belief about a proposition which different amounts of knowledge authorise us to entertain. All propositions are true or false, but the knowledge we have of them

depends on our circumstances; and while it is often convenient to speak of propositions as certain or probable, this expresses strictly a relationship in which they stand to a corpus of knowledge, actual or hypothetical, and not a characteristic of the propositions in themselves. A proposition is capable at the same time of varying degrees of this relationship, depending upon the knowledge to which it is related, so that it is without significance to call a proposition probable unless we specify the knowledge to which we are relating it. To this extent, therefore, probability may be called subjective. But in the sense important to logic, probability is not subjective. It is not, that is to say, subject to human caprice. A proposition is not probable because we think it so. When once the facts are given which determine our knowledge, what is probable or improbable in these circumstances has been fixed objectively, and is independent of our opinion. The Theory of Probability is logical, therefore, because it is concerned with the degree of belief which it is rational to entertain in given conditions, and not merely with the actual beliefs of particular individuals, which may or may not be rational (Keynes, 1921, p.3–4).

We shall discuss expectations and risk at some length in Chapter 7 and Chapter 8, in particular with reference to Knight (1921). As will become apparent, the only way to explain the existence of real-world entrepreneurship—including the entrepreneurial creation of new capital— is to allow for the existence of Knightian or "structural" uncertainty. While there is often a great deal of year-on-year stability in the value of economy-wide capital, this is not necessarily the case at the micro level of the firm. The most innovative firms tend to be those with the least predictable capital values. This relative instability reflects the uncertainty associated with the introduction of new capital. "New capital" is here a shorthand expression that refers to entrepreneurially created attributes that may change the value of the pre-existing resources that embody these attributes, for example a building, a group of people or a new combination of well-known ingredients that result in a new type of cake.

3. Space in economic analysis— from discrete to two-dimensional continuous theory

The classical economists Adam Smith and David Ricardo were the first to theorize about economic phenomena with an explicit—although mostly rudimentary—consideration of space. Ricardo's theory of how the principle of comparative advantage allocates production to countries that trade with one another is a prominent example of the discrete subdivision of space. This approach led to the development of trade theory with two factors, two goods and two regions (nations) as the starting point.

The history of the treatment of space in spatial allocation models is somewhat similar to that of time in dynamic models. Over time economics has moved from implicit space, via discrete systems of regions toward continuous one- and two-dimensional space. When Smith and later Ricardo proceeded to analyze international trade they limited their analysis to interactions between pairs of countries, with almost no consideration of how transport and transaction networks influence space-bridging costs. The classical economists made explicit two factors that had an impact on the location choices of economic actors:

1. Comparative (relative) rather than absolute advantages would determine the structure of production in a country and its trade with other countries.
2. Economies of scale would reinforce the comparative advantage of specialization and the division of labor.

Eli Heckscher's analysis as elaborated upon by Bertil Ohlin (1933/1967) was a reformulation of the classical theory, in the sense that Heckscher and Ohlin saw comparative advantage as a consequence of the size of fundamental and spatially trapped factor resources in a location as compared with other locations. Thus, countries with relatively abundant labor would gain from exporting goods requiring large inputs of labor in exchange for capital-intensive goods from countries with relatively abundant capital resources. Leontief (1956) would later show that a narrow definition of capital would not support the factor proportions theory because it would be incompatible with the empirics of the matter. Another related theorem with more empirical support is that imports of labor-intensive goods act as a substitute for the immigration of workers.

It was a small step to develop this type of trade theory into a programming model for any finite discrete number of locations (that is, nations or regions). The simplest and most common approach is to maximize the sum of profits subject to a pre-specified set of linear production capacity or factor availability constraints in each location. If the objective function is linear, there will then exist primal (quantitative) as well as dual (pricing) solutions. This type of model often defines profits as the difference between the price minus unit cost of a good and the distance-dependent marginal transportation cost. The dual solution requires that the price is less than or equal to the sum of the shadow prices associated with the use of different factors of production such as land, labor and capital. Time has remained implicit in most of this theory and usually only appears in the form of comparative statics; the movement between the initial conditions and the final solutions seems straightforward since it avoids any real consideration of dynamic processes.

In recent decades there has been a reorientation of trade theory toward dynamic network analysis in the form of dynamic and regional "variational inequality models" (Dafermos and Nagurney, 1987; Nagurney, 1999/2013). These models posit that movements toward general dynamic equilibrium requires all (observed or expected) price differences between different locations or points in time to be less than or equal to the sum of the transport and transaction costs associated with interregional or intertemporal trade. The more advanced versions of these models determine all prices and costs endogenously as part of the equilibrating process.

CONTINUOUS ONE-DIMENSIONAL REPRESENTATION OF SPACE IN ECONOMIC THEORY: THE CLASSIC VON THÜNEN MODEL OF THE ISOLATED STATE

Thünen (1826/1930) is the first explicit representation of space in an economic model. The Von Thünen Model assumes that a featureless plain surrounds a central marketplace. The transport of goods gives rise to a uniform level of spatial friction in all directions. Any point on a circle that is equidistant from the marketplace is then associated with the same transport cost, which is proportional to the distance to the center.

The unit revenue from selling an agricultural good would then equal the price at the market minus the distance-dependent unit transport cost. Different goods would have different unit transport costs and different prices. Some goods would combine relatively high market prices with rapidly increasing transport costs with increasing distance to the market. Such distance-sensitive high-priced goods would then be produced closer to the market than goods with the opposite characteristics. The implication of this model is that an optimal spatial arrangement of agricultural production is to have specialized concentric zones. The zones have equidistant borders so that the unit net revenue of each good determines the location of its zone. An unstated implication of the original model is that the marginal transport cost determines the decline in the price of land with increasing distance to the center.

Formally, the Von Thünen Model is based on maximizing land rent in the equation:

$$R = Q(p\text{-}c) - QTd; \tag{3.1}$$

where R = land rent per unit land area; Q = produced quantity per unit land area; c = average production cost; p = market price per unit of good; T = transport cost per unit of good per unit of distance; d = distance to the central marketplace. The validity of the model depends on the following assumptions:

- The marketplace is at the center of the Isolated State.
- Wilderness surrounds the Isolated State.
- The Isolated State is completely flat with equally fertile soil everywhere.
- Farmers in the Isolated State transport their goods to the market across land.
- Transport friction is everywhere the same.
- Farmers maximize profits.

Thünen (1826) offers an illustrative example with four concentric zones or "rings," where each zone specializes in a distinct agricultural good. The zone closest to the center specializes in goods of short durability with high transport cost per unit of weight. In agriculture, dairy products are a class of goods with these characteristics. Figure 3.1 shows how spatial separation of agricultural land uses emerges as an outcome of the Von Thünen Model. In Figure 3.1, the black dot is the marketplace, which is followed by different land-use zones at increasing distances from the center. In the illustrative example, the white zone corresponds

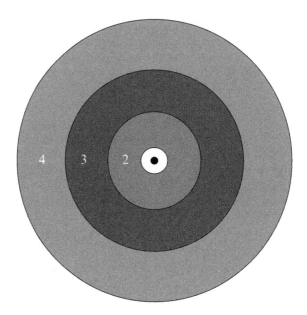

Figure 3.1   A map of the Isolated State of the Von Thünen Model

to dairy and gardening goods. These high-priced distance-sensitive goods are followed, in turn, by forest fuel (2), grains and field crops (3) and ranching (4). The area beyond zone 4 is wilderness because there are no profitable production opportunities in the most peripheral locations.

The Von Thünen Model also shows how land rent depends on the distance to the marketplace and gives rise to a monocentric rent-distance gradient. Figure 3.2 shows the relations among production zones, bid-rent curves and the rent-distance gradient.

The envelope of the highest bids yields the land rent and is a non-linear curve that approaches zero when the distance to the center becomes sufficiently great. Hence equilibrium in this type of land market requires decreasing land rent with increasing distance to the marketplace.

In addition, Puu (1997) shows that the rings around the central market should widen with increasing distance to the market. Puu's result contradicts most popular illustrations of the model. The Von Thünen Model thus not only explains the steep rent-distance gradient close to the center but also the high density of economic activity in the most accessible zones of a functional urban region. Figure 3.3 illustrates the typical "density-distance gradient" that characterizes regions with well-functioning land markets. In

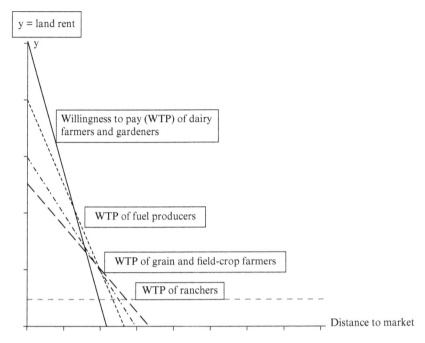

y = land rent

Willingness to pay (WTP) of dairy farmers and gardeners

WTP of fuel producers

WTP of grain and field-crop farmers

WTP of ranchers

Distance to market

Figure 3.2   Bid rents for different agricultural land uses as a function of distance to the marketplace

this case the region in question is the Toronto Census Metropolitan Area (CMA).

Advantageous specialization is an outcome of all theories of trade and location. However, the Von Thünen Model shows that specialization at different distances from the market is advantageous *even if* production technologies or resource availabilities are the same everywhere. Hence it is a more general theory of location and trade than the more widely disseminated theory of international trade as developed by Ricardo, Heckscher and Ohlin. Tõnu Puu explains just how general the Von Thünen Model is:

> Accordingly, only one commodity is produced and transported at each location, except at boundary points. This Specialization Theorem generalizes von Thünen's result, and it was presented by Martin Beckmann and the present author in a joint work in 1985. . . The commodities both produced and traded are in a special relationship to land rent, as the profits from these, the unique best activities at each location, determine the land rent. Constancy contours for land rent thus coincide with constancy contours for the prices of those commodities, and the trade accordingly flows in the direction of land rent gradient. (Puu, 1997, p. 153)

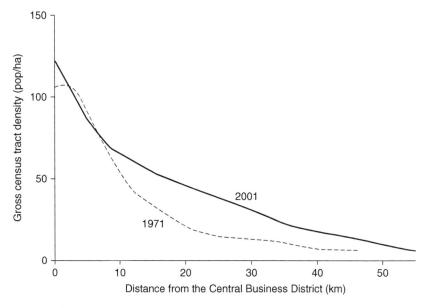

Source: Millward and Bunting (2008).

Figure 3.3   Density-distance gradient for the Toronto CMA

Beckmann (1952; 1953) generalizes the Von Thünen Model—which is a one-dimensional spatial theory of location and trade—into two-dimensional space. Appendix 3.1 is a summary of Beckmann's generalization.

Although the Von Thünen Model is about the best use of agricultural land, later elaborations of the model have mostly concerned the location choices of utility-maximizing households (Alonso, 1964; Muth, 1968; Fujita, 1989; Fujita and Thisse, 2002). Such extensions spell out what is already implicit in Thünen (1826/1930), and introduce households' utilities as analogous to firms' profits. The likelihood of heterogeneous consumption preferences makes examples involving spatial separation of households from other land uses much less persuasive as an approximation of real life than the original example with agricultural goods. Residents may choose their locations for all sorts of reasons. They may want to commute to workplaces as in the model, but they may also want to "consume" neighborhood character, social interactions and many other location attributes. These location choice factors are addressed in Chapter 11.

TWO-DIMENSIONAL REPRESENTATIONS OF SPACE IN ECONOMIC THEORY

Geographers have always been interested in maps: two-dimensional representations of space. Launhardt (1885) is the first attempt to analyze resource allocation in space with such a two-dimensional representation of space. Building on Launhardt's analysis, Weber (1909/1922) popularizes the "locational triangle model." That model addresses the problem of finding the best location of a production facility, assuming that two kinds of raw material must be purchased from two different locations on the map, before selling the resulting output in a marketplace in a third location (for a summary of Weber's theory, see Puu, 1997 or Bröcker, 2014).

Market prices, unit transport costs and the weights of inputs and outputs uniquely determine the optimal location within the two-dimensional location triangle. Early computations of optimal Launhardt/Weber locations made use of mechanical devices such as the "Varignon frame" (see Figure 3.4).

Beckmann (1952; 1953) offers path-breaking contributions that extend the economics of two-dimensional space. Beckmann and Puu (1985) is the final version of that approach in the form of a general equilibrium model of allocation in continuous two-dimensional space. The first equilibrium condition states that the sum of divergence and excess demand equals zero, given that local excess supply is added to—and local excess demand withdrawn from—the flow of traded goods across two-dimensional space (see Appendix 3.1). The second equilibrium condition states that trade flows in the direction of the price gradient and that prices increase with

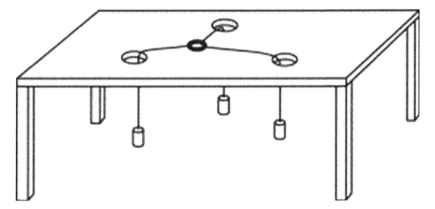

Figure 3.4   The "Varignon frame" method for solving the continuous two-dimensional Launhardt/Weber location problem

the accumulation of transport cost in the direction of the flow. A general competitive equilibrium also implies zero (economic) profits.

The question is why trade and location theorists have neglected this theory of location and trade, which is much more general than all the conventional models of discrete space. Puu (2000, p. 407) argues that this neglect "[m]ost likely . . . is a consequence of a general shortage of PDE (partial differential equations) and vector analysis tools in the analytical equipment of the average economist."

Beckmann (1976) and Puu (2000) extend the two-dimensional continuous space model to encompass continuous time dynamics. They prove that such a dynamic version of Beckmann's theory exhibits unique and stable equilibrium properties under reasonable model assumptions.

Puu (ibid.) employs structural stability theorems to show that only three different geometric layouts of a spatial economy are compatible with regular flow patterns that are structurally stable. One layout is to have squares with an equal number of sinks and sources. The other layouts are triangular or hexagonal ones, with either twice as many sinks as sources or twice as many sources as sinks. All other regular geometric patterns are structurally unstable. A transformation of one stable pattern into another one could be a consequence of how persistent cumulative changes to the transportation infrastructure affect the spatial system as a whole. Puu concludes:

> We landed a long way from von Thünen, but this is an indication of the great potential of his ideas. His land use theory should be interpreted as a general theory of specialization and trade, and there is no need at all to limit its interpretation to that agricultural model to which it was originally cloaked. By making use of Beckmann's general flow concept, it is also possible to disconnect the von Thünen model from its original linear framework.
>
> Leaving linearity, one can make an "integrated state" model out of Thünen's original "isolated state." Due to transversality, the specialization theorem still holds true under the most general assumptions. Finally, a couple of mathematical tools: structural stability for differential equations in the plane, and the elliptic umbilical catastrophe, can be used to characterize the spatial patterns that have the property of structural stability, and to study the transitions between them. (Puu, 2000, pp. 178–9)

Structural stability therefore becomes more important than optimality for explaining the formation of spatial economic or biological patterns. The hexagons of beehives with their six-legged bees are thus a consequence of structural stability rather than some all-encompassing optimality principle. Figure 3.5 shows the three structurally stable regular tessellations (Puu, 2005).

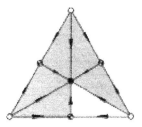 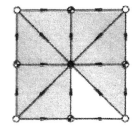 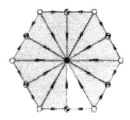

Figure 3.5   Flow tessellations with a white basic triangle; any topologically
equivalent deformations are also allowable forms

SPATIAL INVARIANTS AND URBAN STRUCTURES

Almost all countries have a stable hierarchical regional size distribution of their centers of population and economic activity. The number of large city regions is almost always quite limited. For example, the Nordic countries of Denmark, Finland, Norway and Sweden only have one functional urban region (FUR) each with a population of more than one million. The largest FUR is usually twice the size of the second largest in terms of total population or income, and there tends to be a systematic size reduction with each increase in the rank-ordered number of a FUR.

George Zipf (1949) estimated a rank-size order function for American cities based on data from 1790 to 1930, as Figure 3.6 illustrates. He assumed that the logarithm of a city's population would be linearly related to the logarithm of its rank-ordered number. Figure 3.7 shows the results of an estimation of the rank-size distribution of American metropolitan areas in 2006 to 2008.

The recent logarithmic rank-size curve for US metropolitan shows that large cities are below the regression line. This means that large metro areas are smaller than the rank-size rule would lead us to expect.

Zipf assumed that a minimum energy principle explains this empirical regularity. Later hypothesized explanations have tended to be of the "probabilistic mechanism" type. One example is Simon (1955). In its simplest form this argument proceeds in the following way. At the outset we have a finite number of towns of equal size, say 100. Assuming equiprobable growth prospects, the probability of reaching a larger size that transforms a town into a "subregional service center" may, for example, be 20 percent. Twenty of the initial 100 towns will then grow to become such minor centers. But then there may be a conditional probability of 20 percent of growing even more to reach the next level and become a true "regional center." With 100 towns to begin with, only four will become

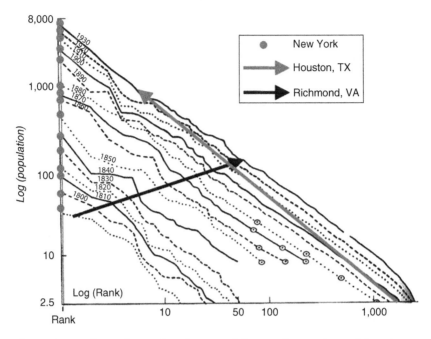

Figure 3.6 The rank-size distribution of the population sizes of American cities as calculated by Zipf (1949) for the 1790–1930 period

regional centers. And using the same probability for the next population threshold level, the most likely outcome will be that only one city will eventually reach the population necessary to qualify as a "national center." The probability for a town to reach the highest level is in this example $(.2)^3$, which equals .008. See Appendix 3.2 for a more general stochastic process generating a power law.

Fonseca (1988) proposes an explanation based on the Fibonacci sequence of numbers, which approaches the golden ratio of 1.618 in terms of relations between successive numbers. The golden ratio has been seen as a relation between all growth parts of some biological forms, for example conical shells with their spiral growth. At any level of resolution the parts of these shells are self-similar. Applying the same principle to the rank-ordering of metropolitan areas in the United States, Fonseca arrived at the following table for the 11 large regions.

There are however other explanations that make more economic sense. As already shown by von Thünen, the role of transport infrastructure and associated costs of trading differ among locations. On any contemporary network there are considerable and stable differences in the accessibility of

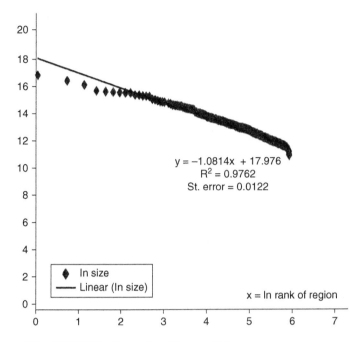

Source: B. Ruett (Jönköping International Business School).

Figure 3.7   Rank-size distribution of US metropolitan areas, 2006–08

different cities to markets and to knowledge. The most centrally located nodes of any country with a large surface area have accessibility advantages that are several orders of magnitude greater than the most peripheral ones. An example is accessibility to scientific knowledge among Swedish regions, which has been estimated to be 6,000 times greater in central Stockholm than in the small town of Kiruna in the extreme north of the country.[1]

If economies of scale in production reinforce such dramatic accessibility differences, the implication would be that the population sizes of the different regions would also be very different. Once established, there are good reasons why steep rank-size distributions of city size persist over time; the historically contingent and relatively stable infrastructure constrains the distribution of people and economic activities to stick to the beaten path that leads again and again to favored locations.

Time, space and capital

Table 3.1   Population of the 11 largest US metropolitan areas in 1980
according to the Bureau of the Census and Fibonacci-predicted
values

Metropolitan Statistical Area (MSA)	Fibonacci rank (f)	Actual population	Fibonacci-predicted population
New York-NE New Jersey (NY-NJ)	0	15,590,274	
Los Angeles-Long Beach (CA)	1	9,479,436	9,635,522
Chicago-Northwest Indiana (IL-IN)	2	6,779,799	5,955,205
Detroit (MI)	3	3,809,327	3,680,596
Boston (MA-NH)	4	2,678,762	2,274,782
Minneapolis-St. Paul (MN)	5	1,787,564	1,405,922
Denver (CO)	6	1,352,070	868,926
Sacramento (CA)	7	796,266	537,037
Albany-Schenectady-Troy (NY)	8	490,015	331,914
Colorado Springs (CO)	9	276,872	205,138
Lancaster (PA)	10	157,385	126,785
Elkhart-Goshen (IN)	11	83,920	78,359

Source: Fonseca (1988).

THE SPATIAL DISTRIBUTION OF THE TRANSPORT INFRASTRUCTURE AND OF POPULATIONS

The most important factor that influences the distribution of economic activity is the initial establishment and the subsequent incremental changes to the transportation infrastructure. Map 3.1 shows the distribution of the American population across 49 of the 50 states and Puerto Rico. There are clear patterns that seem to favor locations in the northeast and, more generally, the eastern half of the contiguous 48 states.

Already by the end of the nineteenth century, the railroad infrastructure had created one of the primary conditions for the distribution of economic activity a century later, as Map 3.2 illustrates.

The role of the northeast and the Great Lakes regions had been established even earlier. The Atlantic seaports had been the conduits for European settlement and trade and the construction of canals connecting the Atlantic to the Great Lakes reinforced the accessibility advantages of the northeastern quadrant of what is today the continental United States. Subsequent investments—first in railroads and later in turnpikes—reinforced the initial infrastructural advantages of the northeast.

Urbanized Areas and Clusters

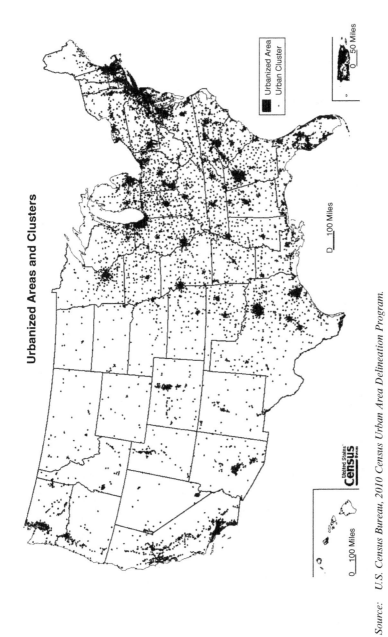

Source: U.S. Census Bureau, 2010 Census Urban Area Delineation Program.

Map 3.1 The spatial distribution of the American population in 2010

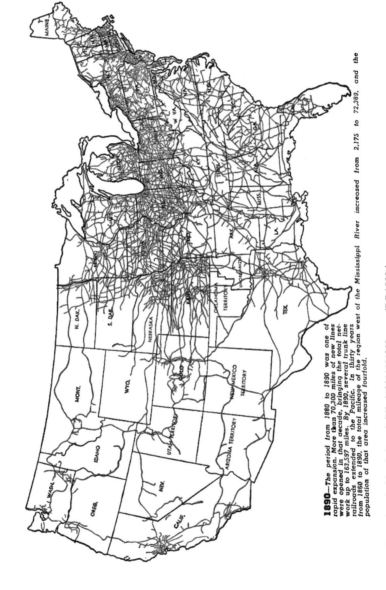

1890—The period from 1880 to 1890 was one of rapid expansion. More than 70,300 miles of new lines were opened in that decade, bringing the total network up to 163,597 miles. By 1890, several trunk line railroads extended to the Pacific. In thirty years from 1860 to 1890, the total mileage of the region west of the Mississippi River increased from 2,175 to 72,389, and the population of that area increased fourfold.

Source: http://users.humboldt.edu/ogayle/Hist%20111%20Images/RR1890.jpg.

Map 3.2   The US railroad network in 1890

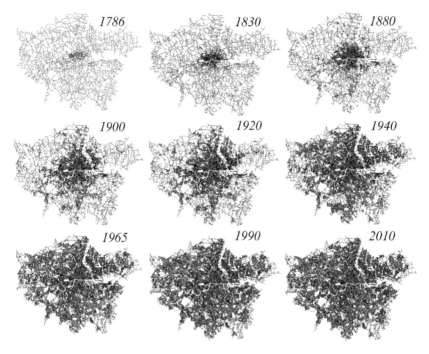

Source: Masucci et al. (2013).

Map 3.3   Roads and population densities in London, 1786–2010

Throughout the twentieth century, investments in both roads and in complementary capital—ranging from power plants to theaters—reinforced the dominance of the northeast and in particular the Boston-NYC-DC corridor (Lakshmanan et al., 2015).

Map 3.3 offers another illustration of how an initial road network shapes the evolution of later incremental additions to it. In the case of London, it is possible to track transport infrastructure and population distribution changes over a period of well over 200 years. This example also demonstrates that path dependence and structural stability characterize transport networks and population patterns at both the interregional and intraregional levels. Map 3.4 shows a similar evolution of population patterns over a period of 80 years in the Philadelphia metropolitan area.

The pattern of internal population growth in FURs tends to follow the main transportation arteries from the first half of the twentieth century, as Map 3.5 and Map 3.6 illustrate for the cities of Berlin and Sydney. These maps not only show that population grows along transportation corridors,

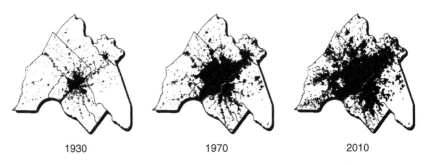

Source: http://philadelphiaencyclopedia.org/.

Map 3.4   Population distribution in the Philadelphia MSA, 1930–2010

Source: Bertaud (2001); Bertaud and Malpezzi (2003).

Map 3.5   Spatial population distribution, Berlin, 2000

but they also hint at how these same corridors extend outward and become links to other cities in the same and other nations. The basic spatial pattern is thus a function of transport plans, some of which may have been formulated several centuries ago.

One of the clearest manifestations of how such regional planning shapes urban population outcomes is the Copenhagen Capital Region in Denmark, where the road-and-rail corridors show up as fingers on a map (Map 3.7). In that region, the planners reinforced and codified pre-existing patterns with the help of an easy-to-visualize image. The vision behind the Finger Plan of 1947 was to create a planned spatial structure that

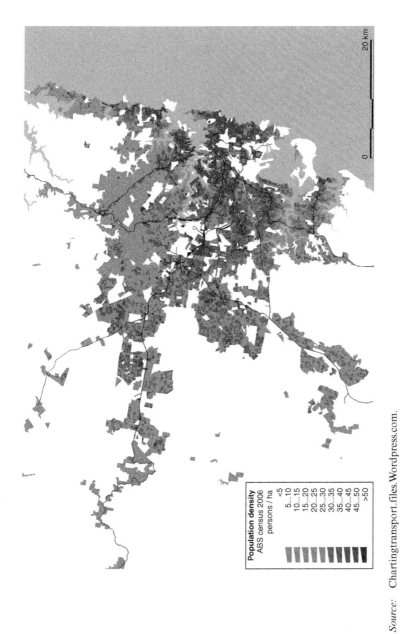

Population density
ABS census 2006
persons / ha

<5
5...10
10...15
15...20
20...25
25...30
30...35
35...40
40...45
45...50
>50

20 km

0

Source: Chartingtransport.files.Wordpress.com.

Map 3.6   Spatial population distribution, Sydney, 2012

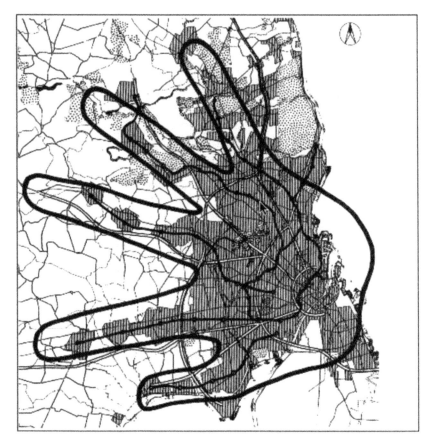

Source: Dansk Center for Byhistorie (2015).

Map 3.7   Copenhagen's Finger Plan of 1947

promoted both access to a central marketplace (downtown Copenhagen) and access to leisure destinations along the coast and on the rural outskirts of the region. Map 3.8 shows how the Finger Plan is still visible on much later maps of the commuter rail network.

While transport corridors shape the expansion of cities into their hinterlands, the baseline densities differ across cities. The initial density of a city has a lot to do with the level of economic development at the time of its foundation. The main transportation mode 1,000 years ago was walking, and the predictable consequence is that the oldest cities have downtown street layouts that are dense and feature short blocks. The goal was to have access on foot to all nodes within the original town.

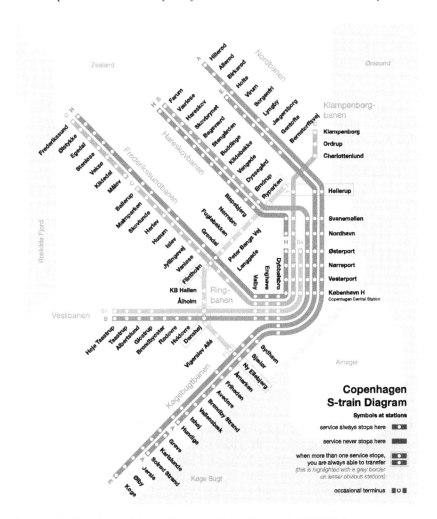

Source: By Electricnet, with contributions by heb – Own work, CC BY 3.0, https://commons.wikimedia.org/w/index.php?curid=8770026.

Map 3.8   The S-train network in the Copenhagen Capital Region

Nineteenth-century planners envisioned lower time distances associated with traveling a given distance, since transportation technology had by then improved to the point where the widespread adoption of railroads and horse-drawn carriages and trams was possible. The twentieth century, finally, saw the rise of much faster modes for the masses such as the automobile and metropolitan rapid transit. Consequently, nineteenth-century downtowns have medium-density grids of streets, while the world's newest large cities feature ubiquitous wide boulevards and plenty of parking. Thus urban densities and relative auto use follow predictable patterns that relate to both the age of a city and its attained development levels in subsequent periods.

Asian cities are old and most are located along waterways on densely populated plains. These cities also industrialized late. Thus it is unsurprising that Asian cities exhibit the highest densities, not only in their cores but also throughout their inner suburbs. Europe represents an intermediate case: its cities are also old, but most of Europe industrialized in the nineteenth century, and saw the mass adoption of the automobile as a means of transportation in the decades following World War II. Hence dense downtowns give way to inner suburbs of medium density and more expansive low-density developments on the urban outskirts. The overall population density of European FURs tends therefore to be lower than is the case in Asia.

The least densely populated city regions are in rich parts of the New World such as Australia, Canada and the United States. Again there is a distinction between relatively old cities and the newest ones. Cities such as Boston, New York and Philadelphia are much older than cities in other parts of North America, and thus they have downtowns of medium rather than low density. This has in turn facilitated the use of mass rail transit systems as compared with cities with lower-density cores. It is no coincidence that it is in cities with dense downtowns that sizable shares of workers commute by mass transit. Commuters make heavy use of public transportation in most Asian as well as in the largest European FURs. In North America, low densities make mass transportation prohibitively expensive in most cities, and it is only in the cities with the densest downtowns that the commuting share accounted for by rail-based modes exceeds 10 percent.

It is however noteworthy that old cities become less dense as they expand outward. Empirically, suburbanization and ever-lower population densities are universal. This has a lot to do with empirical regularities across populations in terms of consumer preferences. Consumers' demands for personal space and for car transportation tend to be income-elastic across a wide range of incomes and demographic categories. Asia and Europe's cities started out as much denser environments than their North American and Australian counterparts. But Asian and European cities have for the past 60 years been suburbanizing and thus lowering their densities at an even faster rate than US metro areas (Gordon and Cox, 2014).

Even in the United States it is possible to observe similar tendencies, with relatively dense cities slowly "catching up" by building wider roads and larger lots. New York has a denser center than Los Angeles, but the New York MSA is on the whole actually *less* dense than the Los Angeles

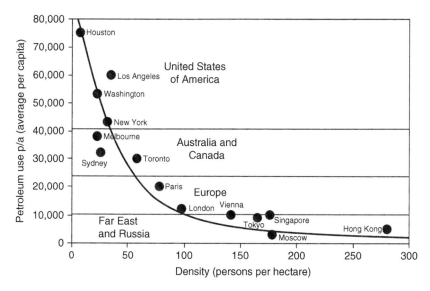

Source: Newman and Kenworthy (1989).

Figure 3.8 Population density and per capita petroleum use in 14 urban regions

MSA (this is no doubt a reflection of the spectacular twentieth-century economic success of LA, so that its metro area has in effect become the world's first "medium-density sprawl").

The most interesting aspect of this long-run suburbanizing tendency is that it has often been the opposite of the stated aims of the urban planners. Most planners favor high population densities and public transportation. And yet the empirical tendency everywhere is toward lower densities and more private transportation. Even the most drastic measures, such as London's Metropolitan Green Belt, were unsuccessful at stopping suburbanization. In the London case, the main effect was suburbanization *beyond* the Green Belt and even longer commutes than what is likely to have happened without it.

Figure 3.8 shows the relationship between metropolitan population density and petroleum use in a sample of world cities. As expected, low densities encourage residents to commute by car, which leads to high per capita petroleum use. It is of course not only density that influences the relative attractiveness of private as opposed to public transportation. Other factors include the density of the downtown area and its relative importance as a regional employment center, as well as various taxes and subsidies that aim at influencing residents' transportation choices. While most cities are close to the estimated regression curve, Melbourne and Sydney are clear outliers. These two Australian cities have lower petroleum use than their low population densities would lead us to predict. Possible reasons could be higher downtown-periphery density ratios, more monocentric workplace structures and/or transport policies that penalize drivers *but not* large suburban lots.

THE INTERNAL STRUCTURE OF TOWNS AND CITIES

The slow and steady expansion of the transport network shapes the development of urban structures. This network connects the city internally as well as toward the external world. The first stage of agglomeration is the transformation of a few scattered houses into a small village. At this stage, accessibility considerations require all buildings to be placed along a single village road as illustrated (see Figure 3.9, Stage 1). With continued economic growth, it can become worthwhile to invest in another road. In the generic case, this results in two cross-shaped intersecting roads, both of which are lined with houses (Figure 3.9, Stage 2).

The third stage sees the emergence of a typical medieval pattern: a market square at a crossroads. It is common for this stage to set the stage for a first division of land use into land for residences, commerce and farming (Figure 3.9, Stage 3). Stage 4 represents a typical nineteenth-century urban plan with a rectangular grid of the type that is most clearly visible in American downtown areas, with their straight numbered streets and uniform block sizes (Figure 3.9, Stage 4).

Stage 5 in Figure 3.9 is the most recent development. In many cities, increasing auto ownership rates caused frequent congestion on their medium-width urban streets and rare radial roads. The most common planning remedy was the high-capacity ring road, such as the Orbital Motorway (M25) that encircles greater London and the Capital Beltway (I-495) around Washington D.C.

In the early twenty-first century, most new high-capacity circumferential ring roads are being constructed around China's cities. Beijing had six ring roads in 2016, with a seventh one under construction. Table 3.2 gives the length of each of Beijing's ring roads and its dates of construction. A consequence of China's high rate of economic growth from the 1990s onward has been a dramatic increase in automobile ownership rates. In Beijing, the car ownership rate quintupled between 1992 and 2014, growing from 51.2 per 1,000 residents in 1992 to 250.6 in 2014.

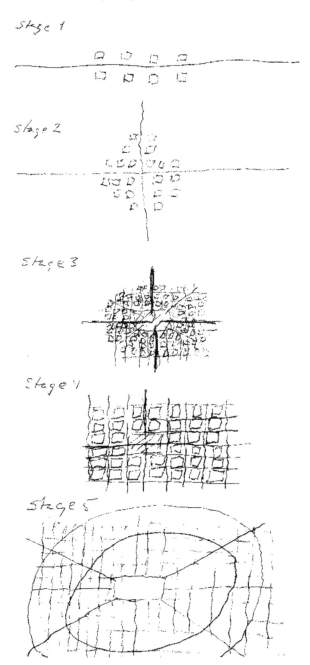

Figure 3.9   The evolution of a settlement from village to metropolis

*Table 3.2   Length and completion of ring roads, number of cars and
              population size in Beijing, 1949–2014*

Ring road	Length (km)	Construction period	Distance to downtown	Year	Number of cars	Population size
1st	17.0	Before 1949	Downtown	1949	2300	2,092,000
2nd	32.7	1960s–1992	Downtown	1992	564,000	11,020,000
3rd	48.3	1980s–1994	Downtown	1994	1,000,000	11,250,000
4th	65.3	1990–2001	8 km	2001	1,698,000	13,851,000
5th	98.6	2000–2003	10 km	2003	2,000,000	14,564,000
6th	187.6	1998–2009	15-20 km	2009	4,000,000	18,600,000
7th	940.0	2015–	N/A	2014	5,300,000	21,148,000

Source: South China Morning Post (2014).

THE RECTANGULAR INNER STRUCTURE OF HISTORICAL TOWNS AND CITIES

A pattern of rectangular city blocks is the dominant tendency in most downtowns, as Maps 3.9 through 3.13 illustrate. Map 3.9 is a medieval map of the town of Ypres in West Flanders, Belgium. Ypres first emerged as a town on the banks of the Ieperlee River at about 1000 AD, when it established itself as a center for the northern European cloth trade. The dukes of Burgundy fortified the town as early as in the thirteenth century.

The larger Flemish city of Antwerp exhibited a similar rectangular structure, as Georg Braun's and Frans Hogenberg's map from 1572 clearly shows (Map 3.10). As was usual at the time, a city wall enclosed Antwerp and limited its potential for growth. This rectangular wall-enclosed structure was typical of cities all across medieval Europe, as Map 3.11 of medieval Ferrara in Italy illustrates.

This rectangular structure of city blocks persisted over the centuries, as Maps 3.12 and 3.13 both show. Map 3.12 shows Ildefons Cerdà's famous city plan for the *Eixample*, which was the nineteenth-century extension of Barcelona. It is in many ways typical of its time. Rapid population growth necessitated massive investments in new streets and roads and the typical design principle was a traditional rectangular grid with a new complement in the form of a small number of radial avenues.

Cerdà's plan was an unusually stringent version of this type of plan. The connections from the periphery to the center consisted of five diagonal boulevards, while all blocks were squares that were surrounded by

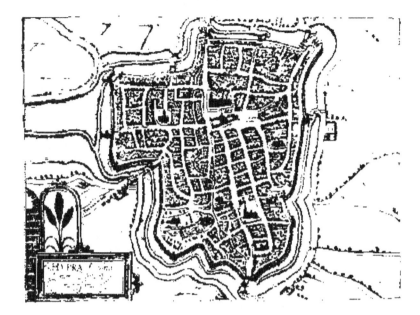

Map 3.9   Medieval map of Ypres

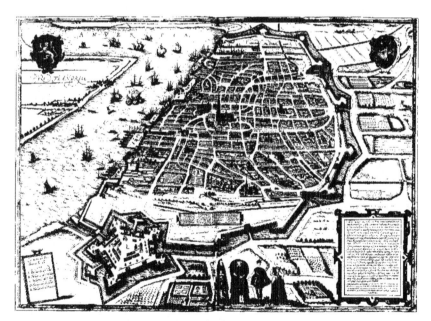

Map 3.10   The rectangular block structure of medieval Antwerp

Source: Wikimedia.

Map 3.11   Medieval Ferrara

four streets. Cerdà's plan was consistent with the traditional rectangular layout of European towns, and there is also an evident connection to the nineteenth-century plan for Manhattan (see Map 3.13). Manhattan was planned as a grid of north-south avenues and west-east streets, which were superimposed on the pre-existing Indian trail that the original Dutch colonizers had called *Bredeweg* and which became known in English as Broadway. Broadway had been the main thoroughfare in New Amsterdam, and it was later extended northward to encompass all of Manhattan and further north into the Bronx and Westchester County. Broadway had the same diagonal relation to a dominant rectangular structure that Cerdà's boulevards had to Barcelona's nineteenth-century grid.

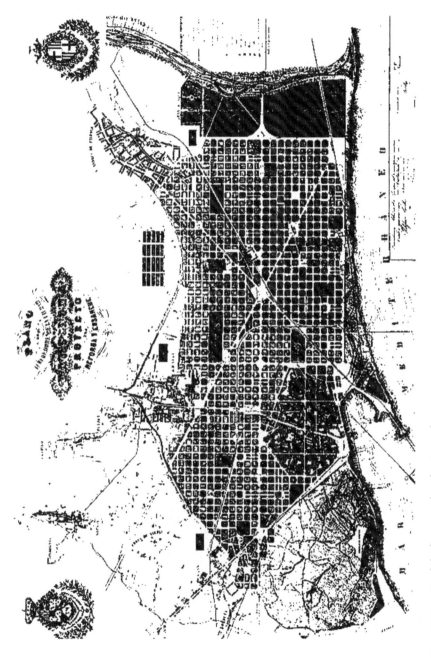

Map 3.12   Cerdà's famous plan for Barcelona

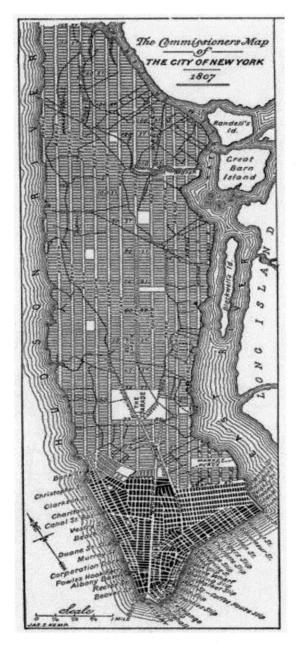

Map 3.13   Nineteenth-century map of the Borough of Manhattan, New York City

NOTE

1. Accessibility, a, is in this example measured as $a_i = \sum_{j=1}^{n} e^{-\beta d_{ij}} R_j$, where d_{ij} = time distance from node i to node j; R_j = stock of scientific knowledge in node j; and $\hat{a}$ = distance friction parameter estimated with the help of Swedish commuting data. The rank-size distribution is much steeper in Sweden than in the United States, which reflects the unusually oblong shape as well as the small population size of the former country.

APPENDIX 3.1: BECKMANN'S GENERAL SPATIAL ECONOMIC EQUILIBRIUM THEORY[1]

Two definitions:

$\text{grad}(f) = \nabla f$

This measures the rate and direction of change in a scalar field; it maps scalar fields to vector fields.

$\text{div}(\mathbf{F}) = \nabla \cdot \mathbf{F}$

This measures the scalar of a source or a sink at a given point in a vector field; it maps vector fields to scalar fields. The theory is developed for a closed region with space coordinates (x_1, x_2). There are four scalar fields defined as:

1. The local price distribution $\lambda(x_1, x_2)$.
2. The local excess demand distribution $z = f(\lambda, x_1, x_2)$
3. The local transport rate distribution $k(x_1, x_2)$.
4. The flow of traded goods $\theta = \theta(\theta_1(x_1, x_2), \theta_2(x_1, x_2))$.

z is a function of price with a first derivative less than 0. The transport rate is assumed to be independent of the direction. The unit direction vector in each one of the locations is $\frac{\theta}{|\theta|} = \left(\frac{\theta_1}{\sqrt{\theta_1^2 + \theta_2^2}}, \frac{\theta_2}{\sqrt{\theta_1^2 + \theta_2^2}} \right)$. This gives the direction of trade, while the norm $|\theta| = \sqrt{\theta_1^2 + \theta_2^2}$ is the volume of the trade flow. The divergence $\text{Div} \cdot \theta = \frac{\partial \theta_1}{\partial x_1} + \frac{\partial \theta_2}{\partial x_2}$ denotes the change of the goods flow volume.

The first Beckmann law (the divergence law of equilibrium of trade flows) states that the sum of flow divergence and excess demand should be equal to zero: local excess supply should be sent into the flow and local excess demand should be withdrawn from the flow. It is the condition of equilibrium of interregional trade flows: $\text{Div}\,\theta + z = 0$.

The second Beckmann law (the gradient law of prices in space) states that trade flows should move in the direction of the price gradient: $k\frac{\theta}{|\theta|} = \nabla \lambda$. Traders should thus send goods in the direction of the largest price increases. Puu (2000, pp. 427–31) proves that the general equilibrium of Beckmann's model is globally and asymptotically stable.

NOTE

1. Puu, 2000, pp. 408–13.

APPENDIX 3.2: STOCHASTICS AND THE POWER LAW

Mikhailov and Calenbuhr (2002 p.91) propose a stochastic differential equation

$$dx/dt = (-a + f(t)) x + b;$$ (A2.1)

where a and b are small constant terms and $f(t)$ is a Gaussian white noise function. With no noise the equilibrium solution would be $x = b/a$. The white noise is of importance for the final distribution. If $f(t)$ becomes larger than a, the growth would become exponentially large, while $f(t)$ smaller than a implies exponential decline towards the small number b. This means that the dynamic process is asymmetric above b. The distribution approaches: $p(x) \sim \frac{1}{x^{1 + \frac{a}{\sigma}}}$; in the limit.

4. Dynamic theories and models— problems and creative potential

Dynamic economics is concerned with observable events, theories about the relations between various processes of change and models that predict what is likely to happen if certain conditions are met. Sometimes such analyses are used in the formation of governmental or corporate long-term strategic plans. Studies of economic change and other dynamic processes are therefore intended to fulfill at least the first three of the following five requirements:

- Use of observable variables and factual conditions
- Logical consistency
- Understanding of processes
- Predictability
- Controllability

These do not only apply to economic dynamics. In a different context, control engineers and applied physicists formulate similar requirements.

The main objective of modeling is to provide a better understanding of how various independent variables directly or indirectly influence the dependent variables of a system. This objective may at first sight seem unobjectionable, but it does not command unanimous support among economists. One noted example is Friedman (1953), which stakes out the contrasting epistemological position that economic theories and models should only aim at good predictive performance.

THE CONSEQUENCES OF INTERACTIVITY

An economic model is generally not reducible to a chain of causality that only involves one or two independent variables causing changes in a dependent variable. Even so, it is common among applied policy-oriented economists and financial analysts to use simple technical charts to forecast the future. They do this by relating the uncontrollable entity of time as an independent variable to their dependent variable of choice. Examples of dependent variables that the elapse of time allegedly "explains" include share prices, gross domestic products and population sizes. Using more or less advanced numerology, these analysts often use historical observations to forecast the future demand for a wide range of goods. Whether the demand is for an important general-purpose good such as energy or a peripheral one such as a specific type of energy drink does not really matter to them. So-called "econometric systems" are of this type whenever the focus is on the elapse of time as the determinant of future changes.

To make economic models more realistic and credible, it is necessary to introduce conflicts of interests and other factors to complicate matters. Models of biological systems and interactive conflicts are examples that go beyond the elapse of time.

It is sometimes possible to model interactions between bacteria and humans from a conflict perspective. Let us assume that an Ebola epidemic suddenly appears in an isolated region with a given population. The number of people who are already infected, the number who are still uninfected and a parameter that represents the *contagiousness* of the epidemic then jointly cause the growth in the number of infected individuals at any point in time.

If the number of infected, the number of uninfected and an infection-propensity parameter determines the growth in the number of infected, we may use the following simple model:

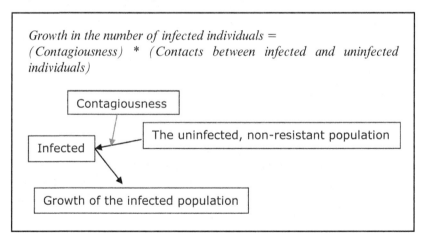

Growth in the number of infected individuals =
(Contagiousness) * (Contacts between infected and uninfected individuals)

Contagiousness

Infected

The uninfected, non-resistant population

Growth of the infected population

Formally, this can be expressed as

Growth in the number of infected = $dp/dt = \dot{p} = rp\,(1-p)$; (4.1)

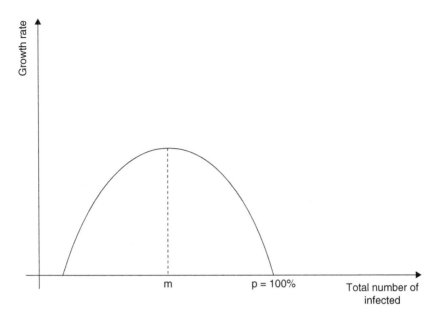

Figure 4.1   The growth rate of an epidemic disease

The number of uninfected is in this case the total population minus the number of people who are already infected. It is obvious that if nobody is infected, the growth in the number of infected will equal zero. The equation also shows that when the whole (non-resistant) population is infected, there will be no further growth in the number of infected. A diagram can illustrate the main features of the equation, where the growth in the number of infected is seen as a function of the total number of infected.

If the contagiousness parameter is greater than zero, the epidemic will grow at an increasing rate until it reaches the point m in the diagram (Figure 4.1). Thereafter the growth decelerates until the total number of infected reaches its maximum value. A diagram with the x-axis representing time and the y axis representing the total number of infected people can also illustrate this process. Such a representation shows that the spread of the disease resembles an s-shaped curve that goes from zero to its maximum value.

Hotelling (1921) suggests a population growth model of the same type as (4.1), and Puu (2000) adds a spatial diffusion equation to (4.1) in order to extend its domain of applicability to migration among locations.

It is also popular to use this type of model for analyzing the growth in demand for fashionable goods or innovations. It has been quite successful as a theoretical starting point for studying various kinds of social interactivity. Interactive phenomena of the diffusion type are common in economic life. Veblen (1899) first introduces the interactive phenomenon of "conspicuous consumption" and Duesenberry (1948; 1949) elaborates on this in a model where consumers are preoccupied with "keeping up with the Joneses." Such models assume that the utility of each individual depends not only on what she herself consumes, but also on the consumption of others. From a perceived disequilibrium, individuals may choose to take part in a "consumption race" that only ends after a "multiplier process" enables them to reach a new equilibrium.

Suppose that a rich household moves into a poor neighborhood. This may cause the original residents of the neighborhood to "compete" with their new rich neighbor and lead them to engage in status-enhancing economic actions such as repainting their houses and buying better cars until they reach a new social equilibrium. If instead a group of bikers sets up a meth lab in the same neighborhood, they may initiate a downward multiplier process where neglect rather than upkeep spreads through a population.[1]

The theory of cumulative growth has been used to model social phenomena such as residential segregation. An early example is Myrdal's (1944) analysis of segregation processes in *An American Dilemma*. Schelling (1969; 1978) proposes a more formal dynamic process that leads to residential segregation; this model shows how positive feedback loops may create self-reinforcing racial segregation of the type that is common in many American cities.

Granovetter (1978) and Watts and Dodds (2009) extend the analysis of such processes by looking at triggers of collective behavioral phenomena such as riots. Granovetter (1978) assumes that each person pays attention to every other member of the relevant population. Each individual has a *threshold*, Φ_i^*, according to some probability distribution $f(\cdot)$, where the value of Φ_i^* represents the preferences of individual i. The distribution in Figure 4.2(b) is an example of a population with heterogeneous preferences.

In Figure 4.2(c), the intermediate value 0.5 represents an unstable equilibrium point. If the average level of Φ_t would be slightly lower the riot would peter out after a short time, while if the average level of Φ_t would be slightly higher there would be rapid growth toward maximum intensity. Equilibrium solutions with segregated behavior are also possible with a version of this model that allows for multimodal probability distributions.

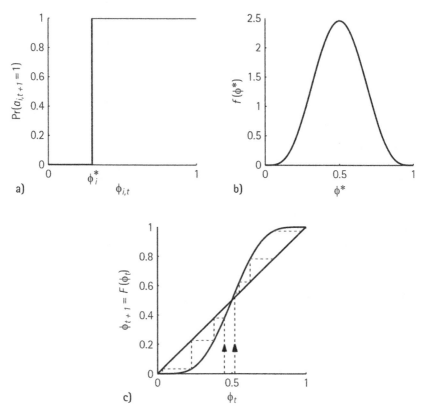

Source: Watts and Dodds (2009).

Figure 4.2   Threshold values and dynamics of clustering

AUTOMATIC PATHS TO EQUILIBRIUM

There is an abundance of examples from engineering and economics of
how dynamic systems with negative feedback automatically reach equilibrium positions. One classical mechanical example is the centrifugal regulator of the steam engine (Thurston, 1878). This regulation with a so-called
"governor" is effected by letting a steam vent open or close with the help of
two revolving balls. The centrifugal force and velocity of the steam engine
decide its rotation velocity and height. A steam engine with greater velocity
than the desired equilibrium causes the balls to rise to a higher level due to
the centrifugal force. This higher position of the balls causes the steam vent
to close, thereby reducing the velocity of the engine. When the velocity has

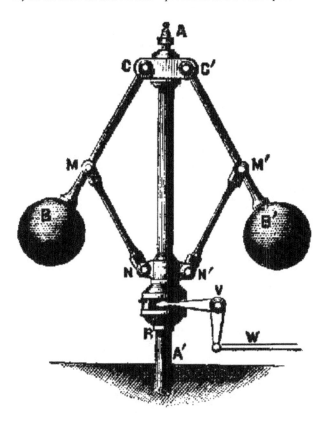

Figure 4.3   The "governor" (centrifugal regulator) of a steam engine

decreased to a below-equilibrium level, this will cause the balls to fall to a lower position, which again opens the vent. The opening of the vent will then make the steam engine accelerate. Disequilibrium thus triggers negative feedback—that is, a countervailing force—so that the system gradually approaches its equilibrium position. In this example, the balls must have an appropriate weight and the slope must be smaller than 45 degrees if the negative feedback is to be successful (see Figure 4.3).

Biomedicine and psychology make use of similar conceptual mechanisms for the modeling of disequilibria in order to understand or guide behavior. In this context, a homeostatic mechanism represents a human being. Every deviation from the biochemical balance triggers hormonal and other reactions in the signaling system of the body. It is these reactions that regulate human chemistry. They are usually sufficient for restoring the biological equilibrium of the body. If this were not so we would not survive for any length of time.

Ecologists and economists have studied macroscopic versions of such dynamic self-stabilizing processes. This requires a theory of the ecological or economic nexus as an often-gigantic system of dynamic interdependencies. *Negative feedback* then plays a decisive role in enabling the system to return to equilibrium after more or less random changes involving different parameters.

Theil (1964) is an example of an alternative interventionist (or social engineering) approach to the problem of stabilizing economic policy. Ecologists and economists tend to oppose political interventionism when a system seems to have self-equilibrating forces. Heavy-handed interventions can destroy the spontaneous or intrinsic ability of such systems to approach equilibrium.

MULTIPLE EQUILIBRIA

Conventional models of general equilibrium focus on ensuring the existence of equilibrium using some fixed-point theorem. Economists have been able to show that there are conditions that yield unique and stable equilibria. However, interdependencies among agents that cause a sufficient degree of non-linearity generically lead to multiple-equilibria solutions. These equilibria are sometimes stable and sometimes unstable.

Kaldor (1940, pp. 78–92) is an example of a simple Keynesian model with non-linear total demand functions (Figure 4.4).

According to Kaldor we should expect a business cycle with shifting and multiple equilibria. There are a number of stages where the national

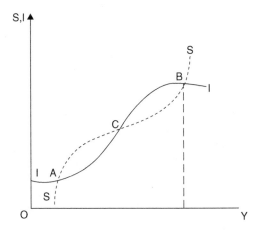

Figure 4.4   The Kaldor model of multiple macroeconomic equilibria

income (Y) may fluctuate between unstable equilibrium C and two stable equilibria A and B.

The national income (Y) is in stable equilibrium during the initial stage of the business cycle. But there is the possibility that the capital stock is growing too fast. If it is, there will be a downward shift in the propensity to invest during the subsequent stage, while rapid income growth among consumers leads to a higher propensity to save. The B and C equilibria are unstable and the system can therefore drop into a temporary recession.

Mees (1975) is another influential application of a highly non-linear model to economic phenomena. It attempts to explain the spatial intricacies of urbanization processes. But it is game theory that offers what is perhaps the most influential economic application featuring multiple equilibria. The well-known prisoner's dilemma model has both stable (suboptimal) and unstable (optimal) equilibria if played once. Conversely, repeated play makes it possible for a stable equilibrium to emerge that is also optimal.

COMPOUND INTEREST, POSITIVE FEEDBACK AND CUMULATIVE GROWTH

As discussed in Chapter 2, anyone with a savings account, a bond or a mortgage has had to learn how to calculate compound interest and to understand the importance of interest in the growth of capital values. If you lend $1,000 at an agreed annual interest of 10 percent, your claim will have increased to $1,100 after one year. Two years later, it will amount to $1,210, and after three years, you can demand $1,331 from the borrower. This is an example of a process that is subject to *positive feedback*. The principle of compound interest illustrates a *divergent positive feedback*, which means that the resulting values are increasingly distant from a conceivable equilibrium position.

In biology, there are many examples of growth patterns that initially exhibit positive feedback and thus resemble compound interest. When a spatially confined bacterial culture grows by consuming a fixed supply of nutrients per unit of time, it will lead to a progressive increase in the number of bacteria during the initial phase of its growth. However, as is shown in Figure 4.1, congestion phenomena will emerge after a specific period of time. This will lead to a gradually diminishing growth rate that will eventually reach zero. The first point in time where there is no more growth is then also the time when the quantity of bacteria has attained its stable equilibrium.

Some unorthodox theories of long-term economic growth assume positive feedback loops, which imply protracted cumulative or progressive growth. One example is Knut Wicksell's theory of the constant inflation rate, where investors' cost of borrowing is lower than the natural interest rate. Analogously, analyses of economic growth show that aggregate income grows at a rate that depends on the rate of investment in relation to the capital requirements per unit of income, as long as there are no natural limitations and no congestion phenomena. Classic growth theories of the von Neumann (1938/1970) and Leontief (1953) type as well as more recent modeling such as Arthur (1983), Romer (1994) and Krugman (1997) all assume similar processes of positive feedback. In Romer's and Krugman's models, increasing returns reinforce growth; however, these two models lack realism since there are no spatial limitations or transport network capacity constraints.

Most demographic forecasts and extrapolations are based on similar conceptions of cumulative growth. The United Nations produced forecasts as late as the 1980s that predicted cumulative unconstrained growth of the world's population for centuries to come. Such unconstrained and unlimited growth has never occurred anywhere. Better returns to investments in human capital, improved education of women and school congestion all provide disincentives to traditional childbearing behavior. Nowhere has the resultant reduction in the population growth rate been more dramatic than in Asia, which is where more than half of all human beings live.

MINOR EVENTS MAY HAVE MAJOR CONSEQUENCES

In the 1960s and 1970s, economists generally assumed that it was possible to achieve economic growth under conditions of a lasting stable equilibrium. A catchphrase of the period, "balanced growth," appealed to this assumption. Economists and politicians thought that restructuring would occur only slowly and without abrupt leaps between alternate multiple equilibria. They pictured society as a structurally stable entity, in the sense that minor changes to the infrastructure would lead to minor economic and social changes.

Meanwhile, some mathematicians and natural scientists had turned their attention to systems with structural instability. In such systems, a minute change of a critical parameter may lead to a thorough transformation of the entire structure. It was no longer evident that a small change in the conditions would result in small consequences. Concepts such as "bifurcations" and "catastrophes" became increasingly prevalent in the scientific literature on dynamic systems during the 1960s and 1970s.

In chemistry and biochemistry it had for a long time been established

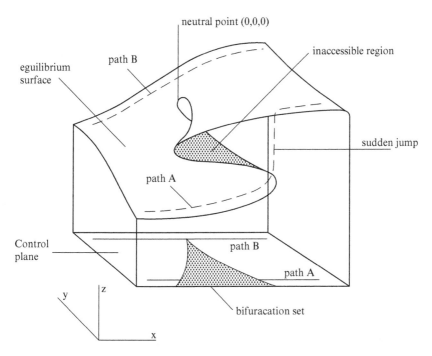

Figure 4.5   A three-dimensional illustration of a catastrophe manifold

practice to study sudden restructuring as a result of increasing the amount of some catalyst to a critical level. A common phenomenon in chemical systems is that the approach of such critical levels is accompanied by divergent and unstable systemic attributes and a subsequent leap to a new equilibrium, which however remains stable even if one increases the quantity of the catalyst beyond the threshold.

Figure 4.5 illustrates a cusp catastrophe in which path A at low levels of variable y leads toward a point where it bifurcates, which means that there is a sudden "jump" between the lower and higher parts of the equilibrium surface. Path B is different because it allows for a smoother transition of z at high levels of y, given similar increases of the x variable.

Most economists were slow to accept the theory of bifurcations and rapid structural change, and saw these phenomena as destructive of their cherished general equilibrium theory. Mees (1975), Varian (1979), Varaiya and Wiseman (1984), Puu (1989; 2000) and Rosser (1999; 2007) are contrarian examples of economic modeling that do incorporate the possibility of bifurcation jumps and thus allow for both dramatic and incremental structural changes.

Structural instability is not only problematic. It can also be the means to realize creative solutions to apparently impossible problems.

THE CREATIVE USE OF STRUCTURAL INSTABILITY

At the end of the nineteenth century, a number of engineers with an interest in aviation tried to create a maneuverable, motorized airplane. In spite of considerable expertise in aerodynamics and other disciplines, all early attempts at creating a maneuverable motor-powered flying vehicle failed. The ambition had been to combine dynamic controllability with aerodynamic equilibrium and stability. The Wright brothers, in contrast, constructed an airplane that was structurally unstable. To the surprise of many, their construction proved maneuverable without superhuman strength, even if it demanded very rapid reactivity on the part of the pilot.

Structural instability is a precondition for much of creativity in the arts and in architecture. It is in general only possible to achieve stable equilibria in conjunction with the completion of the creative process. The initial phase of the process amounts to a search with several equilibria as potential outcomes. Figure 4.6 shows how a stable hexagon is transformed into an unstable cube by means of only minor changes. The two points A and B of the unstable cube are perceived as sometimes being closest to and sometimes furthest away from the observer. The remarkable thing about this cube is that it is perceived as increasingly unstable the longer one observes it.

However, such a high degree of instability creates a creative potential. By generating various minor changes it becomes possible to make a perceptually unstable figure unambiguous, but which stable figure that will result is not predetermined. Hofstadter (1997/1999) shows how the artist Maurits Cornelis Escher made use of ambiguous and unstable structures as a creative tool.

We can also illustrate the importance of structural instability with a decision tree. Apparently immaterial initial choice changes can have dramatic effects on later outcomes. Origami, the Japanese art of paper folding, is an example of a creative process that depends on this type of structural instability. The origami artist folds and refolds a blank sheet of paper, with each new fold building on the preceding ones until she attains the desired object. Even small changes in the sequence of folds—especially early changes—can result in totally different objects.

Figure 4.7 shows a number of possible objects that an origami artist can attain by folding a quadratic sheet of paper. In this picture, all objects share the same initial folds. Every resulting object has a structurally

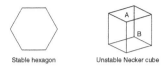

Figure 4.6   Stable and unstable patterns

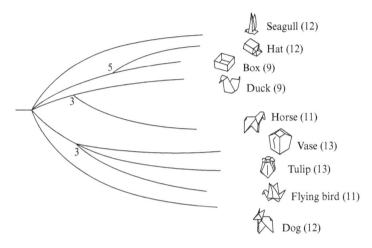

Figure 4.7   Origami as a creative decision tree

stable composition of forms and folds. The transformation paths from an unfolded paper with numerous potential outcomes to the nine final objects run via a few strategic bifurcation points. After three folds, out of nine or eleven, respectively, one has to decide whether to make a duck or a horse. The vase and the tulip are the most complicated objects in terms of the number of folds.

The process also demonstrates that the originally quadratic sheet of paper contains an increasing number of characteristics. The sequencing of the folds is decisive for the final result, even if the intermediate steps do not reveal anything about the actual resulting object. It is that stage of the folding process where it is impossible to guess if the sheet will become, say, a seagull or a dog, which is the first structurally unstable stage. That stage is fundamentally uncertain and is therefore also the critical point in the creative process. This type of process is not unique to origami. We may also think of scientific theories or musical compositions as being the end result of an increasingly determinate step-wise decision tree. Perhaps less obvious is that we may conceive of the entrepreneurial process as the development of ever-finer attribute combinations using resources that are a priori akin to a blank sheet of paper (see Chapter 8).

EQUILIBRIUM OR LONG CYCLES

Scholars with an interest in long-term economic and social development have often concluded that the development of diverse social or economic phenomena— including phenomena as different as gross domestic products, demographic pyramids and political power structures—exhibit long-term cyclical patterns. This is a recurrent idea in the intellectual history of the past three centuries. Hegel, Marx, Kondratieff, Jevons and Schumpeter were all early theorists of long-term cycles (see Schumpeter, 1954).

When economic statistics became more generally available by the end of the nineteenth century, this led to a concurrent increase in the number of such theories. One early example was the business cycle theory (Jevons, 1875) that focused on correlations between the frequency of sunspots and economic output and prices in Britain.

Schumpeter (1934) is one of the more influential theories about how long-term cycles accompany long-term economic development. Schumpeter's theory focuses on the psychological and social characteristics of entrepreneurial innovators and their role in development. The starting point is that general equilibrium (Schumpeter's "circular flow") entails the equalization of yields from equivalent production factors. When an economy approaches general equilibrium, there will therefore be no more actual or expected profits. This is not a desirable state of affairs to potential entrepreneurs since their objective is to earn profits. Hence Schumpeter (ibid.) views general equilibrium as a repellent rather than as an attractor. As soon as the economy makes its approach toward equilibrium, entrepreneurs will have an incentive to make use of existing extra-economic information and knowledge in a way that makes possible new innovations. In its Schumpeterian conception this implies profitable new combinations of pre-existing resources.

The Schumpeterian view is thus that general equilibrium is a condition that the production structure may temporarily approach, but it is never a stable condition. Since general equilibrium is strongly repulsive, the system assumes cyclical characteristics because of repeated cycles of disruptive disequilibrating innovations that attract swarms of equilibrating entrepreneurial imitators—although the equilibrating imitators move the system in the direction of a new and "higher" equilibrium than the preceding one.

Schumpeter (1942) extends the theory by considering politicians' preference for economic stability; politicians then become the anti-entrepreneurs.

If these two groups coexist under conditions of equal power, they will jointly cause a limit cycle, which determines the actual economic development trajectory of a society.

Schumpeter (ibid.) also contends that politicians are bound to become too powerful and numerous relative to the power and number of entrepreneurs. The limit cycle would then become confined to small swings in the proximity of general equilibrium. Such a society would have an inherent tendency to develop repressive traits and a stagnant general economic equilibrium.

Schumpeter (1934) is one of the main theories of entrepreneurship, which by its very nature forces the theorist to go beyond the confines of equilibrium constructs. As noted earlier, entrepreneurship aims at profits, and all dynamic—that is, entrepreneurial—profits have been competed away when the economy is in equilibrium. Schumpeter (1934) and Kirzner (1973) are the two main theories that relate entrepreneurial profits to equilibrium, but they reach conclusions that at first sight may seem to contradict each other. Schumpeter (1934) claims that entrepreneurship is disequilibrating, whereas Kirzner (1973) states that it moves the economic system in an equilibrating direction. But the differences between the two theories are more apparent than real.

Schumpeter (1934) uses a Walrasian "circular flow" as his starting point, which is the type of equilibrium with which early twentieth-century economists were most familiar. It is an economy in which households demand the same goods and supply the same production factors in each period; there is coordination of production and consumption plans. These features resemble later equilibrium models, but there are three key differences. In the "circular flow," people have given knowledge rather than perfect knowledge; different people interpret the same (exogenously given) information in different ways; and trades refer to the current period rather than to all future time periods. Hence there is room for a small minority of disruptive and innovative entrepreneurs who can see profit opportunities where duller minds stick to entrenched habits. Indeed, Schumpeter had a rather elitist view of society, in which entrepreneurial "captains of industry" were responsible for most of the material betterment of the masses.

So, the circular-flow equilibrium is in essence a suboptimal equilibrium of unreflective popular habits. Schumpeter (1934, p. 80) contends that, "the assumption that conduct is prompt and rational is in all cases a fiction. But it proves to be sufficiently near to reality, if things have had time to hammer logic into men." For Schumpeter, it is the role of the entrepreneur to step into this stagnant pool of plebeian monotony and, using his superior perception and leadership, to introduce new products or processes using already available technological knowledge. These entrepreneurial innovations have greater value and the entrepreneur is thus able to outbid traditional resource users. A disequilibrating "creative destruction" takes place, forever redirecting resources to more valuable uses. Entrepreneurs thus lead the development in the direction of a new and more efficient equilibrium as imitators "swarm" the market and gradually bid up resource prices while simultaneously engaging in output price competition. In the eventual new circular flow, factors are more valuable and consumer surpluses greater than in the abandoned old flow. So, there is an unending progression of cognitively limited equilibria involving gradually improving combinations of pre-existing resources.

Kirzner (1973) defines both entrepreneurship and equilibrium in different ways. Entrepreneurship is not the exclusive domain of a cognitively privileged elite; it is an everyday activity that normal people occasionally engage in. Like Schumpeter, the superior perception necessary to identify profit opportunities that others have missed plays a role here too. Kirznerian entrepreneurs are "alert" to profit opportunities such as those where a priori factor prices are lower than their a posteriori implicit prices as part of a profitable innovative output. But this is for Kirzner just one aspect of entrepreneurship. It is not the whole story. Much of it is incremental and rather commonplace. A profitable business start-up such as a conventional fast-food restaurant in a new location but with old recipes is entrepreneurship for Kirzner but not for Schumpeter. Likewise, someone who notices a higher-income employment opportunity in another country is exercising Kirznerian entrepreneurship (Andersson, 2005). This theoretical "democratization" of the notion of entrepreneurship means that a pre-existing circular flow must be abandoned; it is for Kirzner a type of behavior that everyone may engage in, and thus even ordinary people contribute to economic change from within the system.

When Kirzner (1973) describes entrepreneurial action as equilibrating, he does not refer to a Walrasian circular flow. His notion is much more in keeping with the spirit of the times in the late twentieth century, at which time most economists conceived of general equilibrium as implying both perfect information and perfect interpretation of that information. It is a theoretical utopia where every production technique is optimal, all possible goods have been innovated and everyone maximizes their utility in all future time periods, limited only by their resource endowments.

Kirzner's key point is that if someone finds a cheaper input or combines inputs in a way that commands a higher output price than previously, this will imply dissemination of more relevant *economic* knowledge in the market and thus more efficient resource use and overall market integration. The point is however not that general equilibrium is in any way achievable. According to Kirzner (1973; 1985), general equilibrium is impossible in practice, since the equilibrating entrepreneurial changes would then have to play themselves out within a static structure of unchanged preferences, unchanged technological knowledge and unchanged resource availabilities. And these structural conditions, which consist of typical exogenous variables, can and do change. We should also note that Kirzner's theory assumes a pure market economy with free entry and uncontested property rights. It is a theory of equilibrating entrepreneurial adjustment processes against the backdrop of a utopian equilibrium, which functions as a kind of hidden attractor that propels all successful entrepreneurial acts.

Unlike Schumpeter (1934), Kirzner (1973) focuses on dynamic micro phenomena but remains silent on the topic of macro cycles, which lie beyond its theoretical ambit. Nevertheless, the Kirznerian theory has considerable value as an implicit criticism of Schumpeter's explanation of business cycles. Entrepreneur-driven business cycles depend on the sociological assumption that the great majority of humans are passive (or even feckless) creatures of habit.

While it is easy to criticize Schumpeter's view of cycles, it does have the advantage of a comprehensible theoretical foundation. Most other theories have no foundation other than supposedly observed pattern regularities over time or far-fetched causal factors such as sunspot activity. From a mathematical point of view, it is much more likely that a dynamic system exhibits long-term cycles than that it would approach a globally stable general equilibrium. But even more probable is a dynamic system—with its multitude of interdependencies and other complexity—that is irregular and unpredictable in the sense of The Chaotic House.

THE CHAOTIC HOUSE

Essentially, the problem for ambitious economic forecasting and policy-making is associated with the difficulty of understanding and manipulating *dynamic complexity*. In this context, complexity refers to the set of dynamic non-linear interdependencies in the relevant system. To illuminate the meaning and consequences for predictability and controllability we make use of The Chaotic House as a metaphor.

Let us imagine a big house. It resembles other houses and has several entrances. A person enters through one of the doors. When she steps inside the house she notices that a window moves slightly to the left. When she takes another step, the ceiling moves downward. And an additional step opens one of the windows. When she moves around, the house is gradually being reshaped in various ways. Different experiments may teach her the interrelationship between her movements and the shape and serviceability of the house. She can then predict and influence her environment.

Let us now assume that another person enters the house through a second door. His arrival is unknown to the first person. The movements of the second person also influence the shape of the house. When he opens the door, it unexpectedly causes the floor to rise in the room in which the first person finds herself. And when she tries to counteract this change by her own actions, she cannot avoid influencing the shape of the doors, windows, ceiling and floor in both her and the second person's room. It is of course possible that the two people in the house get to know each other. They may then be able to gradually reveal the joint interdependencies between their movements and the shape of the house.

If we assume that a third person enters the house through a third door, we add another layer of complexity. Each additional person who gets into the house makes it more difficult to observe, predict and influence. Sooner rather than later, the interdependencies among all the people in the house make it utterly impossible to predict and know the exact shape of the house. The people who dwell in The Chaotic House will then have discovered the consequences of complex interdependencies. Complex situations remain unpredictable even if each and every dynamic relation is deterministic.

Neo-Keynesian theorists of social engineering such as Tinbergen (1954) and Theil (1964) were completely ignorant of the association between dynamic interdependencies and unpredictability and the attendant impossibility of effective socio-economic planning. None of them could conceive of a deterministic economic system that is unpredictable in principle, meaning that no innovations in modeling or computing technology *could ever* avoid the intrinsic unpredictability of the system. Even today, most of the "specialists" advising central banks and governments on the consequences of economic policies tend to disregard complexity and go far beyond the time frames of possible predictability when they present their deceptively precise econometric forecasts.

The logistic ordinary differential equation (4.1) is quite well behaved. From an arbitrary starting point, it converges smoothly to the stable equilibrium B. The process is quite different if the logistic equation is a *difference equation* in which the value of each period determines the variable value of its subsequent period:

$$p(t + 1) = r\, p(t)(1 - p(t)) \tag{4.2}$$

This equation is well behaved for small values of *r*. However, when *r* is equal to 3, *p* will no longer converge. Instead *p* will bifurcate and start oscillating between two values. Increasing *r* further means that *p* will bifurcate in periods two, eight and 16; an *r* greater than 4 induces chaotic behavior of *p*.

SLOW AND FAST SYSTEMS—MARKETS, POLITICS AND ECOLOGY

Realistic models of dynamic interdependencies are frequently complex. The Chaotic House is one such example. Another example is the very simple model of the interdependence between crime and punishment. The most typical outcome of a dynamic process is neither stable equilibrium, nor regular long or short cycles. The generic or typical outcome is instead incomprehensible and unpredictable swings. Sustainable dynamic processes—that is, processes that survive in the long run—do however tend to be substantially more ordered. In Chapter 6 we discuss an example first introduced by Brian Arthur.

Even if there are chaotic fluctuations in the day-to-day values of stock market indices these fluctuations tend to cancel out in the year-on-year statistics that prevail at the macroeconomic level. In most countries, the gross domestic product does not change dramatically from one year to the next. Likewise, inflation, growth and unemployment rates tend to fluctuate within reasonably predictable national bounds. In a discussion about chaos theory and its consequences for national macroeconomic aggregates the economist Trygve Haavelmo remarked in a private discussion with one of the authors of this book that, "statistical yearbooks are published once a year and contain few surprises." Why is it that the generic outcome of chaos is superseded by reasonably stable macroeconomic magnitudes?

The physicist Hermann Haken (1978) has proposed a theory of the long-term sustainability of dynamic systems. It is based on the interrelationships between ordering entities which change extremely slowly and which guide the adaptive processes of a great number of rapidly changing variables. Haken's theory enables us to develop formal models that deal with the relations between a stable and collective "arena" and the economic and cultural "games" of society.

Because virtually all firms perceive the physical infrastructure and the level of knowledge to be more or less constant, it becomes possible for the market to approach a type of equilibrium. It is related to the fact that the substitutability of various goods may stabilize in predictable patterns that jointly contribute to a predictable aggregate level of output.

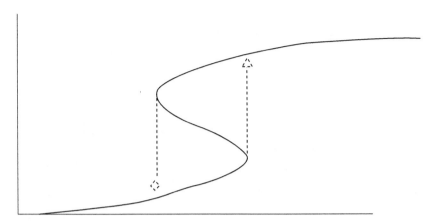

*Figure 4.8   A cusp bifurcation leading to a jump to a higher-level
                 equilibrium at a critical relative level of technological
                 knowledge and/or infrastructure*

It is of course true that neither the physical infrastructure nor the level
of knowledge is set in stone. These factors also grow, although in normal
times at an extremely slow pace. Even if it is possible to conceive of the
system as having the same structural features and structural equilibria in
two consecutive (short) periods, systems of this type will sooner or later
reach a point where changes to the arena have substantial consequences.
At a specific point, the system reaches a critical combination of knowledge and infrastructure that will make it leave its balanced and seemingly
unchangeable structure. A new, almost revolutionary, restructuring occurs
when the normal equilibrium conditions no longer apply. The vertical
arrow at the critical bifurcation point in Figure 4.8 illustrates this stage
of the development path toward a much greater demand for a good that
depends on the accumulated levels of knowledge and infrastructure.

Conversely, the market demand for a good might collapse if the producers of the good cut down on their research and development spending,
while at the same time producers of a substitute intensify their accumulation of technological knowledge. The collapse of both Kodak and Polaroid
after competing Asian and European firms developed IT-enabled photog-
raphy is an example of such a negative bifurcation.

The development before the bifurcation point may of course also be
"somewhat chaotic," but in that case the "chaos" will be confined to relatively narrow limits, in which case the almost unchanging arena conditions
determine the limits.

ON THE STRAIGHT LINE, THE POINT, EUCLIDIAN SPACE AND THE FRACTAL ROOM

For the ancient Greek philosophers and scientists, mathematics was one of many logical general-purpose tools, which could be used both for existential speculations and for practical problem solving. Mathematics, which at that time mainly consisted of geometry, could be used to solve seemingly insoluble problems. It was for example possible to use geometry to calculate the shortest distance across a lake. All one had to do was to construct a right-angled triangle and use Pythagoras' theorem to calculate the hypotenuse, which would equal the distance across the lake. The geometry of a plane dealt with such two-dimensional calculations. Regional scientists and spatial economists have formulated most of their theories using Euclidian one- or two-dimensional space. In architecture and construction engineering, it is necessary to use an additional dimension and its more elaborate three-dimensional geometry includes the three dimensions of width, length and height.

The point, the movable straight line in combination with the point for the construction of the circle, and other concepts eventually resulted in an exhaustive set of theorems for two-dimensional and three-dimensional geometry. Methods for projecting three-dimensional figures onto a two-dimensional plane also appeared in the fourteenth century.

Euclidean geometry has proven very durable. The first substantial addition to this geometry only occurred as late as the seventeenth century. At that time, mathematicians introduced the fourth dimension; the dimension of time. They introduced the conception of time-space in order to make astrophysics more credible: earlier physicists had shown that Euclidean geometry did not work well for predicting processes in the universe. The joint consideration of time and space needed a four-dimensional continuum and a break with the linearity assumptions of Euclidean geometry.

But the elaboration of dimensionality would continue until it reached a critical bifurcation three centuries later. The uncle of the Polish-French-American physicist and mathematician Benoit Mandelbrot once recommended his nephew to focus on developing the French mathematician Gaston Julia's thoughts about the dimensions of mathematics. Mandelbrot later in a conversation (with one of the authors of this book) said that he for a long time was opposed to these seemingly bizarre ideas, which were entirely at odds with traditional mathematical assumptions. Not until several decades after receiving the advice of his uncle did Mandelbrot encounter phenomena that did not fit into Euclidean or any of the proposed four-dimensional spaces. His encounter with these phenomena occurred while he was performing computer simulations as an in-house mathematician for IBM. The motions on the computer screen seemed to exhibit patterns, but these patterns did not bear any resemblance to soft and continuous curves. Abrupt swings were instead prevalent, and one of the most important conventional characteristics was entirely absent: the possibility to draw unique tangents to the curves.

This might seem a minor problem, but this is not so. Most models in use in the quantitative natural and social sciences necessitate a precise measure of how an incremental change in the value of an explanatory variable causes a small change in the value of a dependent variable. An example is the measurement of the change in the velocity of a vehicle as a result of a slight increase in the supply of fuel per unit of time. The tangent to the curve that explains the relationship between fuel supply and velocity is a measure of a local stimulus-response characteristic of the vehicle.

The differential calculus as developed by Newton and Leibniz established the foundation for a revolution in science and engineering that builds on the assumption that functions have locally unambiguous characteristics. What Mandelbrot found in his simulations was that the possibility of drawing tangents was not just absent in certain locations but in every location. The Swedish mathematician Helge von Koch (1904) had encountered similar phenomena in his analysis of snow crystals, but the scientific community had regarded these findings as no more than an anomalous curiosity. In contrast, Mandelbrot envisioned the construction of a new mathematical paradigm as the end result of his similarly anomalous observations. He came to regard his new so-called "fractal mathematics" as a possible theoretical foundation for analyzing biological and social phenomena.

One of the earliest studied examples of a fractal geometric shape is the snowflake (von Koch, ibid.). A snowflake consists of regularly broken line segments. The perception of these line segments is that they become ever shorter and ever more numerous as a result of increasing magnification.

NEW DIMENSIONS

We feel at home in four-dimensional space. Two of these dimensions are necessary to give us building lots, football pitches and maps. Our dwellings and offices require a third dimension. When we travel, we need four dimensions: time becomes as important as the three-dimensional perception of unchanging space.

The line, the square and the cube are representatives of the three dimensions that Euclid so scrupulously analyzed. It is possible to decompose

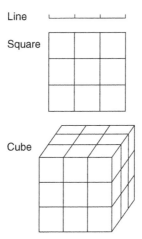

Figure 4.9   Euclidean geometry

each of these geometrical entities into a number of equal parts. Figures 4.9 and 4.10 illustrate such decomposition into congruent parts.

Von Koch (1904) proposes a new geometric construction, building on the same idea about congruence that applies to straight lines, squares and cubes. He starts with a triangle; successive subdivisions allow von Koch to eventually attain an image of a snowflake as in Figure 4.10.

Table 4.1 shows how differences in the number of segments make fractal entities such as snowflakes much more complex than conventional geometric ones such as cubes and squares.

Figures 4.9 and 4.10 represent the general function that the number of segments equals 1 / (reduction factor)^D. If the number of segments is three and the reduction factor is 1/3, it follows that the dimension (D) must be one (the case of the line). Similarly, the dimension must be three if the number of segments is 27 and the reduction factor is 1/3 (that is, the cube).

If we apply the same equation to Koch's figure we find that

$$4 = \frac{1}{(1/3)^D} \tag{4.3}$$

The only D that approximately solves this equation is 1.2619. This strange broken or fractal dimension is the dimension of Koch's figure. This is one starting point from which to approach fractal geometry. Rivers tend to have dimensions of between 1.2 and 1.4. In the same way, there are fractal dimensions for organic bodies, mountains and other natural formations

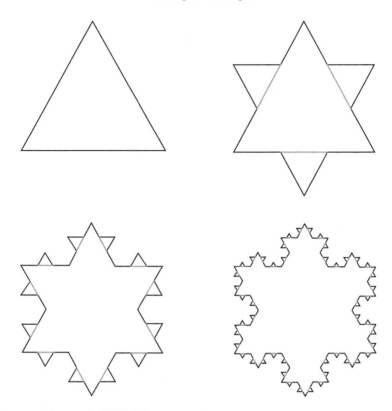

Source: Peitgen et al. (1992/2004).

Figure 4.10   Stepwise construction of a fractal structure

Table 4.1   Segmentation and reduction factors of Euclidean and fractal space

Entity	Number of segments	Reduction factor
Line	3	1/3
Square	$3^2 = 9$	1/3
Cube	$3^3 = 27$	1/3
Koch's figures	$4^1 = 4$	1/3
	$4^2 = 16$	1/9
	$4^3 = 64$	1/27
	4^k	$1/3^k$

that lie between 2 and 3. Another example consists of transport networks ranging from large-scale to progressively finer links all the way down to the paths that animals create. The interior of the human body might seem like a three-dimensional object, but it is a fractal structure with the network of blood vessels serving as a pertinent example.

A large-scale example of fractal geometry is the British coastline. We all know that it is possible to contain Britain within an ellipse with a certain minimum circumference and area. At the same time, it is possible to show that a careful measurement of the circumference of Britain is an infinite and thus Sisyphean task. A yardstick with a length of 10 meters will yield one definite metric magnitude. A one-meter yardstick will however result in a different and greater metric distance. Reducing the length of the yardstick to one decimeter will result in an even greater estimate of the circumference of the coastline. It will in fact approach infinity if we were to continue the process toward an infinitesimally small measuring device. Apparently, it is possible to store an infinite object in a finite container. Mandelbrot (1977) draws the even bolder conclusion that a dynamic process that differs from conventional scientific dynamic models must have generated natural phenomena with fractal dimensions.

Interestingly, very simple discrete dynamic models can give rise to fractal results. The first interactive steps of the following simple model cause an entirely unpredictable and chaotic pattern:

$$z_{t+1} = az_t^2 + c \qquad (4.4)$$

Let us now use this recursive model for an experiment. We will start with different values for the *complex number c*. If the process diverges to infinity after a couple of hundreds of iterations, we will disregard it. If it does not diverge, we will show the combined value of a and c in a diagram. In this example, all combinations of a and c that do not result in divergence form a remarkable picture: The Mandelbrot set (Figure 4.11).

The patterns in the Mandelbrot set repeat themselves on an ever-smaller scale. If we create a similar dynamic model in three-dimensional space, it results in a structure that resembles a cauliflower. In other words, the structure will look the same regardless of the level of disaggregation.

It has now become possible to use fractal geometry to generate a multitude of forms, which sometimes can easily be mistaken for fractal natural phenomena such as coastlines, snowflakes or clouds. An example of a commercial application of such a dynamic system is the creation of credible landscapes in science fiction films. In these films, computer-generated fractal landscapes embed imagined Euclidean spaceships.

In earlier times, scientists conceived of the human being as a sophisticated

Figure 4.11   The Mandelbrot set with its self-similarity at all levels of resolution

machine with construction principles akin to those of classical physics. It has now become possible to show that humans or animals could not even theoretically be constructed with Euclidean geometry. Dynamic systems in fractal geometric spaces generate the nervous system, the cardiovascular network, the brain and other organs in the human body. This is the only way in which a finite body can contain organs with such extreme levels of complexity.

Attempts to use fractal geometry in economics have so far met with limited success. The most influential applications of fractal structures to real-world economic observations are Mandelbrot's analysis of capital markets, to which we shall return in Chapter 7.

SIMPLE RULES CAN GENERATE COMPLEX STRUCTURES

The technological advances of the past decades have transformed the opportunities for exploring the new dynamic theories. Increasingly powerful computers have become virtual laboratories for simulation, long-term optimization and other dynamic experiments involving large-scale economic, social and biological systems. Early computer models were often oversimplified into linear relations because this was necessary in order to achieve calculable results. But the increasing capacity of computers has made it possible to test the dynamic consequences of strong interdependencies.

The biologist Jean-Louis Deneubourg (Deneubourg et al., 1990), who was involved in Ilya Prigogine's research program in Brussels, has demonstrated how two extremely simple behavioral mechanisms explains the dynamic growth of complex termite hills. The instinct to produce building materials and the propensity to imitate the neighboring termite are in his model sufficient behavioral mechanisms. The ability of simple interacting dynamic mechanisms to generate extremely complex patterns is the crucial new insight from fractal modeling and chaos theory. Theories and their associated metaphors will probably move in the direction of simple assumptions having complex dynamic consequences in accordance with the northeast corner of Table 4.2.

Perhaps our institutions, organizations and even cities have reached their complexity by adhering to a small number of rules, which would make these dynamics similar to biological and ecological growth processes. Maybe it is even possible to trace the emergence of a city to a few behavioral rules involving the creation and maintenance of capital and imitation of neighbors, all of which are subject to institutional constraints, which are negative rules—"do not do A"—rather than the more prescriptive "do A."

Table 4.2   How different theories connect processes with outcomes

Causal Processes	Outcomes	
	Simple	Complex
Simple	Dialectical materialism; Mechanical engineering; Social engineering	Biology; Ecology; Spontaneous order theory
Complex	Classical theoretical physics; Four-dimensional geometry; Neoclassical equilibrium theory	Anthropology; History; Sociology

In economics as well as in social theory there is however a minority intellectual tradition that prefers the use of *simple process/complex outcome* theories over the widespread twentieth-century preference for *complex process/simple outcome* models. We are referring to the view that markets, science and democracies are best analyzed as spontaneous-order processes rather than as outcome equilibria.

The modern version of spontaneous order theory is most strongly associated with the work of Friedrich Hayek (1964/1967; 1973) and Michael Polanyi (1962), although Adam Smith's (1776/2012) "invisible hand" is a clear antecedent of this way of viewing the interplay of individual behavior and social consequences. The idea of a spontaneous order consists of three parts. First, there is no individual or organizational designer of the resultant complex structure, and yet the structure exhibits order and stability. Second, there are rules of behavior with which all participants in a particular order must comply. Third, there is order-specific feedback consisting of a systemic resource that participants wish to accumulate. Examples of systemic resources include the role of money in markets and votes in democracies (diZerega, 1989).

A limited number of rules as well as feedback that rewards order-advancing actions among interdependent equals can create very complex structures, both as regards the diversity and number of actors and the network that connects participating individuals and organizations. Even more significant is the fact that two participants in the same spontaneous order may have strictly contradictory aims in a more general non-systemic sense, and yet both may succeed in systemic terms. For example, *Free to Choose* and *Capital in the Twenty-First Century* may both have been profitable books that enabled their authors to accumulate the systemic resource of money, but this does not imply that the world views of Milton Friedman and Thomas Piketty are compatible.

According to Polanyi (1962), science is also an order where simple rules guide interdependent participants and where the sum of all individual actions creates a structure— "the Republic of Science"—that is at the same time complex, orderly and unplanned. The systemic resource is scientific reputation, which reflects the prevailing criteria that jointly make up "scientific opinion." Polanyi's reasoning of the structure of science bears quoting at length, because he unintentionally shows how its behavioral rules share certain structural similarities with termite hills, albeit at a much higher level of sophistication:

> No single scientist has a sound understanding of more than a tiny fraction of the total domain of science. How can an aggregate of such specialists possibly form a joint opinion? . . . In seeking the answer to this question, we shall

discover yet another organisational principle that is essential for the control of a multitude of independent scientific initiatives. This principle is based on the fact that, while scientists can admittedly exercise competent judgment only over a small part of science, they can usually judge an area adjoining their own special studies that is broad enough to include some fields on which other scientists have specialised. We thus have a considerable degree of overlapping between the areas over which a scientist can exercise a sound critical judgment. And, of course, each scientist who is a member of a group of overlapping competences will also be a member of other groups of the same kind, so that the whole of science will be covered by chains and networks of overlapping neighbourhoods. . ..This network is the seat of scientific opinion. Scientific opinion is an opinion not held by any single human mind, but one which, split into thousands of fragments, is held by a multitude of individuals, each of whom endorses the other's opinion at second hand, by relying on the consensual chains which link him to all the others through a sequence of overlapping neighbourhoods. (Polanyi, 1962)

THE CHOICE OF THEORIES AND MODELS IN ECONOMICS

It is obvious from the short discussion in this and the preceding chapter that economic theories and models differ in their representations of time and space. Economists have a great deal of leeway when they decide which representations to employ. Whenever possible, we believe there are strong reasons for selecting continuous representations. We have also argued that explicit use of multiple time dimensions has the advantage of drawing attention to the contrasting speeds at which different types of change occur. Table 4.3 shows the different ways in which a few representative economists have tended to theorize about time and space.

A point of caution is in order. The previous discussion concerns the problem of choosing a *representation of time and space* in a theory or model. Time and space may also appear at another level as variables of choice *within* a theory or model. A consumer or producer may for example choose between cars with long or short duration of use. A producer may have to decide the *duration of storage* of cheese or wine. Managers make decisions about how much space to use for a housing project or a banana plantation. In the creation of logistical systems there are unavoidable decisions regarding the allocation of vehicles to roads. In the public sector decisions on infrastructure imply simultaneous timing and land use choices with some consequences that are immediate, as well as others that accrue in the distant future.

Theorists therefore face choices regarding the treatment of spatiotemporal factors at two different levels:

Table 4.3   Spatiotemporal theory and modeling choices

Space	Time			
	Static	Periods	Continuous	Different timescales
Implicit	Keynesian macro model; Walrasian equilibrium	v. Neumann growth model	Solow growth model; Leontief growth model	New Institutional Economics; Spontaneous orders; Andersson (1985a)
Regions	Trade theory: Ricardo; Ohlin	Variational inequality model: Nagurney	Neoclassical multiregional growth models: Barro; Sala i Martin	Combined institutional and accessibility model: Andersson et al. (2015)
Continuous: One-dimensional	Monocentric model: v. Thünen	v. Thünen-based models	–	–
Continuous: Two-dimensional	Weber model; Beckmann/ Puu	–	Spatial dynamic equilibrium: Puu	–

1. The first choice concerns how to handle the *dimensions* of time and space in a theory or model.
2. The second choice is about time and space *variables* within a theory or model.

We shall return to this two-stage decision problem and how they affect our understanding of economic development over time and across space in subsequent chapters.

NOTE

1. A matrix difference equation can represent this type of socially interactive consumption: $c(t+1) = Cc(t) + c(0)$; where C is a matrix of consumer interactivity coefficients and $c(0)$ is the initial consumption pattern. If we assume that $c(t+1) = c(t)$, then

$c = (\mathbf{I} - \mathbf{C})^{-1} c(0)$. Moreover, if the principal minors of the matrix $(\mathbf{I} - \mathbf{C})$ are all positive (the so-called "Hawkins–Simon condition"), the equilibrium consumption vector c is non-negative. This vector of equilibrium consumption is approached via a convergent multiplier series.

5. Time in the microeconomics of consumption

TIME AND THE CHOICE OF DURATION OF LIFE

Time is a central aspect of every person's life. There are several long-term decisions that influence the "normal" short-term decisions that an individual makes as a consumer, saver or investor in material or human capital. Among the most important longer-term decisions are various lifestyle choices that influence the duration of life. Living in very poor circumstances has been the historical norm, and low-income countries are still associated with relatively short life expectancies. Preston (1975) hypothesizes that there is a strong causal relation between the per capita gross domestic product of a country and its average life expectancy. Figure 5.1 illustrates the so-called "Preston curve" for 2012. Studies by Deaton (2006) and others show that the positive impact on the mean life expectancy of a general increase in per capita income is smaller at high-income levels, and that individual decisions are more important for health outcomes than the development level in the richest group of countries.

Deaton claims that knowledge gains cause long-term increases in income and health outcomes. Differences in longevity among countries at a similar income level depend on differences in institutional quality; these institutional differences are only partly reflected in income differences.

The Preston curve is composed of one part that reflects the impact of real per capita income as well as an intercept that—according to Oeppen and Vaupel (2002)—is increasing over time. A reasonable assumption, consistent with our general analysis of infrastructure and development, would focus on the impact of *institutions*, *networks* and *public knowledge* on life expectancies.

NETWORKS

During the nineteenth and early twentieth centuries, it was improvements in sanitation and better water supply networks that were the most important factors behind the increase in life expectancy. This in some places was

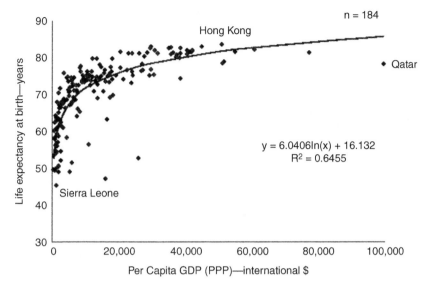

Source: euromonitor.com.

Figure 5.1   Preston curve as estimated on a cross-section of nations in 2012

supplemented by improved general accessibility to primary health care. These factors caused a steady decline in early and mid-life mortality, which is chiefly caused by various infectious diseases.

INSTITUTIONS

Among the worst reasons for a decline in life expectancies are famines and persistent hunger, as experienced in India during World War II and in sub-Saharan regions in more recent times. There are several hypotheses or theory-based explanations that focus on the role of legal institutions. The most noted explanations are associated with the economists Amartya Sen (1976; 1982), Angus Deaton and Daron Acemoglu. In short, Deaton (1976) as well as Acemoglu and Robinson (2012) claim that a combination of non-inclusive states and insufficient state capacity cause poverty, low levels of human capital and persistent hunger.

Sen (1982) claims that insufficient supply—as hypothesized by Malthus and his followers—is not a typical cause of famines. Instead, it is a break-down of the "entitlement structure." According to Sen's model, a person or family has an "entitlement set" that consists of goods that people can acquire by transforming private assets and labor resources via "exchange entitlement mappings." Sen (1982, p. 2) defines the entitlement set as consisting of four subsets:

1. production-based entitlement (growing food);
2. trade-based entitlement (buying food);
3. own-labor entitlement (working for food); and
4. inheritance and transfer entitlement (being given food by others).

Sen's major claim is that geographically related groups of people will experience famine or persistent hunger if any one of these entitlements has drastically declined because of political or other institutional failures.

KNOWLEDGE OF BIOLOGY AND MEDICINE

The development of medical scientific knowledge has been rapid since the late nineteenth century. A major cause of the increase in life expectancies has been research into treatments of infectious diseases, starting from the seminal work undertaken by Louis Pasteur and Robert Koch, who were responsible for the establishment of "the germ theory of disease." This enabled Pasteur to develop vaccines against cholera, anthrax and rabies in the two last decades of the nineteenth century. Between 1890 and 1930, vaccines were developed against tetanus, diphtheria, sleeping sickness, pertussis (whooping cough) and tuberculosis. A second major scientific breakthrough was Alexander Fleming's discovery of penicillin, which motivated massive spending on research that focused on antibiotics as well as on the risks of bacterial multi-resistance. The eradication of many infectious diseases and associated changes in morbidity and mortality patterns eventually resulted in a reorientation of medical research in the direction of therapies for diseases that primarily affect the elderly, such as cancer and cardiovascular diseases.

INCOME, EDUCATION AND LIFE EXPECTANCY

An individual's life expectancy is partly the effect of the general standard of living, including genetic, social and other environmental factors. It is also partly the effect of increasing variation of individual consumption decisions with increasing income. An interesting health-related empirical regularity is the combination of a positive income and negative education elasticity of tobacco consumption (Andersson, 1985a).

A reasonable hypothesis is that this regularity also holds for other goods with negative expected life expectancy effects (intriguingly, the same combination holds for the effects of women's income and education on childbearing).

The perception of risk is an important decision variable. Returning to our tobacco example, it is clear that the decision to smoke tobacco reduces the consumer's life expectancy, other things being equal. While the effect is substantial, it is interesting to note that smokers and non-smokers alike nowadays *overestimate* the actual health risk:

> The public's assessment of the risk of premature mortality from smoking is 0.51. That figure exceeds the available estimates of the death risk based on reports by the U.S. Surgeon General and the National Cancer Institute, which range from 0.18 to 0.36. But do people realize the extent of life that might be lost because of smoking? Scientific estimates of that loss are in the range of six to eight years. However, the public's risk perception is greater, as men believe the life expectancy loss is 10.1 years and women believe it is 14.8 years. (Viscusi and Aldy, 2003, p. 59)

For activities that are less risky than tobacco smoking, such as air travel or terrorism events, people tend to overestimate risks to an astounding extent. The only impactful lifestyle choice where there is a consistent tendency to *underestimate* the mortality risk is the choice to drive a car every day (Andersson and Lundborg, 2007), which is in fact much closer to the mortality risk of daily smoking than to the risk of being killed by terrorists or dying in a plane crash.

While most people are aware of—and in most cases overestimate—actual mortality risks, some people smoke and most people drive, fly and visit potential terrorist targets. People make at least some choices that increase their perceived risk of death to attain other objectives, leading to higher levels of expected utility. Conversely, sometimes individuals make decisions that reduce their risk of death, typically by avoiding consumption choices that are associated with high-perceived health risks. A decision to change one's diet from one that is rich in red meat to one centered on polyunsaturated fats, fruits and fish is one way to reduce one's risk of premature death from coronary diseases.

Formally, the expected utility of a consumption choice depends directly on the consumption of health-improving goods as well as on goods that are health neutral or health reducing. But the effect on the expected utility also depends on the expected duration of life, which partly depends on the consumption of health-affecting goods. This implies that the expected utility depends both directly and indirectly on the composition of the consumption bundle. The indirect effects are further reinforced if there is a positive effect of health-improving consumption on the individual's lifetime income.

Table 5.1   *Top ten occupations with the highest work-related mortality*
                rates and the general homicide rate; annual deaths per 100,000
                full-time equivalent workers, 2011

Occupation	Number of deaths	Mortality rate
Fishers and related fishing workers	40	121.2
Logging workers	64	102.4
Aircraft pilots and flight engineers	72	57.0
Refuse and recyclable material collectors	34	41.2
Roofers	56	31.8
Structural iron and steel workers	16	26.9
Farmers, ranchers and other agricultural managers	260	25.3
Drivers/sales workers and truck drivers	759	24.0
Electrical power-line installers and repairers	27	20.3
Taxi drivers and chauffeurs	63	19.7
All workers	4,609	3.5
Homicide rate (per 100,000 population)	14,610	4.7

Source: US Bureau of Labor Statistics (2012); Bureau of Justice Statistics (2013).

But eating, drinking, smoking, exercise and drug habits are not the only lifestyle choices that influence life expectancy. Educational and occupational choices can also have a substantial impact, as can the choice of marital status, social activities and geographical location. Table 5.1 shows the ten most dangerous occupational choices in the United States, in terms of work-related mortality risks.

Table 5.1 hints at the relationship between spatially mobile occupations and the increased risk of work-related fatal accidents. Most of the risky occupations have above-average proportions of young male workers, which is exactly the same group that is most overrepresented among homicide victims (as well as among perpetrators).

Why do some people choose dangerous jobs when other jobs are available? Why do some people choose to work on an oil platform in the North Sea when they could work as janitors in Aberdeen or Stavanger? To answer these questions, we should consider the relations among wage rates, risks, attitudes to risk and educational attainment. Generally, men tend to be less risk-averse than women, and young men tend to be less risk-averse than older men. We should therefore expect the average young male to be disproportionately attracted to dangerous occupations, given that all workers receive the same risk-adjusted wage.

John Maynard Keynes famously noted that we are all dead in the

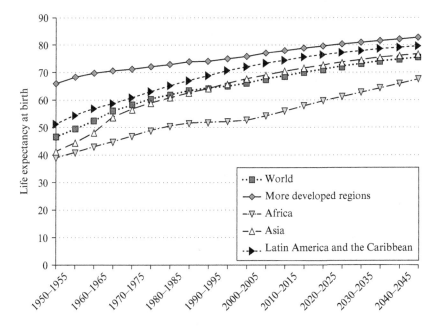

Source: United Nations (2008).

Figure 5.2   Life expectancy at birth by world region

long run. Every human being has a finite life expectancy, but this finite time period has been increasing in most parts of the world. Globally, the increase in life expectancy averages between three and four years per generation, which corresponds to a year-on-year increase of 0.6 percent. Figure 5.2 shows the projected increase over a period of 80 years in five world regions.

The increases in longevity had in 2013 led to life expectancies at birth in excess of 81.5 years in 20 countries. Table 5.2 shows male, female and overall period life expectancies in the top 10 countries with population sizes greater than 300,000.

The country-specific life expectancies in Table 5.2 are so-called "period life expectancies," which means that age-specific mortality rates are those of the period in question. In this case, it amounts to an assumption that the age-specific rates in 2013 will apply over the entire life cycle of a person born in that same year. This is not realistic at all. It is more likely that age-specific mortality rates will continue to fall, as they have for the past 100 years.

Oeppen and Vaupel (2002) present long-run historical trends using very

*Table 5.2   Top ten countries with longest period life expectancies at birth,
              2013*

Rank	Country	Overall life expectancy	Male life expectancy	Female life expectancy
1	Japan	84.6	82.0	87.3
2	Singapore	84.0	82.0	87.0
3	Hong Kong	83.8	82.0	85.6
4	Iceland	83.3	81.4	85.2
5	Italy	83.1	80.4	85.8
6	Australia	83.0	80.5	85.5
6	Sweden	83.0	81.4	84.6
8	Switzerland	82.8	80.4	85.4
9	Canada	82.5	80.4	84.6
9	Spain	82.5	79.5	85.0

Source: World Health Organization (2014).

long time series of observations from six European countries, the United
States and a year-specific recorded global maximum. Figure 5.3 shows the
evolution of life expectancies over a period of up to 170 years.

The problem with forecasting future reductions is that such forecasts
are intrinsically uncertain, since they reflect as yet unknown advances in
medical science as well as unknown future lifestyle choices. Even so, the
Office of National Statistics in the United Kingdom has attempted to estimate "cohort life expectancy at birth," thereby forecasting future declines
in age-specific mortality rates. For males born in the United Kingdom in
2010, the period life expectancy at birth was 78.5 years, but the estimated
male cohort life expectancy ranged from a lower-bound estimate of 81.0
years to a higher-bound one of 102.5 years, with a central projection of
90.2 years (Office of National Statistics, 2011).

A male life expectancy of 90.2 years may seem high, but current period
life expectancies of some population subgroups suggest that the estimate
is realistic. As an illustration, Table 5.3 gives the 20 highest ethnicity-and-
state-specific period life expectancies (both genders) in the United States
in 2010. It is interesting to note that Asian Americans—most of whom
are of Chinese, Filipino, Indian, Vietnamese or Korean extraction—had
life expectancies (in 2010) that exceeded those of Singapore and Hong
Kong (in 2013) in 22 out of 31 states with sizable Asian American populations (the total Asian American population was 17.3 million in the United
States in 2010). It is likely that the higher life expectancy among Americans
of Asian descent as compared with other groups is at least partly tied

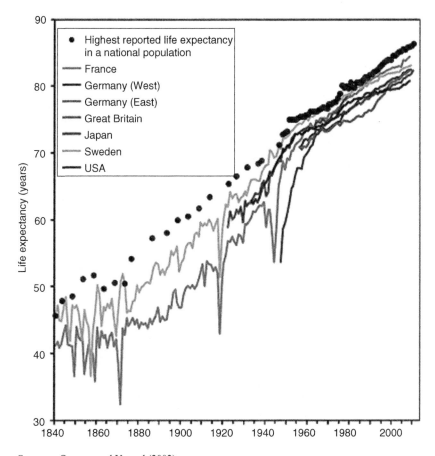

Source: Oeppen and Vaupel (2002).

Figure 5.3   Period life expectancy at birth in seven countries, 1840–2010

to dietary habits. Only 11.6 percent of Asian Americans were obese (BMI>30) in 2010, which is less than a third of the rates of white or black Americans (Center for Disease Control and Prevention, 2010).

Interestingly, the life expectancy of residents in Shanghai, China, was as high as 80.2 years for men and 85.2 years for women in 2013, which means that China's most developed urban region had attained health outcomes that were on par with Canada and Switzerland (Zhou et al., 2016). Apparently, a low obesity rate (about 6.9%) and very low rates of violent deaths (homicides and suicides) more than offset the effects of what are by Western standards a high male smoking rate and a high level of air

Table 5.3 Top 20 state-and-ethnicity-specific period life expectancies and
size of state-and-ethnicity-specific populations, United States,
2010

Rank	State	Ethnicity	Life expectancy	Population size
1	Connecticut	Asian	92.4	157,000
1	Arizona	Asian	92.4	231,000
3	New Jersey	Asian	91.8	795,000
3	Colorado	Asian	91.8	186,000
5	Massachusetts	Asian	91.6	394,000
6	Illinois	Asian	90.7	669,000
7	New York	Asian	90.1	1,579,000
8	Maryland	Asian	89.9	370,000
9	Michigan	Asian	89.8	290,000
9	Nevada	Hispanic	89.8	717,000
11	Georgia	Asian	89.0	365,000
12	Texas	Asian	88.8	1,111,000
13	Virginia	Asian	88.3	522,000
13	Pennsylvania	Asian	88.3	186,000
15	Nevada	Asian	88.2	243,000
16	Illinois	Hispanic	88.0	2,028,000
17	Massachusetts	Hispanic	87.4	628,000
18	New Jersey	Hispanic	87.0	1,555,000
19	Washington	Asian	86.7	604,000
20	California	Asian	86.6	5,557,000

Source: US Census of Population (2010).

pollution. Among the leading causes of death, Shanghai generally exhibits lower age-specific mortality rates than the Chinese average, with the exceptions of lung cancer among men and Alzheimer's disease among women.

Mortality among the oldest age groups has declined almost everywhere in the Americas, East Asia and Europe. This long-run trend elicited the following comments in an official publication of the US Department of Health and Human Services:

> The progressive increase in survival in these oldest age groups was not anticipated by demographers, and it raises questions about how high the average life expectancy can realistically rise and about the potential length of the human lifespan. While some experts assume that life expectancy must be approaching an upper limit, data on life expectancies between 1840 and 2007 show a steady increase averaging about three months of life per year. (National Institutes of Health, 2014, no page numbers)

Table 5.4   The "post-materialist" transformation of the value structure

Materialist values (industrialism)	Post-materialist values (post-industrialism)
Nationalism	Cosmopolitanism or individualism
Collective religion or Marxism	Individual religious choice or agnosticism
Top-down hierarchies	Bottom-up "flat" interactivity
Static productivity	Creativity (dynamic productivity)
Resource exploitation	Resource cultivation
Solidarity/brotherhood	Tolerance

THE DEMOGRAPHICS OF THE VALUE STRUCTURE

In the 1970s the political scientist Ronald Inglehart (1977) predicted a "silent revolution," as rising incomes and an increased sense of security would augur in a shift from materialist to "post-materialist" values. This would be a cohort effect, whereby younger generations with better education and little experience of material deprivation would give priority to softer quality-of-life goals over traditional concerns such as raising economic growth or combating crime. In the long run, Inglehart contended, these new post-materialist cohorts would become the new majority that would shape the political agenda in all parts of the developed world. The transformation from an old industrial, materialist society toward a new post-industrial, post-materialist one would entail a shift in values as in Table 5.4.

There is a strong empirical tendency for the youngest cohorts in the countries that industrialized in the nineteenth century to have the highest levels of post-materialism, as measured by three World Values Survey questions. This tendency obviously supports Inglehart's (1997) main hypothesis, which also has been used to explain the much higher levels of post-materialism among the oldest cohorts in the West as compared with the same cohorts in rich East Asian countries such as Japan and South Korea. We shall return to the "infrastructure of values" in later chapters, in which we also discuss some of the limitations of Inglehart's approach.

We should however at this point note the implication of Inglehart's hypothesis on future consumption habits. Table 5.4 alludes to a shift from imitative to innovative consumption choices as well as more generally from one-size-fits-all toward creative experiments. Such a shift would seem to imply a continued increase in the variety of goods on offer and a continued acceleration of product life cycles. On the production side, the corresponding changes would then be increasing product differentiation and market segmentation among profit-seeking firms and the spread of practices that promote "continuous innovation."

The main caveat is that this culture shift is conditional on positive economic growth. In contrast, economic crises and stagnation would cause the relevant cohorts to adopt values that are *more* materialist than those of their predecessors (Inglehart, 1997, claims that such "backward" shifts had at that point been observed among the youngest adult cohorts in Russia and South Africa).

THE CHANGING TIME BUDGET AND THE LIFE CYCLE

People can use their time in different ways, influencing the perceived utility that they themselves derive, as well as members of their households and—in most cases less dramatically—society at large. An unusually talented individual may have inherited a great deal of money, which enables him to spend his time eating, drinking and sleeping, with unremarkable effects on the lives of others. Or he may choose to develop his specific talents and have a lasting positive impact on countless others, as was the case with those who became famous as great creative "geniuses": think of the lasting impact of the creative outputs of Newton, Mozart or Einstein.

The most important income-generating activity is time spent working. In the nineteenth century, most people in what is now the industrialized world had to work about 3,000 hours per year for about 50 years. With a life expectancy of about 70 years for those who survived their first year, these people had to devote a quarter of their life to work. About 40 percent of their lives would be spent sleeping, eating or preparing meals. Perhaps they would spend 15 or 20 percent on other unavoidable household chores such as raising numerous children and cleaning or repairing their few possessions. In Europe, where people had less freedom of choice in such matters than in America (Stark and Finke, 2000), there was often also a de facto obligation to spend about a tenth of one's time attending various ceremonies of the state-sanctioned religious monopoly, such as masses, processions, holiday celebrations, as well as the weddings and funerals of a much greater number of people—for example, distant cousins or fellow villagers—than is common in the twenty-first century. That left only 5 percent of one's time and (for most people) very little money to be spent on self-selected leisure activities such as sports, reading or parlor games.

Maddison (1982) presents statistical evidence that there has been a continuous reduction in the mean number of working hours per year for well

Table 5.5   *Mean number of working hours per year in 11 developed
economies, 1870–1979*

Country	1870	1900	1929	1950	1979
Australia	2,945	2,688	2,139	1,838	1,619
Belgium	2,964	2,707	2,272	2,283	1,747
Canada	2,964	2,789	2,399	1,967	1,730
Denmark	2,945	2,688	2,279	2,283	1,721
France	2,945	2,688	2,297	1,989	1,727
Germany	2,941	2,684	2,284	2,316	1,719
Netherlands	2,964	2,707	2,260	2,208	1,679
Norway	2,945	2,688	2,283	2,101	1,559
Sweden	2,945	2,688	2,283	1,951	1,461
United Kingdom	2,984	2,725	2,286	1,958	1,617
United States	2,964	2,707	2,342	1,867	1,607

Source: Different sources as given in Maddison (1982).

over a century. Table 5.5 shows the evolution of the average number of working hours in the labor force in 11 developed countries over a period of 110 years.

All advanced economies tend to experience a reduction in the number of working hours per worker over time. In Europe, the decline since the end of World War II has averaged about 25 percent. With a continued reduction of working hours per year, a realistic long-run estimate is that each worker will work no more than 1,300 hours in the not-too-distant future.

In a scenario where the cohort life expectancy has risen to 100 years, we should expect the mean number of working years to be about 50. A mean of 1,300 hours of work per year implies that only 7 to 8 percent of the average person's total lifetime will be devoted to work. The corresponding share in 1900 was 23 percent in both Europe and North America. There will then be a correspondingly radical increase in the share accounted for by leisure activities, with impacts on the structure of consumption and on saving that are likely to be substantial. One of the central consumption and saving strategies is how to distribute consumption budgets over the lifespan and especially how much of savings and loans should go into education and retirement pensions.

LIFETIME CONSUMPTION STRATEGY I: MODIGLIANI'S APPROACH

In the 1950s, Franco Modigliani deduced the *life cycle hypothesis* of optimal consumption behavior over the lifetime of a stylized consumer. Modigliani and Brumberg (1954; 1979) present a path-breaking theory of individual consumption over the life cycle. This theory includes the life cycle hypothesis of saving: "Our purpose was to show that all the well-established empirical regularities could be accounted for in terms of rational, utility-maximizing, consumers, allocating optimally their resources to consumption over their life, in the spirit of Irving Fisher" (Modigliani, 1986, p.163). In analogy to the two-period case, they derive an intertemporal budget constraint by making the present value of lifetime income and initial wealth equal the present value of lifetime spending.

Modigliani and Brumberg assume that the consumer will live for an exogenously determined lifespan of T periods. In each period, the consumer would face a budget constraint.[1] They further assume that the ideal (rational) consumer formulates a lifetime strategy of maximizing total welfare (W), which is the stream of discounted future utilities at the time of strategy formulation; a strategy that does not change in subsequent periods.[2] In this framework, assumptions include a constant level of income for each year that the individual remains in the labor force.

Since Modigliani and Brumberg assume finite known time horizons, they leave behind no assets as bequests to future generations. To simplify matters, assume that individuals earn a constant annual labor income, y, until retiring after R years. Further assume that they earn no additional such income between retirement and the expected end of life at time T. An additional assumption is that individuals prefer a smooth consumption profile over their lifetime. With these assumptions, the marginal utility of yearly consumption should equal the constant marginal utility of wealth and income. This implies that it is optimal for consumption to be a constant share of lifetime income.

Figure 5.4 shows the optimal allocation of consumption and assets over the lifetime of an individual. Such an individual accumulates wealth until retirement, after which she draws on the previously accumulated stock of wealth until her death. She thereby ensures a smooth path of consumption. In more formal terms, the necessary condition of maximum lifetime utility shows that individuals want to smooth marginal utility across time periods. The life cycle model therefore predicts that individuals will borrow money before entering the labor market. They will then accumulate savings as long as they are in the labor force. Upon retirement, they will start spend-

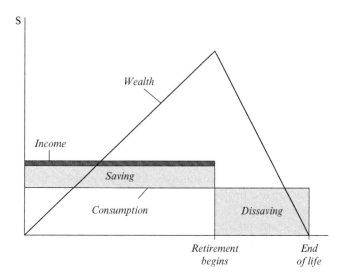

Figure 5.4   Modigliani's life cycle hypothesis

ing their accumulated savings (a process of "dissaving"). The objective is to maximize lifetime utility as seen from the initial time period (t). Thus, the marginal propensity to consume is relatively high in early adulthood, low during the working years and high again in the golden years.

Modigliani (1986, p. 154) provides a summary of the somewhat surprising macroeconomic implications of the Modigliani-Brumberg microeconomic life cycle model. There are six important implications:

1. The savings rate of a country is entirely independent of its per capita income.
2. The national savings rate is not simply the result of the relative thrift of its citizens, since different national savings rates are consistent with identical individual (life cycle) behavior.
3. Among countries with identical individual behavior, the aggregate savings rate will be an increasing function of the long-run growth rate of the economy. It will be zero in zero-growth economies.
4. The wealth-income ratio is a decreasing function of the growth rate, thus being at its maximum level when growth equals zero.
5. An economy can accumulate a very substantial stock of wealth relative to income, even if no one inherits wealth.
6. The main parameter that controls the wealth-income ratio and the savings rate at a given growth rate is the prevailing length of retirement.

The Modigliani-Brumberg life cycle hypothesis has other important implications. For example, consumption responds little to temporary changes in income and proportionally to permanent changes, as in the Friedman (1957) model. Another implication is that the marginal propensity to consume out of current income depends on age.

LIFETIME CONSUMPTION STRATEGY II: FRIEDMAN'S APPROACH

Milton Friedman (1957) approaches the life cycle problem in a somewhat different manner: the problem is about finding a consumption strategy for an *infinite sequence of generations* of consumers. He thus assumes that each generation cares about the next generation. Consequently, all generations from generation one to infinity become linked in the search for an optimal intergenerational consumption process. This amounts to a maximization problem.[3] The key assumption is that $\omega = 1/(1 + r)$, where r is the constant real rate of interest in the credit market. If income (y_t) is constant, the optimality condition implies equal marginal utility of consumption in all time periods. Thus, annual consumption equals an individual's *permanent income*, which is the annuity value of her wealth.

LIFETIME CONSUMPTION STRATEGY III: CHOOSING THE USE OF TIME FOR THREE PHASES OF LIFE

A perfect capital market would permit spending to exceed income from work during early adulthood, enabling young individuals to buy homes and start families. In this phase, the individual will have to fund her expenditures by borrowing in the credit market. In the mid-life phase, spending begins to level off at the same time as wage income enters the picture. At this stage the individual repays her outstanding debt and begins to save for retirement. After retirement, past savings fund expenditures until death.

In modeling a simplified version of this dynamic process, we subdivide the lifespan into three equally long phases, where phase 1 refers to education and some part-time simple work, phase 2 to ordinary working life after completed education and phase 3 to retirement. The assumption of equal phase length makes it possible to use the same rate of discounting for all three periods.

During each phase, we assume that the representative individual's utility depends on the consumption level, C_t, in that period. We further discount the stream of utility over the finite life cycle to its present value, K, at a given discount rate r (including compensation for risk):

$$K = \Sigma_1^3 U(C_t)(1/(1+r))^{t-1}; \tag{5.1}$$

We assume that the individual—who in the normal case can rely on support from family members or other sources—maximizes the present value of K, subject to relevant institutional constraints. In this model, we only consider private income and consumption and exclude the potential impacts of taxes and subsidies. We further assume that educational loans are available for phase 1 and that the duration of schooling is proportional to the size of the educational loans, L. Thus, working time during phase 1 is $T - kL$ and wage income is $w(T - kL)$, where w is the wage rate for unskilled labor. Consumption in phase 1 thus equals the sum of loans (including family support) and wage income.

During phase 2, C_2 equals income from work (Y) minus repayment of loans $(1+s)L$ and savings for retirement in phase 3, S.

Assuming that the duration of schooling—which equals kL—determines income in phase 2 and that income is a concave function of that duration, we obtain the following equation:

$$C_2 = Y(L) - (1+s)L - S; \tag{5.2}$$

During phase 3, C_3 is equal to the retirement pension, P, which we assume is a monotonously increasing function of the savings in phase 2:

$$C_3 = P(S). \tag{5.3}$$

The best lifetime consumption strategy is then the one that maximizes the present value, K, subject to temporal constraints:

$$Max\,K = U(C_1) + U(C_2)\left(\frac{1}{1+r}\right) + U(C_3)\left(\frac{1}{(1+r)^2}\right); \tag{5.4}$$

subject to:

$$C_1 - L - w(T - kL) = 0;$$
$$Y(L) - C_2 - (1+s)L - S = 0;$$
$$C_3 = P(S).$$

Appendix 3.1 gives the necessary conditions for an optimal lifetime consumption strategy. These conditions imply that the discounted marginal return from education (funded by loans) should equal the marginal opportunity cost of studying plus repayment of loans, provided that the marginal utility of consumption is constant over time. A savings strategy for retirement is optimal when the marginal increase of the retirement income per time period due to increased savings equals $1 + r$.

HOW TO SPEND YOUR TIME: WORK VERSUS LEISURE

A persistent empirical regularity in growing economies is the decline in the hours an average member of the labor force devotes to work within a fixed time period. An econometric estimate based on Maddison's (1982) data for advanced industrialized countries shows that there tends to be a reduction of average working time by about 0.3 percent per year in growing economies. This result supports the old hypothesis of the "backward-bending" labor supply curve. The reduced supply of working time (per period) as the consequence of increasing real wages is consistent with standard models of an optimizing consumer.

The number of working hours will decrease with increases in the wage rate if the consumer sees consumption and leisure time as complements. If this complementarity exists, economic growth will be associated with both more leisure time and more consumption per person.

The long-run trend in the advanced economies is consistent with complementarity (see Figure 5.5).

CONSUMERS' TEMPORAL AND SPATIAL DECISIONS

The use of time is intimately related to the choice of where to locate one's home relative to one's social contacts and workplace. There is always a trade-off between the spaciousness of one's home and access to people, services and job opportunities. The following function is one way to represent overall accessibility from a location i:

$$A_i = \sum_{j=1}^{n} a e^{b d_{ij}} z_j; \tag{5.5}$$

where
b = a *time distance* friction parameter;
a = a constant (>0);
d_{ij} = the distance in *travel time* from location i to location j;

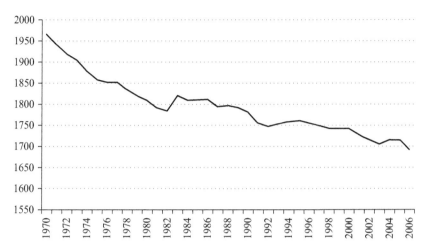

Note: No data available for South Korea.

Source: OECD (2008).

Figure 5.5 *Per capita working time in OECD member states, 1970–2006*

z_i = the magnitude of the attraction in location j (for example, number of jobs, shopping opportunities, number of workers).

Generally, each consumer will have a positive valuation of the two relevant attributes associated with location i—accessibility (A_i) and land area per person (S/z). Thus the utility that a typical consumer derives from residing in location i, $u_i = u(A_i, (S/z)_i)$, increases with increases in location-specific accessibility as well as with increases in the available space per person. We could further assume that each consumer's indifference curves are convex or, more formally, that the intermediate position $\alpha(A_i^0, S_i^0) + (1 - \alpha)$ (A_i^1, S_i^1) is always preferred to (A_i^0, S_i^0) or (A_i^1, S_i^1).

All consumers therefore face a trade-off between travel time and personal space. Consequently, the price of space must increase with travel-time savings, so that more accessible locations are more expensive per unit of land area. Using linear as well as non-linear Eigenvalue equations, Andersson and Karlqvist (1976) show that a general spatial equilibrium exists if all consumers search for utility gains from better combinations of accessibility and personal space (see Appendix 5.2).

NOTES

1. $\sum c_i (1+r)^{-t} - \sum y_i (1+r)^{-t} - W(0) = 0$
2. Max $W = \sum (u(c_i)(1+r)^{-t}$; subject to $\sum c_i (1+r)^{-t} - \sum y_i (1+r)^{-t} - W(0) = 0$; where $u(c_i) =$ utility from consumption in time period t; $y_t =$ income in period t; $W(0) =$ initial level of income-generating wealth.
3. Maximize $L = \sum_1^\infty \omega^{t-1} u(c_i)$; subject to: $\sum_1^\infty \omega^{t-1} y_t + b_0 (1+r) = \sum_1^\infty \omega^{t-1} c_t$.

APPENDIX 5.1

The consumer allocates her total time per year (T) between leisure (L) and work (W). T is of course given, so that $L + W = T$. We then assume that the preferences conform to a CES utility function: $u = (aY^{-\rho} + bL^{-\rho})^{-1/\rho}$; $Y = wW$; where w = the wage rate, hence $Y = wW$ and $L = T - W$. It then becomes possible to express utility solely as a function of labor time (W). Maximizing utility with respect to W requires that $\delta u / \delta W = 0$. This implies that $W = T / (1+(b/a\ w^\rho))^{1/(1+\rho)}$.

APPENDIX 5.2

Assume the attainable utility in subregion i to be $u_i = u(A_i, (S/z)_i)$. Further assume that $u_i = (A_i^*(S/z)_i)$, which is a Wicksell-Cobb-Douglas function with equal exponents. This implies that the indifference curves are convex with respect to accessibility and space, and that utility increases with increased accessibility and personal space in each subregion i. Let the size S_i of each subregion be equal to 1, which implies that $u_i z_i = \sum_{j=1}^{N} ae^{-bd_{ij}} z_j$; ($i=1,\ldots,N$). We thus have an Eigenvalue equation in which each element of the accessibility matrix $\mathbf{A}$ is positive. We can then use the Perron-Frobenius theorem with the following properties:

1. There exists a unique maximum Eigenvalue or utility $u^* = u_i$ for all i and an associated Eigen vector z^*.
2. The u^* increases and the z^* changes if there is a decrease in any time distance, d_{ij}.

The dynamic adaptation to the new Eigenvector continues until all spatial subregions generate the same utility level (which is also the maximum general utility level). Increasing the speed of travel by infrastructural or vehicular improvements increases the maximum equalized utility level.

Andersson and Ferraro (1983) apply this model to spatial population and accessibility data when simulating the population distribution among a large number of spatial subdivisions in the Stockholm region. They show that the Eigenvalue-equation-generated spatial distribution is close to the observed distribution.

6. Durability, duration of production, growth and location

> There are certain products of man's labour which have a very high and sometimes unlimited durability. Examples are provided by houses, streets, railways, canals, certain improvements in land, certain kinds of machines. While by origin, having regard to the manner by which they are obtained, they have the attributes of capital and of other capital goods, they play a part in further production which comes nearest to that played by land. (Wicksell, 1898/1936, p. 126)

> For example, I regard a house, not as a capital good, but as a rent-earning good, which, with or without the co-operation of labour and other factors of production, supplies the consumption good "shelter." (Wicksell, ibid., p. 127)

All goods are durable and in this respect they are by definition capital goods. As a consequence, the latter quotation points in the wrong direction. Wicksell's error was probably a consequence of his preoccupation with Marxian economics, according to which the majority of the population belonged to the proletariat who could not own any capital goods, such as owner-occupied dwellings. In many parts of the world most workers own their homes, have a substantial educational capital and they are thus both capitalists and wage earners.

Frank Knight—in contrast to Wicksell—had concluded that every good is capital and even saw land as capital, because land that had not been connected to networks or had been left without other infrastructure would yield no returns and would therefore be valueless:

> All sources are properly productive agents, and are also "capital goods" in the most inclusive meaning. In practice, it is often useful to restrict the notion of capital goods in various directions, and the definition will depend on the problem considered in any particular piece of exposition. (Knight, 1947/1982, p. 388)

Later in the same publication, Knight notes that:

> [t]he distinction between human beings and property and that between personal and real property are important in law and human relations, but no fundamental economic differences correspond to them. . ..Realistic economic

analysis must avoid any general classifications of productive agents and make distinctions on the basis of facts that are significant for the problem at hand. For general analysis, it would be desirable to drop also the traditional classification of income forms, and to speak of the yield and "hire" of productive agents, irrespective of kind. (Knight, 1947/1982, pp. 394–5).

Some consumer goods have a durability of (that is, are useful for) a few days, for example fresh fruit and vegetables. Other consumer goods, such as cutlery, clothes and computer games, are more durable and are useful for years if not decades. But a sizable portion of the typical household budget comprises consumer goods with a durability that is measured in decades or even centuries: examples include houses, jewelry, paintings and vintage wines. Choosing the desired durability and depreciation of such capital goods is a major decision problem for consumers.

Several factors influence the consumer's choice of the durability of a desired good. Among the most common factors is the price of the good, the cost of loans, maintenance costs and replacement needs. There are obviously trade-offs among the different types of cost, since a specific durability is associated with specific factor costs. A buyer of a bicycle can choose a high-priced titanium bicycle with extreme durability and low maintenance costs or a cheap mass-produced plastic one with low durability and high maintenance costs.

Disregarding interest costs and differences in usefulness for the consumer, it is possible to calculate the cost-minimizing durability of a good using a simplified model (Brems, 1968). The cost of repairing most goods increases with the age of the good. Hence the number of repairs over the lifespan (T) of the good increases more than proportionally over time. A convenient way to model the cost of repairs is:

$$\log n = \alpha \log T \qquad (6.1)$$

where:
n = number of repairs during the lifespan of the good;
T = the durability (lifespan) of the good;
α = an elasticity parameter greater than 1.

Replacement need or depreciation is then the reciprocal of the chosen durability of the product:

$$D = 1/T \qquad (6.2)$$

where:
D = replacement need or depreciation.

The yearly rental cost of the good is then:

$$R = PD + np/T;$$ (6.3)

where:
R = rental cost per year;
P = price of the (capital) good;
p = price of repair (assumed to be constant in this model).

Substituting (6.1) and (6.2) in (6.3) we obtain rental cost:

$$R = P/T + pT^{\alpha - 1}$$ (6.4)

Minimizing rental cost R with respect to durability leads to the necessary and sufficient condition:

$$\ln T = (1/\alpha) \ln (P/p (\alpha - 1))$$ (6.5)

The optimal durability thus increases with decreases in the elasticity α, reflecting the increased physical durability of the good. T is an increasing function of the price of the good and a decreasing function of maintenance costs.

As an example, the optimum durability would be approximately 12 years if the price of the good is $1000, the annual maintenance cost is $50 and α is 1.50.

FIRMS' DEMAND FOR DURABILITY

Most studies of firms' durability choices draw upon Terborgh's (1954) seminal study. In all these studies the trade-off is between initial investment costs and annual maintenance costs. Typically, there is a choice between a durable piece of equipment such as a machine with low maintenance costs and a set of less durable machines with higher maintenance costs.[1]

A practical illustration of this approach is to compare two machines with the same function. Assume that a firm can choose between buying machine A with a durability of five years and machine B with a durability of ten years. The advantage of machine B is that its annual operating cost is lower. Table 6.1 gives the cost structure of the two machines.

The cost-minimizing strategy depends on the prevailing interest rate. Let us assume that the real credit-market interest rate is 20 percent, reflecting the lender's judgment that the risk associated with the project is relatively

Table 6.1   Investment and operating costs of two alternative machines

Year	Investment cost		Operating cost	
	Machine A	Machine B	Machine A	Machine B
0	5,000	15,000		
1			1,200	1,000
2			1,200	1,000
3			1,200	1,000
4			1,200	1,000
5	5,000		1,200	1,000
6			1,200	1,000
7			1,200	1,000
8			1,200	1,000
9			1,200	1,000
10			1,200	1,000

high. The present value of the cost of using machine A is then $18,784, whereas the corresponding cost of machine B is $20,810, which implies that choosing the less durable machine is preferable. Conversely, a lower real interest rate of, say, 10 percent would imply that it would be less costly to choose the more durable machine.

Technological improvements leading to lower investment and operating costs would also influence the optimal durability of a capital good. Technological improvements mean that it would become more advantageous to avoid using durable (and expensive) equipment, since this would imply a delay in the adoption of cost-reducing process innovations such as new and more cost-efficient machines.

THE DEMAND FOR DURABILITY AND ITS SUPPLY

The preceding section showed how consumers and producers demand durability in a market with a given supply of goods that differ in their durability. That is a very partial view of the matter. In reality, an interdependent process of adjustments to durability and other quality attributes of a good shape the supply of and demand for the durability attribute. The cost of a good—including interest charges—increases with increasing durability, while it is reasonable to assume that a normal consumer's willingness to pay is a concave function of the offered durability of an otherwise identical good. In equilibrium, durability would then occur when marginal cost equals marginal willingness to pay.

However, most firms supply a range of models of each type of good, with each model having different durability and other associated attributes. Examples are the broad range of cameras supplied by Canon, Leica or Nikon, ranging from inexpensive and short-lived "point-and-shoot cameras" at a price of about US$120 to professional high-durability cameras that command market prices in excess of US$8,000. In this as in many other markets there is a natural segmentation of consumers into groups, with the members of each group having similar preferences and ability to pay for durability and other product attributes. This makes it possible for numerous equilibrium magnitudes of durability (among other attributes) to coexist in the same time period.

DURABILITY, THE CAPITAL-OUTPUT RATIO AND THE RATE OF ECONOMIC GROWTH

According to the accelerator theory, the product of the difference between the expected and realized demand for goods and the capital-output ratio determines investments. The capital-output ratio is measured as capital value at a point in time divided by value-of-output flow over a period of time. Hence it is possible to measure the capital value at the end of the year while measuring output as a flow (of value) during the year. This would imply that the "dimension" of capital/output is value/value/time and that the one of capital-output is time. As Hawkins (1948), Lange (1957) and Bródy (1970) all point out, an inter-sectoral capital-output ratio, $b_{ij} = \Delta x_{ij}/x_j$, also has the dimension of time or economic durability.

Thus $b_{ij} = T_{ij}\, a_{ij}$; where T_{ij} = the economic durability of good i when used in the production of good j and a_{ij} = the current use of input i in the production of one unit of good j. Assuming a one-good economy we would then have:

$$x = ax + gTax; \qquad (6.6)$$

where:
g = the rate of growth of the economy.

The equilibrium rate of growth, g^*, is $(1-a)/Ta$. Preserving equilibrium at a constant rate of growth—while increasing durability—requires substitution by reducing the use of current inputs per unit of output. A technological improvement that causes a *ceteris-paribus* reduction in the coefficient a induces an increased equilibrium growth rate.

Leontief (1953) generalizes this result to a multi-good economy, with households supplying working time to producers in exchange for consumption goods (Appendix 6.1 presents the details of this model). The main result of Leontief's model is that the maximum growth rate equals the minimum interest rate at a deterministic saddle-point solution. Another result is that an increase in the savings rate raises the growth rate. John von Neumann (1938/1970) proves this property of the saddle point for a more general growth model.

SAVINGS AND GROWTH IN THE STANDARD NEOCLASSICAL MODEL

In a one-sector growth model based on the assumption of diminishing returns to capital per unit of labor, Tinbergen (1942) and later Swan (1956) and Solow (1957) show that a higher propensity to save would not increase consumption growth per unit of labor. This is grossly at variance with the result of the Leontief model. The reason for this difference is that the latter model has constant returns to capital because of the unlimited supply of labor. Thus, in the Tinbergen-Solow model an increase in the savings rate (corresponding to reduced unit inputs of consumer goods) would not lead to a higher equilibrium rate of economic growth. Figure 6.1 is a

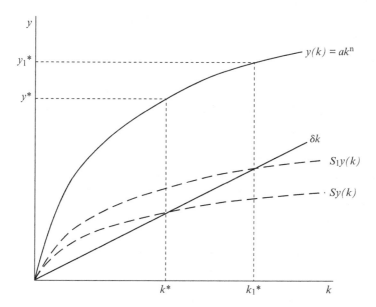

Figure 6.1   Increases in the savings rate and capital equilibrium

diagrammatic representation of the results of this model; y is here output per unit of labor while k is real capital per unit of labor. The production function is a Wicksell-Cobb-Douglas function with an exponent greater than zero and smaller than one, while s is the propensity to save and δ denotes the rate of capital depreciation.

The growth rate of income per worker does not increase in the long run in the neoclassical growth model, because the growth rate converges to the given capital depreciation rate, which is a depreciation rate where δ is equal to the inverse of the durability of capital.

DURABILITY AND RATES OF DEPRECIATION IN VON NEUMANN'S MODEL OF GROWTH

Equations (6.4) and (6.5) are special cases of von Neumann's (1938/1970) general equilibrium theory. Von Neumann (ibid.) and Wald (1936) present mathematical dynamic and static general equilibrium theory, respectively. They had initially collaborated when they took part in a mathematical colloquium in Vienna in the 1930s, which allowed them to base their analyses on the simplified general equilibrium theories of Walras (1874/1896) and Cassel (1918/1932). Wald proved the existence of a static general equilibrium, whereas von Neumann proved the existence of a dynamic general equilibrium in a theory of growth that was based on a simple growth model from Cassel's economics textbook. Von Neumann then proceeded to generalize this model into a theory of an economically sustainable dynamic general equilibrium with any finite number of commodities. His proof of a general equilibrium made use of Brouwer's fixed-point and his own saddle-point theorems, with proofs from the 1920s.

Von Neumann (1938/1970) introduces time into equilibrium growth theory in two ways:

1. The basic model uses discrete period dynamics.
2. The durability of all products enters the theory in its inverse form as constant rates of depreciation between periods (Lev and Theil (1978), show that this is consistent with the assumptions of a deterministic economic system).

This theory, also known as "the Von Neumann growth model," assumes joint production in order to achieve efficient treatment of depreciation and durability. For example, paper production makes use of energy and machines as inputs at the start of the production process. The end of that process yields a *joint product vector* of outputs. This vector represents paper, buildings, energy, machines and other equipment, each of which has depreciated and diminished in capacity (Appendix 6.2 gives the relevant equations).

The Von Neumann growth model allows for joint production and substitution of inputs, assuming a rectangular structure of the **A** and **B** input and output matrices. The producers are thus able to choose which input and output vectors to use in order to increase the productivity and returns of the production processes.

Von Neumann (1938/1970) proves that a sustainable equilibrium exists for the economic system (see Appendix 6.2). It is a saddle-point solution and it determines the equilibrium price and quantity vectors. The equilibrium point equalizes the minimum rate of interest and the maximum sustainable rate of growth.

In Figure 6.2 the saddle point equilibrium combines a maximized growth rate with minimized interest cost. The model assumes that firms

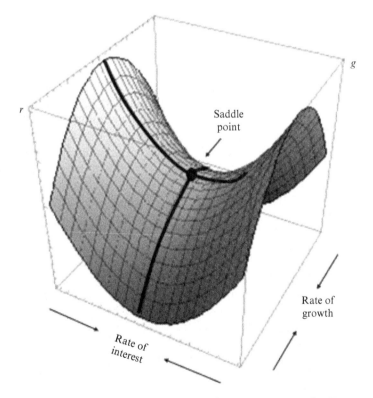

Figure 6.2   The saddle point of growth and interest rates in the Von Neumann growth model

seek to adopt optimal production techniques as well as optimal production scales so as to maximize their growth rates, while minimizing the costs of borrowing and production. At the saddle-point solution relative prices as well as production intensities are in equilibrium.

Von Neumann's and Wald's theories of general equilibrium do not presume that economic agents maximize utility functions. This deviation from standard neoclassical practice probably stems from Cassel's dismissal of individual utility functions as unmeasurable and thus unnecessary for the existence of demand functions. Even so, von Neumann and Wald were the initiators of modern mathematical economics with their use of saddle points and fixed-point theorems. Noted later uses of these ideas include the creation of game theory (von Neumann and Morgenstern, 1944) and the reformulation of general equilibrium theory in utility-maximizing terms (Debreu, 1959).

A related development that also proved influential was von Neumann's introduction of inequalities in the formulation of saddle-point theory. This became one of the two main preconditions for the development of linear and non-linear programming. The other important precondition for LP and NLP was a set of mathematical theorems as presented in a book entitled *Inequalities* by Hardy, Littlewood and Pólya (Hardy et al., 1934/1988). Hardy et al. (ibid.) prove theorems that form the basis of the popular constant-elasticity-of-substitution function (CES), which much later would shape the development of both micro-econometric models and neoclassical models of economic growth (albeit mostly without references to the 1934 book).

DURATION OF PRODUCTION

Böhm-Bawerk and Wicksell were the first economists to draw attention to the choice of duration of production processes. Böhm-Bawerk did this by considering the case of a producer facing the choice between immediately starting production with the capital and knowledge at hand and choosing a longer time of preparation by means of producing better capital goods and improving the producer's own knowledge. This second choice would obviously not only require a longer time horizon but also greater expenditures. As is shown in his numerical example in Chapter 2, the marginal returns from extending this "roundaboutness" of the production process would eventually diminish toward the rate of interest on loans. Optimality would then require equalization of the marginal return from extending the duration of the process and the interest rate.

In the meantime, Wicksell had directed his gaze to the maturation of wine and other biological production processes, concluding that a requirement that the marginal rate of growth in value equals the interest rate yields the optimal duration of the production process. Many economists regarded Wicksell's conclusion as referring to a special case of point-input/point-output production. They were wrong. Wicksell's conclusion is applicable to a wide range of decisions involving the choice of the duration of a production process, as the following model of harvesting a biological resource demonstrates.

MANAGING THE DURATION OF ECOLOGICAL PRODUCTION AND THE OPTIMAL VALUE OF CAPITAL

So far, we have looked at value growth as a function of time in a couple of typical cases. The first was the maturation of wine as an example of how the elapse of time may cause the value of capital to increase, although it is of course true that biological factors are in an implicit sense employed as "production factors" during the maturation process.

The second case, which we discussed in Chapter 4, was the increasing value of a work of art, even though nothing really happens to the good during the period when its value is increasing. Instead, the growth in value may be a consequence of expectations of a future continuation of the growth in value among connoisseurs or speculators. In this latter case time is an even more crucial determinant of value. In both these cases we have the optimal stopping rule: the seller should aim for the sale to take place at the exact point in time when the rate of value growth equals the interest rate (that is, the required real rate of return). This result harks back to the economics of both Wicksell and Jevons. It is also possible to show that this rule is of far greater generality than the special case of the optimal time in storage for a good that is subject to a biological maturation process.

This kind of analysis obviously applies to all those biological and ecological goods that undergo a growth or maturation process as a consequence of the ubiquitous availability of natural resources that contribute to their growth or maturation. Trees in primeval forests and ocean fish are examples of such biological goods. What decision rules should apply to such goods if they are transformed into managed resources? In this section, we present some of the relevant rules of how to manage biological and ecological capital in a dynamic sense. Important contributions to our understanding of this economic management problem include Faustmann (1849/1968); Wicksell (1893/1970; 1901/1934), Ohlin (1921/1995) as well as more recent contributions such as Löfgren (1983), Anderson and Seijo (2010) and Clark (2010).

In this context, it is important to remember that there are obvious differences between the strategic management rules that apply to small-area and large-area resources. For small areas, the problem is often the simple one of choosing the right time to harvest. For large areas, this is not enough. Instead the problem is to find the right harvesting time trajectory. A management rule that is popular in forestry and ocean fishing is that one should harvest at the time that yields the maximum sustainable output. From an economic point of view that rule does not make any sense, despite its widespread adoption. To show why, we need to introduce some realistic assumptions.

The first assumption is that harvesting (h) is proportional to the total capital stock (k) so that $h(t) = u(t)k(t)$, where $u(t)$ is the harvesting rate, which is the control variable of our dynamic control problem. We assume $u(t)$ to be real-valued, semi-positive and below maximum harvesting capacity ($u(max)$). We further assume net revenue per harvested unit (p) to be given at the outset and independent of time and the scale of harvesting.

Biological growth is normally logistic; meteorological conditions, productive inputs in the biotope and other such location-specific factors determine the upper limit of growth. A typical biological growth process consists of a positive linear part (with the parameter a) and a quadratic dampening (with the parameter b), leading to the logistic growth equation (see chapter 4):

$$\dot{k} = ak - bk^2; \tag{6.7}$$
$$\dot{k} \geq 0.$$

This growth equation is the factor that constrains the solutions to our problem.

We assume the market can absorb the harvested volumes at all points in time, implying that there is no terminal date of the optimization problem to be formulated below. We now assume that the manager of the renewable biological resource wants to maximize the total returns. These derive from the chosen harvesting trajectory. In this context, one must discount the returns using the constant internal rate of return or the best alternative rate of interest to be earned in the capital market. It is then possible to formulate an optimization rule. The rule is that the optimum equals the maximum of an integral of the continuous flow of returns from harvesting at different points in time, subject to the logistical growth constraint (see Appendix 6.2). The optimum harvesting trajectory ($u(opt)$) should therefore equal the maximum ($u(max)$) whenever k is greater than $k(opt)$

and otherwise equal zero. The optimal harvesting trajectory must satisfy the equation:

$$uk(opt) = ak(opt) - b(k(opt))^2; \tag{6.8}$$

which implies that:

$$u(opt) = 0.5(a + \rho), \text{ if } k > 0. \tag{6.9}$$

Hence the optimal harvesting rate, $(ku(opt)) = (a^2 - \rho^2)/4b$, is always less than the maximum sustainable yield, which equals $a^2/4b$. The relative difference is $(\rho/a)^2$. If, for example, the interest rate is 4 percent and the growth rate, a, is 10 percent, then the relative difference between optimal harvesting and harvesting at the maximum sustainable yield will be 16 percent. The general implication is that the optimum harvesting strategy leads to an equilibrium state; this equilibrium state is stable as long as a is greater than ρ (see Appendix 6.2). In addition, the growth rate of the capital value must equal the interest rate at the optimum rate of harvesting (this is also Wicksell's rule). This optimum rate is also associated with a stable equilibrium of the stock of the relevant renewable biological resource.

The behavioral interpretation of this optimum is quite straightforward. If the value of the biological stock (k) is growing at a lower rate than the rate of interest it makes sense for the manager to invest in a different resource with a higher rate of return. Conversely, if the rate of value growth is greater than the interest rate, it will make sense for the manager to invest in resources that make it possible to increase the harvesting rate. The rate of value growth must be kept in line with the interest rate, which implies adjusting capital to its equilibrium level.

Whether renewable biological resources become endangered is a question that relates to the required rate of interest, ρ. A magnitude of a that is smaller than ρ implies a collapse. In this case, it is an elementary catastrophe of the fold type. In countries such as Brazil and China with high economic growth rates, the interest rates will be correspondingly high. There is then a clear possibility that the interest rate, ρ, may exceed the growth rate, a, of many species that make up part of the total stock of biological capital. Species are thus more likely to become extinct if their habitats are to be found within high-growth rather than low-growth economies.

DURABILITY, DURATION AND PATTERNS OF LOCATION AND TRADE

The problem of the spatial structure of production is related both to the sustainable scale of each firm and to the total demand for its products. It is long-term total average cost that determines the sustainable scale of a firm, and this total cost includes interest on capital as well as transaction and transport costs. A firm in long-run equilibrium will have output prices that correspond to minimum long-run average costs. The basic idea is that firms will enter markets as long as there are profit opportunities with the prevailing cost structures.

In order to determine the impact of product durability on the spatial structure of production, we need to specify the long-run average production cost function (APC) and its dependence on the scale of production, x. A simple but often realistic assumption is to subdivide the total production cost into fixed cost (FC) and variable cost ($VC(x)$). The fixed cost is that of all the capital in the production unit and is independent of the scale of operation as soon as the production unit has been established. For simplicity, we assume that the production unit is identical to the firm.

Such an analysis can provide a straightforward connection to our earlier focus on the durability of goods (including services) and the duration of production processes. By analyzing the "roundaboutness" of production and the duration of the production process it is possible to address the question of how much capital is needed and therefore also fixed production costs. Large fixed costs are typical of knowledge-intensive production, since such production requires a long period of research and development before actual production can occur. Typical examples are the pharmaceutical and advanced electronics industries, which regularly invest more than 20 percent of their sales revenues in the creation and innovation of new products and processes. Another example is the production of feature films, which involves an extended production period reaching all the way back to the initial idea in the form of a novel or an original script. Films also involve assembly and contracting of actors, actual shooting, post-production and marketing. Each of these stages of production implies increased duration and thus increased fixed cost, later to be followed by the variable cost of transmitting the final output to audiences around the world. During this sequence of production stages there is an option rule that states that, "it is never too late to give up."

Variable costs are in the generic case monotonously increasing with the scale of production up to the capacity limit of the firm's capital. We consequently assume that the optimal scale of operation is smaller than or equal to that upper limit.

The simplest variable cost function is linear: $VC(x) = vx$. The total production cost function would then be $TPC = FC + vx$; and the average production cost function is consequently $APC = FC/x + v$.

Interaction between a firm and its customers causes transport and transaction costs of various kinds (strictly speaking, all space-bridging costs are relevant, but transport costs tend to approximate these costs in the Internet era). If customers are more or less evenly distributed in the space that surrounds the firm, then total transport and transaction costs associated with firm-customer interactions will increase progressively with increases in the scale of production and in sales. This implies that the average sum of transport and transaction costs, $ATTC$, will also increase with increases in the scale of operations. A simple yet reasonable approximation is the average transport and transaction cost function $ATTC = kx$. The term k can be decomposed into cost per unit of shipment, a, and the frequency of contacts, which depends inversely on the durability, t, of the product. The average transport and transaction cost is thus $ATTC = (a/t)\,x$. Hence more durable products are associated with lower average transport and transaction costs.

The total average cost AC equals the sum of the average production cost APC and the average transport and transaction cost $ATTC$:

$$AC = FC(T)/x + v + (a/t)\,x. \tag{6.10}$$

Minimizing average cost requires that the derivative of AC with respect to the scale of production is set equal to zero. This implies that the optimal scale of production is:

$$x(opt) = \sqrt{\frac{FC(T)_t}{a}}. \tag{6.11}$$

The optimal scale of a firm's production is thus an increasing function of its fixed cost of production (primarily of capital, including "land") and an increasing function of the durability of the product.

Consequently, the scale of production is an increasing function of *both* the duration of production *and* of the durability of the product. It goes without saying that the total size of the market determines the optimal number of firms. The greatest spatial extent of a market is the world market, which necessitates sufficiently integrated and low-cost transport and communications networks. The existence of an accessible world market leads to a more competitive market and more firms than when the largest accessible market is smaller.

Assuming a world market, the total number of firms, N, that produce a specific good is $N =$ Total demand/x(opt), implying that the total number of firms is a decreasing function of fixed cost, which in turn depends on the duration of the production process. The total number of firms is also a decreasing function of the durability of the good being produced.

Increasing the fixed cost—as influenced by the duration of the production process—and increasing the durability of the good being produced both have the effect of reducing the number of firms, if the demand for the good remains the same. In some cases, the number of firms becomes so constrained that assumptions of near-perfect or "atomistic" competition cannot be upheld even if the good is globally traded. Examples of such goods are trains, ships, airplanes and nuclear reactors, all of which are produced in a handful of locations that serve a global market.

We should keep in mind the rapidly decreasing costs of conveying some goods from producers to their customers. One example is the cost of transmitting movies, music, texts and other media that can be digitalized without any substantial quality losses. For some of these goods the high fixed costs of long-duration production interact with lowered space-bridging costs to thereby increase the optimal long-run scale of production; the maximum number of economically sustainable firms will then drop. To some extent agglomeration economies may reduce firm-internal scale economies, as in the case of the Los Angeles or Mumbai film industries. However, such firm-external scale economies do nothing to increase the number of advantageous locations. Instead, there will be one or a handful of clusters that allow small firms to take advantage of industry-specific agglomeration economies, at the expense of competing firms—of whatever size—in the "wrong" locations.

The combined impact of production duration and product durability on firms' fixed costs determines the maximum number of firms that are economically sustainable in the long run (*ceteris paribus*), but it does not determine the maximum number of locations in geographical space. For that we need a connection to the theory of location and trade.

A combinatorial process shapes the location pattern of a given number of production units. In this process, firms choose locations to minimize total transport and transaction costs for the set of firms as a whole, subject to the demand and supply constraints of the constituent nodes.

This entails finding a location pattern of production units that ensures that the sum of the marginal production cost of the traded output plus the marginal transport and transaction costs of reaching consumers is less than or equal to the marginal value to the potential buyers in the receiving location. We should however bear in mind that competition tends to make long-run average production costs equal the supply price of a good in the originating location. The implication is that the optimal location pattern is such that the price in each receiving location minus the price in the originating location is less than or equal to the long-run marginal transport-and-transaction cost (in other words, the marginal cost of transmitting the output between the supply location and consumers in various demand locations).

As von Thünen first showed in the nineteeth century and Beckmann and Puu (1985) elaborated upon more than a century later (see Chapter 3), trade emerges because of differences in product durability and transport costs. Dafermos and Nagurney (1987) formulate a variational inequality model that summarizes these earlier contributions as a theory of location and trade in a discrete network of regions. In their computable network equilibrium models, prices that are announced in various locations represent the demand and supply in each location. An increase in the export flow of a good from one location to another requires the price difference to be greater than the sum of the transport and transaction costs that are associated with a unit trade flow between the two locations. This basic idea is not new; the classical economists allude to this conclusion in their writings about the reasons why merchants engage in trade. The pattern of trade flows reaches equilibrium when the endogenously determined price difference between two locations equals (or is smaller than) the sum of all relevant marginal transaction and transport costs.

As we have seen, the durability of a good affects its transaction and transport costs. The greater the durability of the good is, the smaller this trading cost will be, other things being equal. Trade will keep expanding until there are no price differences between different locations for the limiting case of extremely durable goods. For goods with extreme durability and low transportation and transaction costs, the law of one price will prevail. This condition nowadays applies to the trade in currencies and is also increasingly valid for the type of digital information services that lend themselves to web-based payment and service delivery.

Table 6.2 summarizes our conclusions regarding the impacts of scale economies and combined transport and transaction costs on location patterns.

DURABILITY, FIXED COST, DENSITY, POPULATION SIZE AND SUPPLY DIVERSITY

Launhardt (1885) offers an early account of the connections between production cost, transport cost and the spatial extent of the demand for a good. There is however no attempt to address the impact of the durability

*Table 6.2   The effects of scale economies and combined transport and
transaction costs on location patterns*

Combined transport and transaction costs	Economies of scale in production	
	Small/negligible	Large/substantial
Small/negligible	Highly dispersed spatial distribution of production units in a highly competitive global market.	Global network of R&D and production centers in knowledge regions. Dispersed retail and repair.
Large/substantial	Dispersed spatial distribution of production with monopolistic competition between firms in different regions.	Very small number of R&D and production centers in knowledge regions. Highly dispersed retail and repair.

of the good, the duration of the production process or the impact of high fixed costs on the choice of location.

Consider a firm that supplies consumer good x within a given region. The total production cost is $TPC = FC + vx$, and the average cost, AC, is then $TC/x + v$. However, in deciding how to supply the region, the firm must consider the cost of distributing the good to the region's population.

The distribution cost (that is, the combined transport and transaction cost) depends on the size and density of the regional population of consumers. The total distribution cost, $TTTC$, will always increase more than proportionally to the volume of sales as it reaches an increasing number of consumers at an increasing average distance. We can represent this as $TTTC = u(\delta)x^2$, in which δ is the density of the consuming population. We stipulate that u is a decreasing function of density. The average distribution cost is then $TTTC/x = u_0(\delta)x$.

The average production cost exhibits increasing returns to scale, but it is necessary to balance lower average production costs from increasing scale against higher average distribution costs. Long-run equilibrium requires the minimization of the sum of average production and distribution cost, implying that the firm exhibits increasing returns in production at its equilibrium scale. Assuming that total demand is proportional to the population size, P, and density in the region, a firm will *not* be established if $P < \frac{1}{k}(FC/(u_0(\delta)))^{-0.5}$.

The probability that someone will establish a firm that produces good A will accordingly increase if the per-capita demand for A goes up, or if the population density rises or if the fixed production cost falls. As

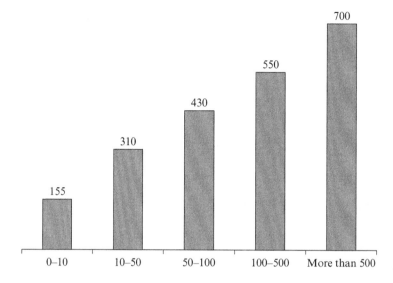

Source: Statistics Sweden.

Figure 6.3   *Population (in thousands) in Swedish labor market areas (functional urban regions) and the average number of represented industries in each population-size category*

these factors differ between different industries and different goods, there will be a positive relation between the region size and the number of represented industries and available goods. Figure 6.3 shows the relation between population and number of industries for Swedish labor market areas.

In the smallest regions, only firms of industries with very low fixed costs, non-durable products and high per capita demand can survive in the long run. Examples of such firms are barbers, cafes, convenience stores and other outlets that sell perishable goods. Examples of industries with the opposite characteristics—high fixed costs, low per capita demand, high durability and long duration of the production process—include aircraft manufacturers, film studios, music producers and knowledge-intensive business services. These industries can only survive and thrive in the largest and most densely populated regions.

According to Swedish data, labor market areas with between 3,000 and 6,000 residents host around 40 different industries on average. In contrast, the labor market area of Stockholm, with about two million residents, hosts 600 of the 750 distinct industries that exist in Sweden. Hence the

Table 6.3   *Production units and employment in private-sector and public-sector service provision, Sweden, 1990*

	Production units	Employment	Employment per production unit
Private services	265,571	1,233,000	4.64
Public services	44,419	1,270,000	28.59
Private/public	5.97	0.97	0.16

Source: Statistics Sweden (1991).

percentage of industries represented ranges from 5 percent in the smallest regions to 80 percent in the largest one.

Johansson and Strömquist (2005) present a function that shows how the number of five-digit industries (according to the SNI classification) depends on the population of labor market areas. The estimated relation between the number of industries, N, and population, P, of Swedish labor market areas in the 1990s was N = -804 + 95 ln P (R^2 = .96).

Firms operating under competitive conditions will in the long run search for locations offering minimum average costs, including transport and transaction costs, irrespective of how these costs are charged. It is noteworthy that tax-funded service monopolies at best have incentives to minimize average production costs, implying that they pay little if any attention to transport or transaction costs. Crucially, this neglect often reveals itself as the waiting-time cost associated with queuing. As the theory that we present in this chapter implies, this minimization of average fixed production cost has the predictable consequence of excessively large production facilities. Table 6.3 illustrates the macro-level implications of this governmental misallocation of productive resources in the case of Sweden in the 1990s.

As Table 6.3 shows, there were six times as many private as public service production units, despite almost identical numbers of workers. One of the main efficiency gains in the following decades—following privatization of pharmacies, health clinics and some schools—was a more dispersed spatial structure of production, smaller workplaces and better spatial accessibility for consumers. It is a little used and yet typical example of how market processes tend to produce more efficient resource use than public-sector planning, even when none of the actors—whether governmental or private—is aware of all of the factors that affect overall efficiency in production.

NOTE

1. Terborgh's (1954) model is as follows:

$$K_0 = I_0 \sum_1^T C_t(1/(1 + r)^t) = I_0 + C(1/r - 1/r(1 + r)^t)$$

Define: $(1/r - 1/r(1 + r)^T) = \alpha_r^T$

which implies that $K_0 = I_0 + \alpha_r^T C$; where C = annual costs (assumed to be constant); α = an annuity factor; t = year; T = duration (lifespan) in years; K = present value of the cost flow; I = initial investment cost; and r = real rate of interest (or discount).

APPENDIX 6.1

$\mathbf{x} = \mathbf{Ax} + g\mathbf{Bx} = \mathbf{Ax} + g\mathbf{TAx}$; where $\mathbf{A} = \{a_{ij}\}$; $\mathbf{T} = \{T_{ij}\}$; $(i, j = 1, \ldots, n)$ and where $\mathbf{x} = \{x_i\}$; $(i = 1, \ldots, n)$;

In a simplified case, the durability of a good would be the same for all users. Then $\mathbf{T}$ is a diagonal matrix with T_i as the diagonal elements of the matrix $\mathbf{T}$. It is easy to prove that with $\mathbf{A}$ and $\mathbf{T}$ greater than 0, there exists an equilibrium structure of production (x^*) with all $x_i > 0$ and with an associated equilibrium rate of growth, $g^* > 0$. Furthermore, a *ceteris-paribus* decrease in *any* of the elements of the $\mathbf{A}$ matrix as a consequence of technological improvements will increase the equilibrium rate of growth and change the equilibrium structure of production.

The equality $p = p\mathbf{A} + r\, p\mathbf{TA}$ determines the dual equilibrium structure of prices (p) and the real rate of interest r. Because $\mathbf{A}$ and $\mathbf{T}$ are the same as in the quantitative equilibrium problem we would have an equilibrium price vector (p^*) greater than zero and an associated equilibrium real rate of interest (r^*). At the general growth equilibrium $r^* = g^*$.

APPENDIX 6.2

The von Neumann model of growth is: $\mathbf{q}^T\mathbf{B} \geq \alpha\mathbf{q}^T\mathbf{A}$; $\mathbf{Bp} \leq \beta\mathbf{Ap}$; $\mathbf{q}^T(\mathbf{B} - \alpha\mathbf{A})\mathbf{p} = 0$; $\mathbf{q}^T(\mathbf{B} - \beta\mathbf{A})\mathbf{p} = 0$; $\mathbf{q} \geq 0$; $\mathbf{p} \geq 0$; where $\mathbf{q}$ = vector of outputs; $\mathbf{p}$ = vector of prices; $\alpha = 1$ + rate of growth; $\beta = 1$ + rate of interest; $\mathbf{A}$ = mn matrix of inputs; and $\mathbf{B}$ = mn matrix of outputs.

Von Neumann proved the existence and uniqueness of equilibrium by generalizing the Brouwer fixed-point theorem. His model of a growing economy considered the linear matrix pencil $(A - \lambda B)$ for the nonnegative matrices $\mathbf{A}$ and $\mathbf{B}$. He further proved the existence and uniqueness of the relative price vector p and the relative quantity vector q and the growth intensity λ of $p(A - \lambda B)q = 0$.

The model and its dual can also be solved as a linear programming formulation. The strong assumption that $a_{ij} + b_{ij} > 0$ was used by von Neumann in his proof of the existence and uniqueness of the equilibrium rate of growth and interest. Kemeny et al. (1956) propose the weaker condition that $\Sigma j\, b_{ij} > 0$ for all i and $\Sigma i\, a_{ij} > 0$ for all j, which implies that each good is reproducible and that each process requires at least one good as input.

APPENDIX 6.3

Maximize $V = \int_0^\infty pu(t)k(t)e^{-\rho t}dt$ dt (A6.1); subject to the growth constraint $\dot{k} = ak - bk^2$ (A6.2)

We can now formulate the Euler-Lagrange equation corresponding to (A6.1) and (A6.2). Inserting uk $= ak - bk^2 - \dot{k}$. into (A6.2) we arrive at the following optimization problem: *Maximize:* $\int_0^\infty p(ak - bk^2 - \dot{k})e^{-\rho t}dt$ (A6.3); with the necessary condition k(opt) $= (a - \rho)/2b$ (A6.4).

The stability of the equilibrium state can be proven with the aid of Lyapunov's theorem. Introduce the new variable $K = k - k^*$, where k^* indicates the equilibrium value of k: $dK/dt = -(a - \rho)/2 K - bK^2$. It is then possible to prove that the solution $K = 0$, if the Lyapunov function V(K) is positive definite. $V(K) = K^2((a - \rho)/2 + bK)^2$. The V–function is positive definite. Thus, the equilibrium is asymptotically stable.

k^* can be seen as an ecologically and economically sustainable equilibrium state. The formulation in equations (A6.1) through (A6.4) can be transformed into the equivalent Hamiltonian maximization problem of equation (A6.5):

$$\text{Maximize } H = puke^{-\rho t} - \mu(ak - bk^2 - uk) \text{ (A6.5)};$$

A necessary condition of a maximum is:

$$\frac{dH}{du} = pke^{-\rho t} + \mu k = 0 \tag{A6.6}$$

Since k is greater than 0 in a sustainable equilibrium solution, the implication is that $pe^{-\rho t} = -\mu$; or $\frac{d\mu}{dt}/\mu = \rho$.

The adaptation of behavior is related to the optimal harvesting effort as is demonstrated by the following optimality condition:

$$-\frac{dH}{dk} = \frac{d\mu}{dt} = -pue^{-\rho t} + \mu\,(a - 2bk - u) \tag{A6.7}$$

By substitution of (A6.5) into (A6.6) we again get:

$$\frac{d\mu}{dt}/\mu = a- 2bk = \rho \tag{A6.8}$$

The rate of growth of the capital value should thus equal the opportunity real rate of interest along the optimal trajectory.

7. Expectations, capital and entrepreneurship

> Persons who like to take great speculative chances are likely to sacrifice a large amount of their exaggerated expectations for the sake of relatively small addition to their present income. In other words, they will have a high degree of impatience. On the contrary agents receiving an income which is risky for all periods of time [may exhibit] a low, instead of a high degree of impatience. (Fisher, 1930, p.79)

Most models of capital value assume that investors in capital make decisions that include elements of risk (also known as "probabilistic uncertainty"). There is also often the explicit or implicit idea that all risk-adjusted expected returns are equal in equilibrium, irrespective of what type of capital was invested in.

The question of how people form their expectations is one of the weakest parts of the conventional theory of capital value. The normal assumption is that the history of returns in the form of observed averages and fluctuations determines future returns. This view does not command unanimous consent, however. There are analysts who remain skeptical about smooth statistical representations of probabilistic uncertainty. They claim that these processes are complex, and that it is possible for large upward or downward leaps to disrupt a period of smooth and undramatic fluctuations.

MICROECONOMIC DECISIONS WITH UNCERTAIN EXPECTATIONS

Ramsey (1926/1931) lays down the foundations for modern decision theory, and proposes three fundamental strategic elements:

1. Expectations concerning variables that influence valuable outcomes.
2. Uncertainty, probability and risk associated with expectations.
3. Utility of outcomes.

Ramsey (ibid.) also proves an important representation theorem. The theorem shows how a utility function that is determined up to a positive linear transformation can represent a person's subjective preferences (Sahlin, 1990). Ramsey's goal is to isolate the conditions under which binary preferences lead to maximized expected utility. The chosen representation makes sure that a probability function exists, that the utility function is unconditional and finally that the probability and utility functions yield expected utilities that reflect subjective preferences. Ramsey (ibid.) uses eight axioms of three different types to prove this theorem. The types are behavioral, ontological and structural.

Behavioral axioms involve rules that "rational" individuals are supposed to comply with when arriving at a decision. The rule that preferences should be transitive is a well-known axiom of this type. For example, an individual exhibits transitive preferences if the following relationships apply: the difference in utility between A and B equals the difference between C and D; the difference between C and D equals the difference between E and F; the difference between A and B therefore equals the difference between E and F.

Ramsey's ontological and structural axioms meanwhile refer to what exists and provide the mathematical tools for the proof of the representation theorem. An example is his first axiom, which states that there "is an ethically neutral proposition p believed to degree ½" (Ramsey, 1926/1931, p. 74).

Rediscoveries of axioms similar or identical to Ramsey's include von Neumann and Morgenstern (1944) and Savage (1954). Figure 7.1 represents the choice model that results from this approach to human decisions.

Figure 7.1 represents an individual such as an investor who faces the possibility of investing in some new capital such as a machine tool, at an

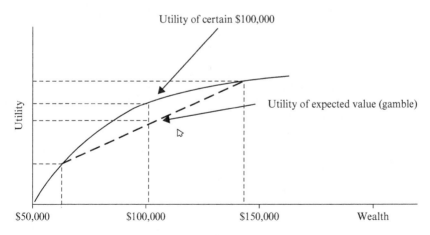

Figure 7.1   Ramsey's approach to decision theory

investment cost of $100,000. We may, for example, assume that the investor finds herself in an expansive economy with full employment and that this implies a gross present value of $150,000 dollars, corresponding to a net rate of return of 50 percent. If the economy had been in recession, we may hypothetically assume a gross present value of $50,000 and a net rate of return of −50 percent. If these were the only two possibilities, then an investor in a state of complete ignorance (regarding which of the two states she will find herself in) would face two states with equal probability and an expected return of $0. With the assumed utility function the wise decision is then to abstain from the investment. However, if she is sure that the full-employment state is the true state she should make the investment.

How to arrive at reasonable expectations is an unsolved problem in this theory as developed by Ramsey and his followers. The importance of even very long time horizons is obvious when decisions refer to long-lived capital such as heavy machinery, buildings, education or new knowledge.

A central aspect of economic decisions is to find methods that help decision makers generate reasonable expectations about the future of the economic variables that influence their decisions. Keynes was quite outspoken about the role of psychological factors such as pessimism and optimism in the formation of expectations and their influence on decisions to invest:

> A conventional valuation which is established as the outcome of the mass psychology of a large number of ignorant individuals is liable to change violently as the result of a sudden fluctuation of opinion due to factors which do not really make much difference to the prospective yield; since there will be no strong roots of conviction to hold it steady. In abnormal times in particular, when the hypothesis of an indefinite continuance of the existing state of affairs is less plausible than usual even though there are no express grounds to anticipate a definite change, the market will be subject to waves of optimistic and pessimistic sentiment, which are unreasoning and yet in a sense legitimate where no solid basis exists for a reasonable calculation. (Keynes, 1936, Ch. 12, Section 5.3)

Optimism bias is not merely hypothetical—it affects both microeconomic actors such as entrepreneurs and macroeconomic ones such as central bankers. Optimism bias is particularly prevalent when the stakes are high, for example when investing in start-ups or planning mergers and acquisitions. Empirical surveys in the United States have found that 68 percent of start-up entrepreneurs believe their company is more likely to succeed than similar companies, while in reality only 50 percent of start-up companies survive beyond three years of activity (Bracha and Brown, 2010). Köllinger et al. (2007) surveyed a large sample of start-up entrepreneurs in 18 countries and found that entrepreneurs in all of these countries tend to overestimate the likelihood of success by relying on subjective perceptions rather than on historical success probabilities for start-ups.

Recently there have been some attempts to formally analyze pessimistic and optimistic views on expectations of the future that are consistent with the models of Ramsey (1926/1931), von Neumann and Morgenstern (1944) and Savage (1954).

Dillenberger et al. (2015) offer one such attempt.[1] They introduce a variable that denotes bias, r. If this r equals one there is no bias and hence no probability distortion. If $r > 1$, there is pessimism bias, which implies a systematic tendency to underestimate probabilities associated with good outcomes, with especially severe underestimates attaching to the very best ones. These pessimistic individuals also overestimate the probabilities of bad outcomes. Conversely, if $r < 1$, the bias works in the opposite optimistic direction, as for start-up entrepreneurs. The resulting choice behavior is indistinguishable from that of a decision model with a Savage-type representation.

Present-value calculations are conditional on expected but uncertain future prices in all investment decisions. Equity prices, interest rates and exchange rates also depend on expected future prices. The classical economists paid some attention to the role of expectations, but their methods were mostly qualitative and referred to an imaginary state in which perfect foresight prevails. Expectations were equated with actual outcomes, which reduced their relevance.

In the 1930s, the "cobweb model"—a one-period supply-lag model with expectations—appeared as the standard dynamic example of decision processes in markets. In this model, observations of prior prices shape producers' expectations and production decisions, while current prices determine current demand. Kaldor (1934) even refers to this model as the "cobweb theorem." Despite all this attention the model failed to generate any important quantitative results.

In the same decade, the Stockholm School—consisting of Erik Lindahl, Gunnar Myrdal, Bertil Ohlin and other young followers of Wicksell— initiated a more sophisticated approach to the study of expectations. They called their approach the temporary equilibrium method. This approach includes an explicit distinction between the *ex-ante* and *ex-post* values of the same variable. *Ex-ante* values are expected values that determine decisions and thus influence realized *ex-post* outcome values. The underlying assumption is that expectations determine market demand and prices. The consequence is that a learning process guides the evolution of prices and production decisions over time.

In his doctoral dissertation *Prisbildningsproblemet och föränderligheten* [The Problem of Price Formation and Change], Myrdal (1927) presents one view of how expectations and risks influence the business cycle. The fact that production takes time and the additional fact that economic agents have imperfect knowledge are—according to Myrdal—aspects of economic life that cause a dynamic pricing problem. Later, Hayek—an opponent of Myrdal on many economic and political issues—came to similar conclusions about the endogenous dynamics of market behavior.

Hayek viewed expectations as deriving from shared habits, norms and traditions (Butos and Koppl, 1997). The rules that govern behavior then give rise to expectations. In Hayek's view, it is a combination of slow biological and faster social evolutionary processes that causes these rules to emerge in human societies (Hayek, 1952; 1973). It is therefore not necessarily true that the uncertainty of the future causes discoordination in the present. Since shared rules—or, in other words, institutions–shape expectations, there is a tendency for these expectations to converge among people who interact within a shared institutional context. There is also a long-run selection process in operation, whereby the market process selects sufficiently "fit"—although not necessarily optimal—expectations at the expense of "unfit" ones. A market with stable rules that govern the behavior of participants will then also coordinate their expectations.

Koppl (2002; see also Koppl and Whitman, 2004) proposes that the tendency toward convergent expectations will only exist if there is sufficient institutional stability. If certain people—so-called "Big Players"—have the ability to change the rules or terms of the game in sudden and unpredictable ways, it becomes much more likely that expectations will diverge. Koppl (ibid.) suggests that a central banker with discretionary powers to change interest rates is a good example of a "Big Player" who may cause discoordination of expectations.

According to the economists of the Stockholm School, the combined effect of the duration of production and market actors' imperfect knowledge is uncertain expectations; leading to dynamic impacts on the endogenous formation of prices of goods and factors of production. This analysis found no guaranteed equilibrium. However, when these ideas were built into macroeconomic analyses of investments, economists of the Stockholm School came to conclusions more in line with Keynes's *General Theory* (1936) than with Hayek's *Prices and Production* (1931/1967). Keynes's macroeconomic theory emphasizes the importance of long-term expectations of prospective yields for capital investment and asset prices. An example of this reasoning is the liquidity preference function, which takes on a hyperbolic form to reflect the impact of expectations of a future increase in the interest rate on the demand for money. Keynes (1936) calls this expectation-derived effect "the liquidity trap" and considers it the main cause of high-unemployment equilibrium. Similarly, a sudden and contagious fall in *expected* demand and profits causes a radical collapse of investments, leading—via a downward multiplier process—to a depression.

Another instance of the macroeconomic use of naive expectations is the expectations-augmented Phillips Curve. One example is Blanchard's (2008) assumption that the expected rate of inflation in one year equals the observed rate of inflation a year earlier.

In the early writings on the role of expectations in economics the focus was thus primarily on the macroeconomy. With the exception of Frank Knight (1921), there was not much interest in formulating a consistent microeconomic theory of investment and capital that accounts for the effects of risk and uncertainty. An exception from the Stockholm School is Ingvar Svennilson (1938), which represents an early attempt to formulate a consistent microeconomic theory of decisions that are subject to risk. However, the Stockholm School as a coherent school of thought disintegrated shortly thereafter.

FRANK KNIGHT'S PATH-BREAKING CONTRIBUTION

In *Risk, Uncertainty, and Profit*, Knight (1921) offers a theory of microeconomic processes that for the first time makes explicit the fundamental difference between risk and true uncertainty. What is usually labeled "uncertainty" in later mainstream contributions is in fact no more and no less than simple risk as Knight defines it. Risk is a state of affairs with more than one possible future outcome, but it is at the same time a well-structured state where the set of possible outcomes is known in advance and where each outcome is associated with an objective probability. It is then a straightforward matter of performing a simple calculation to act in a way that maximizes the *expected* utility or profit. Later "rational expectation" theories use two assumptions that relate to Knightian risk. The first assumption is that there are objective probabilities associated with all possible economic outcomes, and the second assumption is that economic actors know these probabilities and incorporate them in their decision rules in a way that makes them maximize their *expected* utilities or profits. This is what it means to be "rational" according to these theories.

The Knightian view is different. Situations of risk refer to when a structure has been put in place by people or is an emergent property of natural processes. Casino gambling is an obvious example that involves risk on the part of both the casino's owners and its customers, but so is a plane crash due to mechanical failure. Note that in both these cases there are known and well-defined outcome sets. Generally speaking, many processes that may be labeled as biological, medical or technological have well-structured risks and outcomes; the main reason for this is that such processes play themselves out without (endogenous) human creativity. The same is true of the risk of natural disasters and below-average rainfall and their effects on the quantities and prices of various agricultural goods. A stable equilibrium, especially in its original formulation as a circular flow—an economic process that is repeated every year—is a state of affairs which easily incorporates notions of risk but which is subverted by Knightian uncertainty.

Uncertainty in its Knightian sense is a set of possible future outcomes that is open-ended, in the sense that there is no way to know how many possible outcomes should be listed as feasible. It is thus unstructured. And since it is unstructured there is no reliable way of attaching a probability to an outcome, even if it is one that is clearly possible or one that seems "likely." In a well-structured situation with a known set of outcomes, it is not necessary to have access to objective probabilities in order to maximize. An individual who is ignorant of the actual probabilities may simply choose to assign the same probability to each event or even to invent her own *subjective* probabilities. The situation is totally different for an individual who faces a choice involving structurally uncertain outcomes. According to Knight, such a person exercises *judgment* rather than a maximizing strategy.

While it is reasonable to assume maximization of expected utility as the decision rule of rational people in well-structured situations, it is unreasonable to assume the same of rational people facing a genuinely uncertain outcome as the end result of whatever it is that they decide. According to Knight, a decision maker who judges rather than maximizes is an *entrepreneur*. Hence the role of the entrepreneur in the economic system is to "shoulder uncertainty."

While Knight's seminal treatment of risk, uncertainty and entrepreneurship has been almost completely ignored by later economists, it is beginning to have an impact in the early twentieth century, particularly within the interdisciplinary field of entrepreneurship and in some non-mainstream schools of economic thought. Langlois and Cosgel (1993), Foss et al. (2007), Langlois (2007), Andersson (2008) and Foss and Klein (2012) all put the notion of entrepreneurial judgment at the center of their analyses of entrepreneurship and integrate Knightian uncertainty into modern institutional economic theory so as to account for microeconomic change.

Yoram Barzel (1989) offers a theory of economic property rights that is particularly conducive to an integration of Knightian uncertainty and entrepreneurship into a broader framework (Foss et al., 2007; Andersson, 2008). Owners of human and physical capital (including "land") may rent out their resources and in exchange they receive a contractually specified payment. It is easy to think of such people as (at least implicitly) maximizing some sort of expected income or utility and therefore it is no great surprise that standard theory limits itself to such factors. But capital owners may also decide *not to rent out their capital*. If they decide to keep control of the use of their capital, owners thus *do not* receive any pre-specified return; they reserve the right to exercise their property rights in the form of *entrepreneurial judgment*. They then become *residual claimants*, so that any deviation from the sum of all contractual compensation is accounted for as "profit" or "loss."

The owner of a resource under her own direction—that is, one that has not been rented out—must subtract an opportunity cost that corresponds to the market rent (or "salary") from accounting profits or losses to arrive at an estimate of the true entrepreneurial profit or loss. This is obvious. But what is less obvious—and where property rights theory makes a real contribution to our understanding of Knightian entrepreneurship—is that entrepreneurship is really about the *creation of capital* if capital is understood in its broad Knightian sense.

An illustrative example will help to clarify this notion of entrepreneurship. Assume a skilled individual. Let us call him Adam. Adam possesses economic property rights over the use of his skills, which means that he is the person who has ultimate control over the deployment of these skills to productive or consumptive activities. These skills constitute Adam's human capital. His human capital may be conceived of as an open-ended bundle of valuable attributes. For example, one attribute is his ability to teach undergraduate microeconomics, while another attribute is his ability to give an inspirational speech on the importance of creativity to real and aspiring executives.

Several colleges recognize Adam's skills as an economics lecturer, and the highest-bidding college offers him a salary of $50,000. This is then Adam's market "wage" and also his opportunity cost, since this is his best-paying skill as an employee. But Adam thinks that he can earn more by repeatedly offering his spiel to groups of executives in different cities, renting auditoriums and selling tickets to events that he advertises on his website as "the event that will unlock your creative potential and make you rich." This is an attribute of his human capital that potential employers such as colleges have no willingness to pay for, and thus he becomes an entrepreneur, who in effect *judges* that others—colleges, companies, bureaucracies—underestimate his true value. By exercising entrepreneurial judgment, Adam in effect *creates* a new human capital attribute that he thereby *innovates*. (In other words, the human capital attribute of a specific inspirational speech enters the market for the first time.)

Note that it is impossible for Adam to a priori objectively estimate his potential profit, since this is an entirely new type of speech and he might become a celebrity (good for Adam) *or* some other person might successfully capture this market by offering what consumers perceive as a superior imperfect substitute. Alternatively, he might attract imitators who out-compete him by giving lower-priced speeches *or* something entirely unforeseen might happen such as a (speech-induced) opportunity to run in an election (with potential utility gains from the exercise of political power). Indeed, even the range of possible earnings may be unknowable below some extremely high upper limit (and thus irrelevant as a decision criterion), since markets such as these often give rise to "winner-takes-all" phenomena (Andersson and Andersson, 2006).

Such an open-ended list of potential outcomes, all of which result from one initial entrepreneurial decision, does not exist in general equilibrium. The underlying assumptions make such scenarios impossible. In equilibrium, every factor earns the same marginal return and there is no room for entrepreneurial profits or losses. Therefore, equilibrium models are not useful tools for understanding the role of entrepreneurship in the economy. An entrepreneurial action can only be a movement away from or toward some equilibrium, depending on how "absolute" the equilibrium is. There is in this sense no real difference between entrepreneurship theories, whether Knightian, Kirznerian or Schumpeterian. They all by necessity refer to dynamic phenomena that happen when the economy is not yet—or no longer—in equilibrium.

In spite of this system-level agreement, we believe that there are strong reasons for preferring the Knightian approach rather than the main alternatives. While earlier arguments for Knightian theory have stressed its greater realism as compared with other influential theories (see Foss and Klein, 2012), we believe that it is its treatment of asset ownership *and* its potential as an empirical research program that are the key strengths of the Knightian theory of entrepreneurship.

A COMPARATIVE ASSESSMENT OF KNIGHTIAN ENTREPRENEURSHIP THEORY

Schumpeter (1934) and Kirzner (1973) are doubtless the two most influential theories of entrepreneurship in economics. Arguably, they owe their popularity to the clarity of their expositions, which present them as *complements* to general equilibrium models. Schumpeter's complement is a Walrasian "circular flow," while Kirzner's is Debreu's timeless general equilibrium. A property of both theories is a clear separation of the entrepreneurial and capitalist functions. Hence these theories are not about entrepreneurs in the sense of the normal use of the word; it is about a specific type of human action that does not require any resources at all. It is a superior insight about how to combine pre-existing labor and land in a new way (Schumpeter, 1934) or a superior alertness to a pre-existing profit opportunity (Kirzner, 1973). These are "thin" theories about economic life at its highest level of abstraction, but there are—what we consider to be—three serious flaws. First, there is an artificial separation between entrepreneurship and uncertainty. Second, both theories obscure the role of capital. Third, a wide gulf separates the two theories from what most academics would consider to be empirical studies of entrepreneurship.

Schumpeter's and Kirzner's very abstract conception of the "entrepreneur" makes it possible for them to claim that entrepreneurs do not shoulder uncertainty (or risk). How is this possible? Using our example of Adam—the economics lecturer and inspirational speaker—should make their reasoning clear. In the Schumpeterian framework, Adam in his role as entrepreneur combines labor and land (and capital as given mixtures of land and capital) in a new way. Adam's new combination is his labor (now as motivational speaker rather than as a lecturer), land (space for auditoriums) and mixed labor and land known as capital goods (buildings, laptop computers and so on). This new use gives rise to entrepreneurial profits if Adam is successful and if it is sufficiently successful to affect economic development, it will attract imitators who will gradually bid up input prices and bid down output prices. (Admittedly, this is not a very Schumpeterian example, since Schumpeter had a traditional view of development that focused on manufacturing and agriculture.) The key point here is that Adam in his role as entrepreneur has no need for capital. The theory posits that a capitalist provides capital and shoulders uncertainty, but that same capitalist does not earn an entrepreneurial profit. How does Schumpeter (ibid.) accomplish this feat? He does this by assuming that in the case where Adam uses his own money to rent auditoriums and his own labor to produce speeches, he is—in a theoretical sense—borrowing money from himself (Adam in his capitalist role) and hiring himself as a worker (Adam in his role as labor input). Consequently, Adam earns profits in his entrepreneurial role, risk-compensated interest in his capitalist role and wages in his labor role. He may even earn rent if he happens to be the landowner. Hence there are no flesh-and-blood Schumpeterian entrepreneurs.

Kirzner's (1973) treatment is similar, except that Adam "discovers" a discrepancy between the total cost of the land, labor and capital inputs and the output revenue from selling his inspirational speech service. The "entrepreneur" again ceases to exist after the initial and instantaneous discovery, after which all costs and revenues accrue to conventional production factors, apart from the profit which accrues to Adam in a way that does not put "Adam the entrepreneur's" resources in jeopardy—it is either "Adam the capitalist" or an external lender who shoulders a vaguely defined uncertainty or risk in this theory.

The implicit assumption in both theories is that asset ownership is unimportant for our understanding of the economic function of entrepreneurship. This makes for a thinner and perhaps more elegant theory, but at the considerable cost of treating economic development as if access to resources does not matter. But it does. An assumption of asset neutrality distorts our understanding of real-world entrepreneurial processes. An economy with a well-developed banking system where most people have access to credit is more likely to spawn innovations than an economy where most innovative entrepreneurs must rely on their own—perhaps meager— savings (Andersson, 2008).

The argument against "entrepreneurs" without capital is even stronger. If we take Knight seriously and view capital as inclusive of all types of human, physical and other capital, it becomes impossible to conceive of an entrepreneur who is devoid of capital. Even the possibility of discovering a profit opportunity requires—first—that the discoverer has the human capital necessary for recognizing what revenues and costs are and— second—the institutional capital of a system of property rights that make revenues and costs meaningful and worthy of discovery in the first place.

Our third argument for Knight and against Schumpeter and Kirzner is empirical. Since entrepreneurship involves a transitory mental realization or discovery according to both Schumpeter and Kirzner, it becomes impossible to do conventional empirical research on the prevalence of entrepreneurship in different institutional or spatial contexts. The only type of research that may conceivably address the "entrepreneurial function" is asking innovators, speculators or arbitrageurs to describe what they recall about their mental states at the moment when they suddenly realized that there was an unexploited profit opportunity or when they equally suddenly decided to pursue that opportunity. While these are interesting questions, it is nevertheless a very limited type of empirical research.

In contrast, the Knightian approach incorporates most of which goes under the general rubric of entrepreneurship studies. Since Knightian entrepreneurship is judgment under conditions of uncertainty about how to deploy physical or human capital, it is obvious that what we conventionally think of as entrepreneurship belongs to this category. Starting a new firm is entrepreneurship. Introducing an innovation within an existing firm is also entrepreneurship. Even an owner's decision to deploy the human capital of a manager in a new way is entrepreneurship in its Knightian sense. A quantitative empirical study of innovation in firms with different attributes or business start-ups in regions with different business conditions thus deal with different subsets of Knightian entrepreneurship, but have nothing to do with either the Schumpeterian or Kirznerian type.

SLOW AND FAST PROCESSES IN ENTREPRENEURSHIP RESEARCH

The salience of structural uncertainty in the definition of entrepreneurship may seem to imply that it is impossible to make general or systematic statements about the prevalence of entrepreneurship in different contexts. This is however not true. To understand why we can say something with more substance than "entrepreneurship exists," we have to return to the question of timescales—that is to say to the question of slow and fast processes in economic life.

A person's decision to start a business or to innovate is inherently unpredictable and belongs to the fast processes of everyday market activity. There is no way to predict who will introduce a specific product innovation, or for that matter the specification and function of a product that does not yet exist. In other words, disaggregated quantitative forecasts of entrepreneurial activity are indeed impossible because of the presence of Knightian (or structural) uncertainty. But we would argue that despite our irremediable ignorance of individual future events, it is possible to make *pattern predictions* about the relative frequency of various types of entrepreneurship in aggregate contexts, but only if these contexts consist of variables that are changing at a slower rate and affect more people than the type of entrepreneurship under investigation. In other words, we need to use *infrastructural* variables when attempting to explain aggregate entrepreneurial outcomes.

A few examples should illustrate why this is a reasonable view of the matter. We would expect more entrepreneurial activity in the institutional context of Hong Kong than in the context of North Korea. We would also expect more entrepreneurial activity in the accessibility context of London than in that of the Isle of Man. Institutions change slowly by definition and spatial accessibility derives from the position of a node within slowly changing infrastructure networks. We believe that research that addresses the impacts of institutions and/or accessibility on entrepreneurship will improve our understanding. It may also enable us to predict broad patterns of entrepreneurial phenomena such as regional frequencies of start-ups and innovations. Predictions are however bound to be of patterns rather than of exact quantities. A not very daring example would be a prediction of a "high" level of entrepreneurial activity—whether innovation, speculation or business creation—in large cities and a "low" level in remote villages, given the same institutions.

THE INCONVENIENCE OF STRUCTURAL UNCERTAINTY TO THE POST-WAR MINDSET

Since Knightian uncertainty implies an unstructured situation away from equilibrium, later economists almost totally disregarded it, especially in the first decades after World War II. In fact, economics developed in a direction that was the *opposite* of what development along Knightian lines would have implied. Economists came to increasingly favor supposedly exact econometric forecasts, more demanding but less realistic micro-economic assumptions and short-term manipulation of macroeconomic variables. In spite of their disagreements and differences, leading pre-war economic theorists such as Wicksell, Keynes, Schumpeter and Hayek all focused on *understanding* and *explaining* regularities in economic life. The early post-war economists were different, focusing instead on prediction, "operationalization," and—among the more applied ones—technocratic management.

Theories that invoke structural uncertainty and the role of self-directed individual entrepreneurship in economic development would in this context have been the exact opposite of "preaching to the choir." Thus, economists paid lip service to Knight's contributions, but then went on to occupy themselves with unrelated problems that seemed more pressing and relevant even to Knight's two most influential students, Milton Friedman and George Stigler (Knight's third famous student, James Buchanan, was an exception). The treatment of expectations in economics from the 1950s to the 1970s developed in a direction very different from what one may have predicted in the 1930s.

"RATIONAL EXPECTATIONS"

John Muth (1961) returns to Kaldor's analysis and hypothesizes that economic agents normally develop "rational expectations," with the cobweb model as an example. Assuming that the model is stable and generates the equilibrium price p^*, the rational expectation would be $E(p) = p^*$. Surprisingly, this idea of "rational expectations" did not enter microeconomic theorizing. Instead, a contribution by Lucas (1976) that builds on Muth's rational expectations theory as well as the Heisenberg indeterminacy (or uncertainty) principle became a cornerstone of the critique of

Keynesian macroeconomics. In essence, Lucas's claim boils down to the conclusion that if a policymaker tries to control a variable such as the rate of inflation, it will cause other changes that the policymaker does not expect or want. This conclusion brings to mind similar earlier claims by Karl Popper and Hayek. It is also consistent with Schumpeter's analysis of the potential failures of democracy.

INFORMATION THEORY AND EXPECTATIONS

In the eighteenth century, the Reverend Thomas Bayes proposed that any decision having future consequences should be based on *experiences that have resulted in probable belief* and proposed the following formula:

$$P(A|B) = \frac{P(B|A)P(A)}{P(B)} \tag{7.1}$$

in which A and B are events and the probability $P(B) \neq 0$. Then,

- $P(A)$ and $P(B)$ are the independent probabilities of A and B.
- $P(A|B)$ is the probability of event A if B is believed to be true.
- $P(B|A)$ is the probability of event B if A is believed to be true.

The Bayesian approach to decision making is central to information theory (Kullback, 1959; Snickars and Weibull, 1977). In information theory, $ln\ p(x)/q(x)$ is the information in x for discriminating between the distributions p and q; it is the natural logarithm of the likelihood ratio. It is thus the Bayesian factor with the assumption of uniform priors of the distributions.

It is possible to expand this reasoning so as to be compatible with theory-based knowledge. A simple example is as follows. Let us assume that loans fund all investments in different industries and that the central bank determines the loanable funds, L, with the requirement that the returns to the loanable funds should be at the level rL. This implies that the sum of all investment returns in different industries is constrained to equal rL, if this is the only constraint:

$$\sum_{i=1}^{N} r(i)I(i) = rL; \tag{7.2}$$

Rephrasing this as relative proportions yields:

$$\sum_{i=1}^{N} \left(\frac{r(i)}{rL}\right)p(i) = 1; \tag{7.3}$$

Let us further assume that all decision makers know the relative proportions $q(i)$ that have been realized in earlier periods (at what are possibly different levels of rL). The least surprising allocation $\{p(i)\}*$ is the minimum information allocation, which is:

$$\text{Min } I = \sum_{i=1}^{N} p(i) \ln p(i)/q(i) - \lambda\left(\sum_{i=1}^{N} \left(\frac{r(i)}{rL}\right) p(i) = 1 \right); \tag{7.4}$$

The necessary conditions for minimization are:

$$\ln(p(i)/q(i)) = \lambda\left(\frac{r(i)}{rL}\right) - 1; \ (i=1,\ldots,N); \tag{7.5}$$

$$\sum_{i=1}^{N} \left(\frac{r(i)}{rL}\right) p(i) - 1 = 0;$$

The earlier realized (prior) propositions then determine the most likely relative proportions $p(i)*$, possibly as observed one period earlier *and* as a result of the constraint on the required return on loanable funds:

$$p(i) = q(i)e^{\lambda(\frac{r(i)}{rL})-1}; \tag{7.6}$$

a logit function thus determines the investment proportions.

Hence it is possible to use the minimum information principle—that is, the least surprising expectation principle—to determine the expected values of decision variables as soon as information on earlier outcomes becomes available and it becomes possible to formulate reliable outcome-constraining models.

EXPECTATIONS BY REVISING AND LEARNING

In a much-cited study, Brian Arthur (1991) proposes a new way of handling expectations that seems more natural and richer than theories involving supposedly rational expectations: "We could speak of this as a system of temporarily fulfilled expectations—beliefs or models or hypotheses that are temporarily fulfilled (though not perfectly), that give way to different beliefs or hypotheses when they cease to be fulfilled."

His approach to expectations analysis is by way of a parable involving *El Farol*—a bar located in Santa Fe, New Mexico. The bar is of limited size, and when it is fully occupied most potential customers think that it is too crowded to be worth a visit, and they feel equally uninterested if the bar is empty. Most people consider the bar most attractive when it is 60 percent full.

Arthur (ibid.) assumes that all patrons have formed their *initial* expectations according to their own individual model of how to form expectations, for instance: Predict next week's number to be:

- the same as last week's [35]
- a mirror image around 50 of last week's [65]
- 67 [67]
- a (rounded) average of the last four weeks [49]
- the trend in the last eight weeks, bounded by 0 and 100 [29]
- the same as two weeks ago (two-period cycle detector)
- and so on.

Each agent is assumed to learn the new attendance figure, and thus proceeds to update the monitored predictors.

Given starting conditions and the fixed set of predictors available to each agent, the future accuracies of all predictors are predetermined. The dynamics in this case is deterministic, even though the agents revise their expectation-forming models according to their failure or success tendencies. It thus becomes an expectation-based adaption-and-learning model. Figure 7.2 shows the outcome of Arthur's computer simulations.

The average attendance is 60 percent, but the swings around that figure are unpredictable. The model is obviously chaotic—a consequence of the mixture of negative and positive feedback mechanisms among the agents.

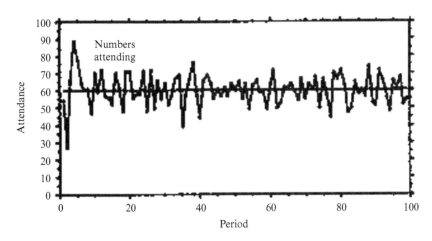

Figure 7.2   Computer output of attendance fluctuations during 100 periods

RETURNS, INVESTMENT RISKS AND THE MARKOWITZ CAPITAL VALUE REVOLUTION

Quite independently of the discussions among macroeconomists, financial theorists and operations analysts had started the development of modern financial economics as a separate field of microeconomics, with contributions first by Markowitz (1952) and later by Treynor (1962), Sharpe (1964) and others. Their approach was based on the idea that investors would have to base their decisions on their perception of expected future returns and risks, for which they could use calculations involving historical returns.

For example, an entrepreneur planning to buy a machine or some other capital equipment is in exactly the same situation as a household planning to buy equity in a firm. There will be an immediate obligation to spend a sum of money, I_0, with the expectation to receive returns in a number of future time periods, $(C_1, \ldots, C_T)$. The initial expenditure is a certain sum while the stream of returns as profits or dividends is uncertain.

An investor expects the stream of returns to occur at given points in time; the simplest expectation is then to assume that what has recently happened will repeat itself in future periods. This would amount to an expectation of stable equilibrium, with C^* occurring in each future period. If the best alternative investment yields a percentage return of r, then the future C^* will have to be discounted at that same rate. An investor should only choose investments where:

$$I_0 \leq C^*\left(\sum_1^T\left(\frac{1}{1 + r}\right)^r \right). \tag{7.7}$$

The right-hand side of this expression is the present value of the invested capital; the definition of the net present value is the present value minus the investment. Such a decision rule may of course turn out to be mistaken if the idea of "rational expectations" is incorrect. It will surely fail if entrepreneurs have an optimism bias and believe in a brighter future than what eventuates.

Markowitz (1952; 1959) approaches the problem of assessing uncertain capital values and investment decisions in a novel way, breaking with the earlier deterministic or mainly qualitative discussions of the impact of risk on capital values. The main assumption is that the only information about the value of a firm is reflected in the recent historical valuation of the firm's shares on the stock exchange. Shareholdings are mostly embedded in portfolios that consist of different securities (shares) and bonds. Each portfolio fluctuates in value, and it is possible to calculate an expected percentage return as an average of past percentage returns, while the standard

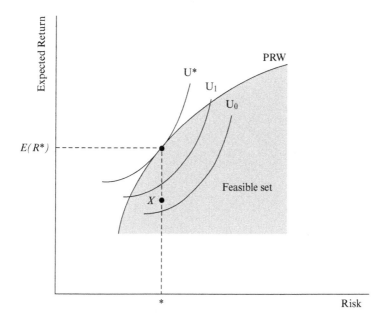

Figure 7.3   Utility curves and feasible combinations of expected portfolio return and risk according to Markowitz (1952)

deviation in percentage terms represents the fluctuations in a similar way. The standard deviation of the returns of a shares portfolio is, according to Markowitz (1952), a measure of the *capital portfolio risk*.

An optimal portfolio is then a set of shares and bonds that minimizes the risk, subject to the required expected returns. Minimizing the risk for a large set of required returns would trace out a risk-minimizing set of port-folios. Figure 7.3 shows this as the border curve PRW. Any portfolio below the border is inefficient. The point R is optimal and maximizes the utility of the investor, since it is the point of tangency between the opportunity curve PRW and the investor's indifference curve, U*.

Figure 7.3 can show the position of any single firm. If a firm's com-bination of risk and return is above PRW, it will trigger a reaction in the form of greater demand for shares in the firm. The share price will then increase until the combination of risk and return has moved the firm to a position on or below the PRW curve. Using reasoning first associated with Irving Fisher, it becomes possible to expand the opportunity set to include a linear combination of a risk-free asset (for example a safe and liquid bank account) and a maximum tangency point with the opportunity set, as Figure 7.4 illustrates.

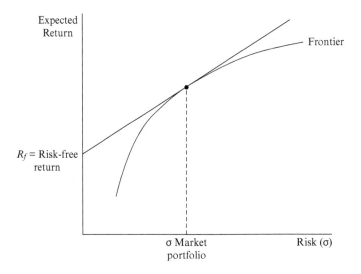

Figure 7.4   The possibility of a linear combination of a risk-free asset and a market portfolio

Building on earlier work by Markowitz and Fisher, Jack Treynor (1961; 1962), William F. Sharpe (1964), John Lintner (1965) and Jan Mossin (1966) all propose or advocate the use of the Capital Asset Pricing Model (CAPM). Fischer Black (1972) is another newer version of CAPM (the Zero-Beta CAPM) that does not presume the existence of a riskless asset. The expected return-risk equation is linear and has the following form:

$$E(R_i) = R_f + \beta_i(E(R_m) - R_f); \qquad (7.8)$$

where:
$E(R_i)$ = the expected return on the capital asset;
R_f = the risk-free interest rate such as the rate on government bonds or savings accounts;
$\beta_i = [\mathrm{Cov}(R_i, R_m)/\mathrm{Var}(R_m)]$ = sensitivity of the expected asset returns to the expected market returns;
$E(R_m)$ = expected return of the market portfolio.

The coefficient β_i is the chosen measure of risk, replacing Markowitz's use of the standard deviation of the portfolio. The basic idea is to expand the investors' choice set by allowing for linear combinations of the risk-free rate of return and the return to the market portfolio, which resembles Fisher's approach to a deterministic choice situation (see Figure 7.5).

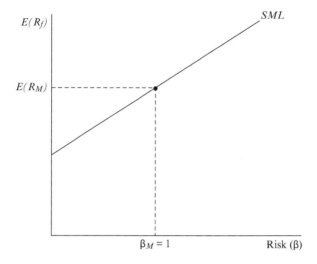

Figure 7.5 β_i *as a measure of the linear combination of expected return and risk* ($E[R_i]$ = *expected portfolio return*)

The equilibrium condition of CAPM states that the risk-adjusted expected excess returns from any pair of securities should be the same if the stock market is in equilibrium.

ARBITRAGE PRICING THEORY AND THE LAW OF ONE PRICE

Stephen Ross (1976) proposes Arbitrage Pricing Theory (APT) to take account of more factors than the beta-value risk. The most important assumption is that the actions of stock market investors will remove all possible arbitrage gains. Each share will then trade at one price in equilibrium and there are then no opportunities for arbitrage gains. Other APT assumptions are as follows:

- All securities have finite expected values and variances.
- Agents can form well-diversified portfolios.
- There are no taxes on security trading.
- Trading is not subject to transaction costs.

APT assumes that there are many possible factors that determine the returns of a security, such as a *surprising* increase in the inflation or unemployment rate; such factors may then also influence the expected returns. However, the no-arbitrage condition requires equilibrium, since two financial instruments or portfolios—even if they are not identical—should have the same price if their returns and risks are identical.

EL FAROL AND CAPITAL PRICING WITH ENDOGENOUS EXPECTATIONS

Arthur et al. (1996) propose a learning approach to the formation of expectations in capital market theory. The basic approach is to apply the same modeling principles as in the El Farol model (Arthur, 1994). The key assumption is that financial investors have a number of models or investment rules that guide their initial investment decisions. The relative success of an investor's decisions makes her retain, discard or amend the initial model. This implies endogenous determination of expectations in parallel with the succession of investment outcomes. Arthur et al. (1996) compared the results of their computer simulation of this process with the results of a rational expectations model. Trading volumes turned out to be much greater under a regime of decision-rule learning as compared with a rational expectations regime. Price differences were very small, but the time series had greater kurtosis and skewness with a much "fatter" tail.

THE IMPOSSIBILITY OF A DETERMINISTIC AGGREGATION OF CAPITAL

Many economists from Böhm-Bawerk (1891) to Hayek (1941/2014) struggled with the creation of a complete theory of the aggregation of capital, starting from disaggregated capital goods and with the goal of finally arriving at a consistent macroeconomic capital stock. The essence of their perceived problem was the heterogeneity of the capital goods and their prices as well as problems related to differences in their time structures. Mainstream neoclassical economists meanwhile approached the capital aggregation problem in a somewhat simplistic manner by assuming that the aggregated capital value is the historically calculated sum of depreciated investment goods valued at their historical prices.

One example is the Keynesian model in which fixed prices are used in the aggregation of national income, total investment and consumption. Another even more problematic example of this procedure is the Tinbergen-Solow-Swan model of growth.

The latter approach became the focal point of Joan Robinson's (1975) devastating critique and the Marxist-influenced capital controversy of the Cambridge (England)/Italy school (Pasinetti, 1969). All these approaches were bound to fail, because they all assume deterministic aggregation. The only escape in a dynamic deterministic world is into the world of Leontief and von Neumann, with their endogenous determination of relative prices, growth, interest rates and capital structure across industries.

The real problem with all these approaches is that capital is not enough to make a dynamic economy work. Expectations are the other necessary component of a theory of economic dynamics and expectations are by definition uncertain. A defensible aggregation of capital requires full consideration of risk and the wider concept of uncertainty.

The solution to the problem of capital aggregation requires acceptance of the *unavoidable uncertainty of expected returns* to investments in capital. It further requires acceptance of the fact that financial markets determine capital prices, with the most important being the stock and real estate markets. Theories such as those by Markowitz or Sharpe are a starting point, but these will need to integrate components from theories of knowledge and learning.

In the financial markets, macroeconomic capital equals the aggregated value of capital at the expected flow of dividends. The aggregate value of capital is therefore a relevant sum of investor-determined share prices. The stock market does not value capital per se—it only values *firms* with their firm-specific aggregations of capital. This means that a publicly listed firm gives rise to an aggregated but intrinsically uncertain valuation of a unique combination of human, physical and even social capital.

The modern theory of financial markets claims that the market for shares and bonds determines the total equilibrium value of each traded firms' capital as an average over an appropriate period of observation, taking expected prices, perceived risk and the real rate of interest into consideration.

The claim is that one can capture the totality of all capital allocation opportunities in the financial capital market, using the expected return, $r(m)$ and the expected "risk," $\beta(m)$. Both measures use what investors consider as a relevant historical time series. Although Markowitz and his followers did not realize this, different investors may use very different time series, resulting in different subjective "risk" estimates for the same firm. The key to understanding why this is so is by noting that investors arrive at a judgment by transforming uncertain future returns into subjective or perceived "risk." The APT value of a firm—seen as an aggregate of its material and non-material capital—will tend to approach its correct value as long as there are unusually knowledgeable investors willing to exploit arbitrage opportunities arising from incorrectly valued firms. Note that a deterministic allocation of capital, devoid of risk or uncertainty, yields $\beta(0) = 0$ and $r\,(0) \geq g$.

This way of analyzing the value of the firm implies that if we divide a firm's total capital value—as given by the stock market—by the scale of production, we obtain the average durability of the firm's capital.

THE NON-RANDOMNESS CRITIQUE OF CAPITAL MARKET THEORY

Some financial theorists have voiced a critique based on the inability of capital market theorists to predict black Mondays, Thursdays and other "black swans." Benoit Mandelbrot (1999/2008) focuses on their assumption of normal distributions, as opposed to distributions with a long or "fat" tail. In a 2008 *Edge* interview, Hans Ulrich Obrist called Mandelbrot "the father of long tails." Mandelbrot argues that:

> [t]he risk-reducing formulas behind portfolio theory rely on a number of demanding and ultimately unfounded premises. First, they suggest that price changes are statistically independent of one another: for example, that today's price has no influence on the changes between the current price and tomorrow's. As a result, predictions of future market movements become impossible. The second presumption is that all price changes are distributed in a pattern that conforms to the standard bell curve. The width of the bell shape (as measured by its sigma or standard deviation) depicts how far price changes diverge from the mean; events at the extremes are considered extremely rare. Typhoons are, in effect, defined out of existence.
>
> Do financial data neatly conform to such assumptions? Of course, they never do. The risk-reducing formulas behind portfolio theory rely on a number of demanding and ultimately unfounded premises. . . .Charts of stock or currency changes over time do reveal a constant background of small up and down price movements—but not as uniform as one would expect if price changes fit the bell curve. These patterns, however, constitute only one aspect of the graph. A substantial number of sudden large changes . . . stand out from the background of more moderate perturbations. . . .According to portfolio theory, the probability of these large fluctuations would be a few millionths of a millionth of a millionth of a millionth. . . .But in fact, one observes spikes on a regular basis . . . and their probability amounts to a few hundredths. (Mandelbrot 1999/2008, no page numbers)

Mandelbrot proposes a theory based on deterministic but complex dynamics—a theory that could be classified as fractal. A fractal theory would allow for stock market crashes as well as dramatic increases in the total capital value, which Markowitz-type models are unable to explain.

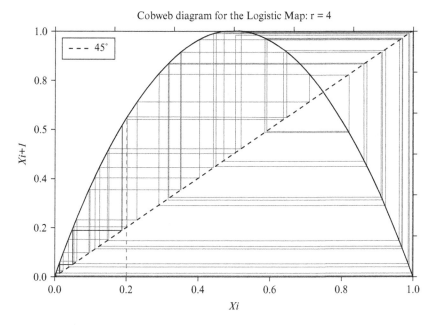

Figure 7.6   A dynamic system with mixed feedback

Fractal models are close to chaos models, in which positive feedback as in Keynesian theory mixes with negative feedback as in general equilibrium theory. Such coexistence of negative and positive feedback in a dynamic model causes chaotic motion as a generic outcome. Figure 7.6 illustrates a dynamic system with positive feedback up to an x-value of 0.5. At this value the agents start reacting in a way that is opposite to their reactions during the expansion phase.

However, it is often hard to determine whether a stochastic or deterministic chaos model has generated an observed irregular time series. Figure 7.7 is an example of such a time series.

A way of detecting deterministic chaos in a time series is by constructing a "return map," which means that the phase variable at a point in time ($x(t)$) is made a function of the variable at an earlier point (say $x(t$-$1)$).

Doing this with the observations of Figure 7.7 leads to the diagram in Figure 7.8, which depicts a logistic map. The seemingly stochastic time series in Figure 7.7 is in fact a logistic map in the chaotic region associated with an r of 3.99.

This procedure is therefore able to detect the structure of the underlying logistic function. Finding a return map is relatively straightforward for one-dimensional systems. On the other hand, systems with more than two

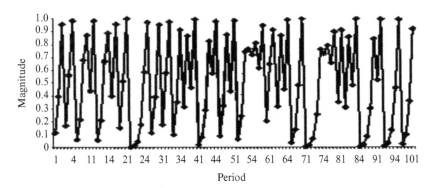

Figure 7.7 A non-stochastic (logistic) time series

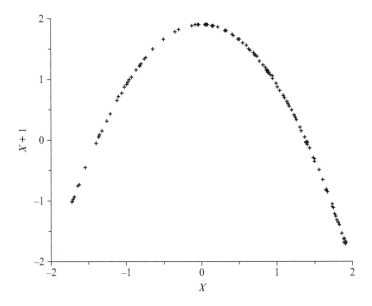

Figure 7.8 Return map from a discrete logistic function with r=3.99

dimensions yield return maps that are much less useful in discriminating between deterministic and stochastic dynamic systems.

The major weakness of the proposed fractal and other non-linear models that lead to chaotic capital market dynamics is the unspecified micro-behavior of the individual decision makers that constitute the onto-logical foundation of all economic models of dynamic systems. In contrast, the most widely used theories make use of testable behavioral micro-level hypotheses about investors' expectations and preferences.

THE FIRM AS AN EMERGENT ORDER OF CAPITAL

Accumulated capital goods—which firms buy at their depreciated book values—provide the standard measure of how capital value determines output and growth. A consequence is that Solowian growth models underestimate the contribution of capital accumulation to the overall growth rate of an economy. Typical econometric estimates of capital elasticities are in these models very low, at approximately 0.3. Hence there is always a very large unexplained residual that is exogenous to standard neoclassical growth theory. The "new growth theory" of Uzawa (1961), Shell (1966), Andersson and Mantsinen (1980), Rebelo (1991) and Mankiw et al. (1992) is different in that it attempts to endogenize knowledge as a component of the accumulation of capital. The resulting capital elasticity estimates tend to be much higher than in empirical studies making use of the Tinbergen–Solow–Swan model.

However, neither of these approaches account for the role of entrepreneurial decisions in the organization of firms as profitable and productive assemblies of physical, human and social capital. The aggregate production function remains a black box with an unknown inner structure.

The transaction cost theory of the firm in the tradition of Ronald Coase (1937) and Oliver Williamson (1985) is a useful starting point for analyzing the formation of firms, but it is at the same time no more than a starting point. Except for the necessary recognition of the role of transactions costs, new institutional microeconomics offers few insights regarding the role of technological and spatial allocations of physical and human capital in making firms more productive and profitable. Resolving this larger problem requires an analysis of how firms search for ways to improve firm-internal interaction networks.

A haphazard arrangement of the carriers of human capital, other knowledge sources, machines and buildings is suboptimal and results in low output value. At the same time, it is in practice impossible to maximize a firm's profitability if its productive activities involve the interaction of large numbers of discrete resources. Access to powerful computers does not mitigate this problem.

If three workers are to be assigned to three tasks there are $3! = 6$ possible assignment patterns. Four tasks involving four workers imply $4! = 24$ possible patterns. The number of possible assignment patterns grows fast. For a firm that must allocate ten workers to ten different tasks there are as many as 3.6 million possible patterns. This number increases with the factorial of the number of workers and tasks. With 20 workers and 20 tasks, the number of possible patterns has already reached $2.43*10^{18}$ (see Appendix 7.1).

The presence of interaction effects usually implies numerous local maxima, making it more difficult to find a global maximum (in a figurative sense, multiple maxima correspond to a map with numerous valleys and peaks, rather than a map of a single-peaked mountain).

Some scholars have proposed solutions that use real values in an attempt to approximate integer values. However, rounding off to the nearest integer value will yield a suboptimal and therefore erroneous assignment pattern. Another widespread idea is that it is possible to search for an optimal solution subject to non-integer constraints by rounding off to the closest value of zero or one, but this procedure is also unable to generate an optimal solution to the problem of assigning quadratic integer values. The impossibility of solving integer quadratic assignment problems has the important practical consequence that it is impossible to optimize the organization of a firm with a complex production process. Satisficing or other heuristic methods are therefore the only ways of dealing with these impossible optimization problems.

A popular heuristic method is to decompose the organization into hierarchical levels and to solve the quadratic assignment problem separately at each level. This method is typical of military organizations, but it has the drawback of neglecting all interdependencies between different hierarchical levels. Another method, which is especially popular in scientific organizations, is the subdivision of research into different faculties, schools and departments, each of which has only limited interactions with other units. We shall return to the problem of how to organize science in Chapter 13 (see also Andersson and Beckmann, 2009 and Hollingsworth, 2007).

A combination of entrepreneurial experimentation and competitive processes seems to be the only way of attaining efficiency gains in the organization of interactive physical, human and social capital. A market where numerous firms undertake a variety of organizational experiments is the only practicable way of reaching positions that are somewhere in the proximity of the global maximum. Competitive experimentation among units *within the same firm* is also useful, because it allows for direct profitability comparisons. Stuart Kauffman and his associates (1995) develop the so-called "patch procedure," which is an example of an evolutionary process of organizational experiments within a firm:

> The results hint at something deep and simple about why flatter, decentralized organizations may function well: contrary to intuition, breaking an organization

into "patches" where each patch attempts to optimize for its own selfish benefit, even if that is harmful to the whole, can lead, as if by an invisible hand, to the welfare of the whole organization. The trick, as we shall see, lies in how the patches are chosen. We will find an ordered regime where poor compromises for the entire organization are found, a chaotic regime where no solution is ever agreed on, and a phase transition between order and chaos where excellent solutions are found rapidly. . ..Therefore, as a general summary, it appears that the invisible hand finds the best solution if the coevolving system of patches is in the ordered regime rather near to the transition to chaos. (Kauffman, 1995, pp. 147 and 264).

At the end of such an evolutionary process, superior firms will have achieved aggregate capital values that are much higher than what the book values of their assets imply.

CONCLUSIONS

Economics as a dynamic discipline concerns itself with decisions on the best size and structure of capital, both as a stock and as a flow of depreciation and investments. The other aspect of dynamic decision making is the formation of expectations. The deterministic theory of capital and investment has been a major theme in economic theory since the nineteenth century, and there is now general agreement that a deterministic dynamic general equilibrium requires the real interest rate to be greater than or equal to the general growth rate.

Ramsey was the first to clarify how the utility of a decision depends on the uncertainty of the associated expectation, as summarized by its probability and risk. However, there is no consensus view on the nature and economic consequences of the formation of expectations. The most popular models of the formation of expectations are *statistical extrapolation, cobweb, adaptive expectations,*[2] *rational expectations* and *learning and genetic programming* models.

Some economists and mathematicians are rather skeptical about the possibility of developing reasonable expectations. Mostly these conclusions derive from the generic property of complex models to imply chaotic outcomes, no matter how careful the modeling or data analysis.

The field of finance—starting with Markowitz's model of the financial market—has avoided getting involved in the debate about expectations among other economists. Instead, the focus has been on analyzing the returns to a large number of shares within a portfolio with different expected returns and expected risk as reflected in historical variances and co-variances. The main conclusion of this school of thought is that the rational investor can select a utility-maximizing combination of returns and risk consisting of a mixture of a portfolio of shares and a risk-free asset.

The financial approach is a starting point for thinking about how to address the problem of capital aggregation, which was the focus of the ultimately unsuccessful theories of Hayek, Keynes and Solow. As pointed out by Joan Robinson and other Cambridge economists, such aggregation is logically impossible unless all prices are fixed during the aggregation process and in the subsequent analysis of the macroeconomic equilibrium. The logical problem is the necessary endogeneity of the interest rate. Thus, they were all traveling down the same blind alley.

We have come to the conclusion that the core of the aggregation problem is the deterministic nature of all the main macro theories, whether neoclassical, Keynesian, New Keynesian or New Classical. The only way to solve the capital aggregation problem is by accepting the uncertainty of subjectively expected returns and risk; the only measure of the aggregate value of capital is to be found in stock and real estate markets. The basic proposition is that the product of capital quantities and their purchasing prices *do not determine* capital values. The real value of these capital quantities depends on their aggregation into more or less well-organized *firms*. Financial investors value the total capital of these firms in various markets, such as in the main and over-the-counter (OTC) stock markets and in real estate markets. The total capital value of the firm depends on all types of relevant capital, including physical, human, social, institutional and locational assets.

The problem of how to organize firms is one of the most complicated theoretical issues. Here lies the thorny issue of how to combine various resources that jointly comprise the firm's capital; the objective is to reap advantages from cooperating capital resources such as machines, skills and rules of behavior. An abstract way of viewing this problem is as a quadratic assignment model with integer values. Solving this type of problem exceeds the capacity of the most advanced computers; organizations must therefore rely on heuristics and trial and error. Planning algorithms that optimize production processes are in practice impossible.

NOTES

1. An example of such a model is as follows: "Consider $x_i \neq x_j$ and the transformation $f(z) = z^r$. Then $\partial p_i(x;p)/\partial x_i < 0$ for $r > 1$, and $\partial p_i(x;p)/\partial x_j > 0$ for $r \in (0, 1)$" (Dillenberger et al., 2015, p. 5). The proof of this proposition is in their appendix (ibid.).
2. An example of adaptive expectations is $p_t^e = p_{t-1}^e + \lambda(p_{t-1} - p_{t-1}^e)$; it is also possible to formulate this model with a distributed lag structure.

APPENDIX 7.1

Koopmans and Beckmann (1957) were the first economists to propose a quadratic assignment model of location. Later their model was adapted to the allocation of employees to tasks. The adapted model assumes indivisible units of machines and workers; the productivity of a machine or worker depends on interaction with another machine or worker. Further assuming that a quadratic form can capture the net benefits from interaction, they claimed that there is no price-based incentive mechanism that provides a route to the global maximum. There has been a substantial mathematical research effort that is oriented to finding algorithms that would solve the quadratic assignment problem for large n x n matrices.

The quadratic assignment model is $Z = \min \sum_{i,j,k,l} f_{ik} \, d_{jl} \, x_{ij} \, x_{kl}$; with the following constraints: $\sum_{j=1}^{N} x_{ij} = 1$; (i=1,. . .,N); all tasks must be performed; $\sum_{i=1}^{N} x_{ij} = 1$; (j=1,. . .,N); all employees must be employed; $x_{ij} = 1$ if task i is assigned to employee j, otherwise 0.

An intractability theorem is stated in Woeginger's (2003) open problem 7.6: In the quadratic assignment problem the input consists of two n x n matrices with real entries, so that $Z = x^{T} \, FD \, x$.

The objective is to find a permutation that minimizes the quadratic cost function Z [alternatively maximizes a profit function] subject to (0,1) integer constraints and the condition that each task is performed and each employee is assigned to one task. "The quadratic assignment problem can only be solved in $O^{*}(n!)$ time. No faster algorithms are known" (Woeginger, 2003, p. 206–7).

Hence this is a super-polynomial-time algorithm problem, which is intractable for large n. For the linear assignment model the optimal permutation can easily be found: "A large number of algorithms, sequential and parallel, have been developed for the linear sum assignment problem (LSAP). They range from primal-dual combinatorial algorithms, to simplex-like methods, cost operation algorithms, forest algorithms and relaxation approaches. The worst-case complexity of the best sequential algorithms for the LSAP is $O(n^{3})$, where n is the size of the problem" (Burkard and Çela, 1999).

8. A general theory of infrastructure and economic development

Economic development has always taken place on an arena of the combined material and non-material infrastructures. The material infrastructure mainly consists of networks for transmitting information and knowledge and for transporting goods and people. The non-material infrastructure consists of scientific, artistic and other generally accessible knowledge as well as formal and informal institutions. Constitutions, legal systems and durable laws are examples of formal institutions. Informal institutions are shared rules and predispositions that constrain individual behavior. We discuss the role of institutions in greater detail in Chapter 10.

The implicit treatment of the infrastructure is as something that remains parametrically stable in general equilibrium theory and in most theories and models of economic growth. Despite occasional references to time, history or space, it seems fair to claim that most of these theories are not general in the deep sense of taking time and space seriously.

The traditional approach is untenable if the aim is to understand long-run economic history or to build theories of the economic development of regions and nations. Economic development spans centuries and continents, and therefore both the material and the non-material infrastructures are subject to change. These changes are so substantial that they sometimes disrupt the basic conditions for economic activities and network interdependencies. There are then often fundamental transformations of production techniques, the organization and location of firms and patterns of trade. Similarly, dramatic transformations of the economic behavior of households tend to occur at the same time.

A handful of economists and economic historians have addressed the important role of the infrastructure on the quantitative size and qualitative structure of economic development over long periods of time. In most cases these economists have also analyzed the spatial economic consequences of long-term changes to the infrastructure. Infrastructural economics and infrastructural economic history include the following seminal contributions: Schumpeter (1934), Pirenne (1936), Heckscher (1935), Braudel (1979), Maddison (1982) and North (1990; 2005).

THE CONCEPT OF INFRASTRUCTURE

The word infrastructure is derived from the Latin *infra* (under) and *structura* (structure). Politicians and planners tend to use the term when referring to physical networks and links such as roads, railways and utility networks. Here we use it in the broader sense of all durable and public (collective) systems that support the activities of more than one firm or household—in other words, systems that are public in their effects. The infrastructure thus includes material public capital such as road and railroad networks, but also non-material public capital, including accessibility to knowledge and markets and formal and informal institutions.

There are two fundamental attributes of the infrastructure:

1. It is a public good that many firms and households can use at the same time.
2. It is much more durable than other capital.

Table 8.1 illustrates the subdivision of different goods for a dynamic analysis of infrastructure as an arena for economic interactions, with examples of deterministic theories associated with each cell.

General competitive equilibrium theory—as most economists have formulated it—presumes an arena of public as well as private capital that acts as a set of constraining and facilitating conditions for the smooth and rapid equilibration of market processes. At some points in time, the stability of these slowly changing conditions is lost and a process of creative destruction takes over. The growth of new industries then causes a disruption of general equilibrium; a search for a new equilibrium structure of production and prices follows.

GENERAL COMPETITIVE EQUILIBRIUM THEORY AND ITS DEPENDENCE ON THE INFRASTRUCTURAL ARENA

While Walras first formulated a theory of general equilibrium in economics in the late nineteenth century, the modern version is from the 1950s and consists of Gérard Debreu's reformulation of equilibrium theory as a set of existence and uniqueness theorems. Alan Kirman (2006) summarizes some of its limitations:

> Debreu was not preoccupied with the problem of how prices might adjust to equilibrium. He was concerned with the existence of equilibrium and only in a

very tangential way, through his work on local uniqueness, with its stability. . ..
There is a rather arid economic environment referred to as a purely competitive market in which individuals receive signals as to the prices of all goods. . ..
Choosing the best commodity bundle within their budget set determines their
demand at each price vector. Under what assumptions on the preferences will
there be at least one price vector that clears all markets, that is, an equilibrium?
Put alternatively, can we find a price vector for which the excess demand for
each good is zero? The question as to whether a mechanism exists to drive prices
to the equilibrium has become secondary, and Herb Scarf's famous example
(1960) had already dealt that discussion a blow. The warning bell was sounded
by such authors as Donald Saari (1996) and [Donald Saari and] Carl Simon
(1978), whose work gave an indication, but one that has been somewhat overlooked, as to why the stability problem was basically unsolvable in the context
of the general equilibrium model. (Kirman, 2006, pp. 249–50)

As Scarf (1960), Hurwicz (1960; 1973) and Morishima (1984) show, it
is obvious that *general* equilibrium theory is a rather *special* equilibrium
theory. These contributions make clear that a fundamental flaw of the
theory is the absence of institutions or more precisely the absence of property rights structures. Such institutions are necessary for the determination
of wealth and income distributions as well as for the creation of mechanisms that ensure the stability of price-setting processes. We would like to
add that this flaw is not limited to institutions. The other infrastructural
components of the arena for market exchange—the networks—are also
prerequisites for a stable and equilibrating economy.

THE FORMATION AND USES OF INFRASTRUCTURE

Table 8.1 implies that inclusion of the infrastructure—material networks,
knowledge and institutions—is a prerequisite for realistic theories, irrespective of whether these theories concern the growth of capital, competitive market equilibria or interactions between information flows and
market processes.

Networks that transport goods, water, energy and other flows have
always been crucial in creating opportunities for specialized capital and
production and thus also for facilitating gains from trade. But networks
are also necessary for communication and information flows such as
phone calls and email messages as well as distribution of—or access
to—books, databases and online games. Theories and models of transport and communication networks have been slow in coming. Leonhard
Euler formulated the fundamental theoretical base already in 1735 (Euler,
1741a), which was when he solved the riddle of the "Seven Bridges of

Table 8.1   Types of capital by rate of change and scope of effects with relevant deterministic theoretical frameworks

Scope of effects	Rate of change	
	Fast	Slow
Individual (private)	**NON-DURABLE PRIVATE CAPITAL:** ordinary consumer goods	**DURABLE PRIVATE CAPITAL:** private capital goods; human capital
	General equilibrium theory: Walras; Cassel; Wald; Arrow-Debreu; Sonnenschein; Beckmann	*Capital/interest/growth theory:* Leontief; von Neumann *Facility location models:* Launhardt; A. Weber; Koopmans; Beckmann; Erlenkotter; Klose; Drexl
Collective (public)	**NON-DURABLE PUBLIC CAPITAL:** information; communication; imitative preferences; fashion	**DURABLE PUBLIC CAPITAL:** material/non-material infrastructures *Networks:* Euler; Dupuit; Launhardt; Beckmann; Dijkstra; Bellman
	Networking/diffusion theories: Rogers; Bass; Hurwicz; Mansfield; Berners-Lee	*Institutional theories:* Adam Smith; Montesquieu; De Borda; M. Weber; Veblen; early Hayek; Buchanan; Olson; Hirschman; Hurwicz *Science:* Euclid; Newton; Gauss; Einstein; Bohr; Turing; von Neumann; Crick/ Watson; Thom; Haken; Mandelbrot

Königsberg." Euler went on to develop the foundation of graph theory based on the following definitions:

1. A network is made up of nodes (vertices) connected by non-intersecting links (arcs).
2. A vertex is odd if it has an odd number of links leading to it; otherwise it is even.
3. An Euler path is a continuous path that passes through every arc once and only once.

The most famous theorem (Euler, 1741b) states that, "if a network has two or zero odd vertices, it has at least one Euler path. In particular, if a network has exactly two odd vertices, then its Euler paths can only start on one of the odd vertices, and end on the other."

Progress in the theory and modeling of networks from graph theory to transport network applications has been slow. In 1844, Jules Dupuit—a French civil engineer—proposed that transport planners should abandon the common cost minimization principle when constructing road links in favor of the principle of net utility maximization. The proposed method was to calculate consumers' surplus, basing it on the marginal utility of the improved transport possibility: "The purchaser never pays more for the product than the value he places on its utility" (Dupuit 1844, p. 89).

This step made it possible to develop systematic calculations of the costs and benefits of network link extensions. But it would take another century before transportation economists adopted network-wide investment models with systematic measurements of costs and consumer as well as producer surpluses. This type of model also includes relevant demand and supply functions. Much of the theoretical and modeling work has been oriented to the problem of finding algorithms for generating optimal solutions to the integer-valued problems associated with investments in airline corridors, road, railroad, electricity, telecommunications and water networks. Bellman (1958) and Dijkstra (1959) are early seminal contributions.

The accumulation of *scientific knowledge capital* in freely accessible forms such as books, scientific journals and other media is for the most part a recent phenomenon. Notable early examples of generally accessible knowledge—at least in Europe—include the theories and models of Euclid, Leon Battista Alberti and Tycho Brahe. In Europe, the medieval Church constrained knowledge growth, particularly in astronomy and other natural sciences, while the Confucian normative ideal of repetitive and imitative learning almost entirely closed off new lines of scientific inquiry in East Asia. The Renaissance in Italy and the Enlightenment in England, France and Scotland were institutional breakthroughs that created a new knowledge infrastructure for the world's first international scientific order. It was this infrastructure that made it possible to create new forms of material capital such as steam-powered machines for use in extraction and manufacturing industries as well as in transport. Probably the most important scientific breakthrough, however, was the discovery (or invention) and development of calculus, as pioneered by Newton and Leibniz and their followers, particularly in Britain, France and the Netherlands.

The infrastructure of science made possible the remarkable outpouring of creativity that has been the hallmark of scientific research since the eighteenth century. This has been especially true of mathematics as applied to natural science and engineering. Examples include the independent discoveries of non-Euclidian geometry by Gauss, Bolyai and Lobachevsky. Non-Euclidian geometry constitutes the foundation for Einstein's relativity theory, which together with Niels Bohr's development of quantum theory generated physics as we know it today. But in spite of these breakthroughs, modern physics is not the science with the most revolutionary economic implications. That distinction is associated with the work of Alan Turing and John von Neumann in the 1930s, who in combination laid the foundations for the computer and information revolution of the late twentieth and early twenty-first centuries.

Another remarkable scientific advance with major economic repercussions was the field of genetics from Mendel to Crick and Watson. Discoveries in genetics—as well as the merger of computer-based mathematics and biology—paved the way for the spectacular rise of the pharmaceutical and biotechnological industries in the late twentieth century.

The growth of science's infrastructure in the form of theorems, models and experiments as disseminated through monographs, textbooks and journal articles would be all but useless in the absence of widespread advanced education. The development of the knowledge base has benefited from the steady increase in human capital associated with the introduction of compulsory secular education, first in Europe and North America and later in many other parts of the world.

According to Maddison (1982), the average level of formal education in the most advanced economies (the OECD countries) was about three years per person in 1900. One hundred years later it had risen to about 12 years per person. This corresponds to an average increase in the supply of educational capital of 1.5 percent per year since 1900, controlling for the size of the population.

The third form of infrastructure is the *institutional framework* that regulates and—ideally—facilitates private decision making. Amartya Sen makes an argument along these lines when discussing Adam Smith:

> Even as Smith's pioneering investigations explained why (and particularly how) the dynamism of the market economy worked, they also brought out the support that the markets need from other institutions for efficacy and viability. He identified why the markets may need restraint, correction, and supplementation through other institutions for preventing instability, inequity, and poverty. (Sen, 2010, p. 50)

In a related vein, Michio Morishima notes:

> If economists successfully devise a correct general equilibrium model, even if it can be proved to possess an equilibrium solution, should it lack the institutional

backing to realize an equilibrium solution, then the equilibrium solution will amount to no more than a utopian state of affairs which bears no relation whatsoever to the real economy. (Morishima, 1984, pp. 68–9)

Introducing institutional details is no simple matter, however. Implicitly, equilibrium models assume that property rights over all resources are perfectly specified and measured, and also that these same rights are uncontested. For a very long time, this made most economists disregard one of the most important problems in economic development, which is the inconsistency between what resources people actually control and what *de jure* property rights the legal system can be relied upon to enforce (De Soto, 2000). The problem here is that the resources—that is to say, capital—an individual controls without formal ownership rights are much less "fungible" than other resources. Such resources are next to useless in impersonal exchange with anonymous strangers, for example when used as collateral to secure funding for a new business venture.

Informal institutions matter in a similar but perhaps even more elusive way. Many Western economists have argued that there will be insufficient demand for education unless the government makes it compulsory, since knowledge externalities improves the functioning of markets and raises productivity in general. Perhaps this is true in some parts of the world, but is it true everywhere? Anyone with real-life experience of Confucian East Asia—China, Japan, Korea, Vietnam—will attest to the fact that the overwhelming majority of parents will, if anything, err on the side of *over*-educating their children. There is an obvious budget constraint that prevents poor people from paying tuition for expensive degree programs, but it is *not* a credible hypothesis that poor people *from this culture* would demand too little education if they were richer. We could make a similar argument about Jewish culture. So, the institutional details matter, even for those economists who supposedly ignore them. An economist who argues that there is too little demand for education from the poorly educated is—perhaps unconsciously—alluding to the informal institutions of some other specific group, such as the English working class.

Modeling spatial economic development in terms of employment, production, capital formation and interregional trade requires a clear understanding of the ways in which the infrastructure is changing—and at what rate. Sometimes the infrastructure serves as a catalyst for economic restructuring. Changes in the infrastructure can thereby trigger sudden transformations of market activities, capital accumulation, location patterns of production and employment and transport, communication and trade flows.

As stated earlier, infrastructural capital may be material or non-material.

The road and rail networks have the greatest economic impacts of the transportation networks, which constitute a subset of the material infrastructure. This network infrastructure is geographically delimited and territorial. It affects the spatial distribution of property rights and private capital values.

Material infrastructural capital has three generic attributes:

1. It is a public good for most people and firms within a geographically delimited area.
2. Its use creates rivalry among consumers or producers to the extent that it becomes congested.
3. Its use may be open-access or limited to individuals, firms or organizations that have been endowed with enforceable property rights.

Transportation and communication networks are useful for most people as long as the flow of traffic or messages does not exceed the capacity of the network. The non-material infrastructure does not have the same physical capacity limitations. An illustration is Euclidian geometry, which countless students and engineers have used for almost three millennia without the congestion typical of the material infrastructure. Even so, some inventors and even more innovators view the absence of natural limitations in the use of knowledge as undesirable. To innovators of new knowledge, an artificial capacity constraint is the prerequisite for the use of new knowledge as a scarce good with monopoly pricing. Intellectual property rights create such artificial constraints. They thus enable property right holders to use monopoly pricing, thereby rationing the use of knowledge and information with intrinsic public good attributes.

THE INFRASTRUCTURE AND THE ECONOMY

Table 8.1 provides a starting point for formulating a general theory of infrastructure and economic development.

Ordinary market goods—goods of low durability—are exchanged in different marketplaces such as shops, auction houses, alibaba.com and amazon.com. Billions of households and millions of firms make the relevant decisions. The time frames of agreements such as contracts, payments and deliveries range from instantaneous to weeks and the stability and enforcement characteristics of the relevant legal system secure and enforce the agreements.

FAST DYNAMICS AND GENERAL EQUILIBRIUM OF MARKET EXCHANGE

The following equation represents individual market-good dynamics:

$$dp/dt = f(p,k,y,z); \qquad (8.1)$$

where p is a vector of non-negative prices of ordinary market goods (including factor services), k is a vector of given quantities of private capital goods, y is a vector of different types of economically relevant information and z is a vector of predetermined infrastructure, including markets, knowledge networks and institutions governing the exchange of goods. Equation (8.1) can be seen as a dynamic version of the price setting of a competitive economy or a Walrasian timeless *tâtonnement* process, which is one noted model for investigating the dynamic approach of equilibrium. Prices are in this model announced (perhaps by an "auctioneer") and agents state how much of each good they would like to sell (supply) or buy (demand). No transactions and no production take place at disequilibrium prices. Instead, prices are lowered for goods with positive prices and excess supply. Prices are raised for goods with excess demand.

Equation (8.1) gives rise to a fixed-point solution under standard conditions as specified in general equilibrium theory. To guarantee that equilibrium exists, it suffices that consumer preferences are convex. With a sufficiently large number of consumers, it is possible to relax this convexity assumption. With a large number of producers, convex and feasible production sets suffice for existence. Convexity implies the exclusion of indivisibilities and other causes of economies of scale. Most extensions of general equilibrium theory to include time and space require the introduction of spatial and temporal transfer mechanisms; most versions of general equilibrium theory do not include such mechanisms. However, Beckmann (1952; 1953), Beckmann and Puu (1985), Dafermos and Nagurney (1987) and Nagurney (1999/2013) formulate general equilibrium theories that are explicitly spatial.

The Beckmann model as formulated in 1952 presumes the existence of a transport infrastructure and technology. The existence of such an infrastructure ensures the existence of a general equilibrium of locations, trade flows, land prices and rent gradients under quite general assumptions regarding preferences and production technologies.

Most proofs of the existence of equilibrium in an excess-demand economy rely on the Brouwer fixed-point theorem for functions. Düppe and Weintraub (2014) provide a fascinating account of the introduction of fixed-point theory into economics. Newer proofs use the Kakutani fixed-point theorem for set-valued functions.

In the 1970s, Hugo Sonnenschein initiated a debate on the scientific standing of general equilibrium theory. Sonnenschein (1973) contends that much of general equilibrium theory is not scientifically refutable. This is so because there is no solution that can be proven to be unique. Although some fixed-point solution can be proven to exist, this is not enough for testing hypotheses about implications at the aggregate level. One author even claimed "anything goes" in equilibrium theory. Abu Turab Rizvi concludes that:

> [m]atters are even clearer on qualitative features of equilibrium such as local uniqueness, stability, and comparative statics. The equilibrium manifold approach employing a finite set of observations does not allow us to refute statements on these features of equilibrium. Thus, many of the problematic outcomes from SMD [Sonnenschein, Mantel, Debreu] theory remain entrenched. Not only are there no results for general configurations of the data in these areas (Nachbar 2002, 2004); we cannot test to see if an economy is poorly behaved. So we still have no progress on these aspects of the theory. In this important area, then, the intuition that general equilibrium theory is devoid of meaningfully general results remains true. It turns out that Arrow [1986, p. 388–9] was correct to conclude that "if agents are different in unspecifiable ways, then . . . very little, if any, inferences can be made." (Rizvi, 2006, p. 242)

SLOW DYNAMICS OF PRIVATE CAPITAL ACCUMULATION

Theories and models of capital accumulation are abundant in economics, as we discussed in Chapters 2 and 6. It was common among the classical economists to assume that earned profits directly determine the growth of capital, so that $\Delta K = \rho K$ or that the rate of growth, g, equals the rate of profit, ρ.

Cassel (1918/1932) proposes an equation that states that the growth rate of capital (and income) equals the propensity to save times the productivity of capital. Domar (1946) and Harrod (1948) reiterate this view. On the other hand, von Neumann (1938/1970) develops a Cassel-influenced multi-good model of equilibrium growth, as we illustrate in Chapter 6.

It is also possible to show that a dynamic Leontief model in equilibrium implies a situation where capital is growing at a rate which is the inverse of the capital-output matrix times the rate of profits, as given by $p(I\text{-}A)$. Increasing productivity or household savings then leads to higher growth rates of capital and output. The neoclassicals assumed diminishing returns to capital per unit of labor and would thus—in contrast to the constant-return theories mentioned earlier—claim that only higher productivity would be compatible with an equilibrium rate of growth of capital and income. Von Neumann's model of economic growth is a reasonable specification of a capital growth process for economists (like us) who accept the hypothesis that human capital services rather than undifferentiated labor is the most important factor that households supply. It is furthermore reasonable to assume that human capital grows as fast as other forms of private capital. The advantage of the Von Neumann Model is that it allows for substitution of techniques and differences in capital durability when approaching the general equilibrium of growth and interest rates. It is here important to remember that the dual prices of the Von Neumann Model are long-term prices that reflect fixed as well as variable costs. This means that the equilibrium prices of the Von Neumann Model are different from the short-term prices of Wald's or Debreu's general economic equilibrium exchange models.

In our framework, the following equation represents capital accumulation:

$$s(k)\, dk/dt = g(\boldsymbol{p},\boldsymbol{k},\boldsymbol{y},\boldsymbol{z}); \qquad (8.2)$$

where $s(k)$ is a constant that represents the timescale conversion between ordinary market goods and durable capital goods, that is, $s(k) = t/T(k)$. If t equals one year and $T(k)$ equals ten years we would have $s(k) = 0.1$. With $\boldsymbol{p}$ in equilibrium and $\boldsymbol{y}$ as well as $\boldsymbol{z}$ at given levels, $\boldsymbol{k}$ will remain approximately constant in the perceptions of agents in the markets for perishable goods.

The location of capital is part of the capital accumulation process, either if extended into continuous space or into a discrete network of nodes of consumption, production and transfer of goods. In operations research, there are several theories and associated models that generate patterns of facility location or location patterns involving other types of material capital.

FAST DYNAMICS OF PUBLIC INFORMATION

A model of information dynamics is:

$$s(y)dy/dt = h(\boldsymbol{p},\boldsymbol{k},\boldsymbol{y},\boldsymbol{z}); \qquad (8.3)$$

where $s(y)$ is greater than or equal to one, signifying a rapid timescale.

Information and communication are central to the creation of a workable general equilibrium. This was however not mentioned as a problem in Debreu's *Theory of Value* (1959). Hurwicz (1960; 1973) gives attempts to address this gap by proposing economic mechanisms that guide the process toward a stable general equilibrium. Don Saari shows that any such mechanism must probably have to be local rather than general, because a realistic extension of the number of products and agents leads to information overload:

> Stated in words, if demands are driven by preferences, why should the economics of prices be the same in Rio as in Chicago, in Moscow as in Stockholm, or in Zurich as in Paris? Maybe the economists' long time goal of a universal price mechanism is an impossible dream; instead, maybe different locales require different mechanisms. To express this mathematically, say that a given mechanism M covers a set of economies (i.e., a set of individual preferences and initial endowments for the agents) if $p(n+1) = p(n)+M(\xi(p(n))$ converges to at least one equilibrium should the prices start sufficiently close to it. So, mimicking the reason it is impossible to represent the sphere S2 with a single chart, maybe the topology of price adjustments requires more than one mechanism to cover the set of all economies. (Saari, 1996, p. 7)

Information would reach its equilibrium state quite rapidly. Information appears in many forms. Channels of dissemination include traditional media such as rumors among decision makers, newspapers and television programs, as well as more recent internet-enabled social networks. Logistic and dynamic interaction models—such as those associated with Mark Granovetter or Brian Arthur—show that much of economic and social information is interactive.

The 1990s saw a major breakthrough in information infrastructure with the launch of the World Wide Web by Tim Berners-Lee at CERN. Berners-Lee insisted that the new information system be a public good: "Had the technology been proprietary, and in my total control, it would probably not have taken off. You can't propose that something be a universal space and at the same time keep control of it."

THE VERY SLOW DYNAMICS OF PUBLIC INFRASTRUCTURE

Finally, the following equation represents infrastructure development in our theory of the dynamics of the infrastructure and other parts of the economic system:

$$s(z)dz/dt = m(\boldsymbol{p},\boldsymbol{k},\boldsymbol{y},z); \qquad (8.4)$$

where $s(z) = t/T(z)$. $T(z)$ is a very slow (although positive) timescale, indicating that $s(z)$ is a very small positive number, possibly of the order of .01 or even smaller. This implies that in the time frame of the other variables in this system, dz/dt approximately equals zero most of the time. We thus have a dynamic system:

$$dp/dt = f(\boldsymbol{p,k,y,z}^*);$$
$$s(y)\, dy/dt = h(\boldsymbol{p,k,y,z}^*); \qquad\qquad (8.5)$$
$$s(k)\, dk/dt = g(\boldsymbol{p,k,y,z}^*);$$

to be solved subject to the constraint:

$$m(\boldsymbol{p,k,y,z}^*) = 0; \qquad\qquad (8.6)$$

For systems of this kind we can apply Tychonoff's theorem (Sugakov, 1998; Tychonoff, 1930). Assume a dynamic system of N ordinary differential equations that can be divided into two groups of equations. The first group consists of m fast equations; the second group consists of $(m + 1,. . ., N)$ slow equations. Tychonoff's theorem states that the system:

$$dx_i/dt = f_i(\boldsymbol{x,g});\ i = 1,. . .,m\ \text{(fast equations)}$$
$$f_j(\boldsymbol{x,g}) = 0;\ j = m + 1,. . .,N\ \text{(slow equations)}$$

has a solution if the following conditions are satisfied:

1. The values of $\boldsymbol{x}$ are isolated roots.
2. The solutions of $\boldsymbol{x}$ constitute a stable stationary point of $f_j = 0$ for any $\boldsymbol{x}$, and the initial conditions are in the attraction domain of this point.

For each position of the slow subsystem, the fast subsystem has plenty of time to stabilize. Such an approximation is called "adiabatic" (Sugakov, 1998; Haken, 1983).

In the very short run, the fixed-point solution to the first two equations—$f^*(\boldsymbol{p,y}) = 0$ and $h^*(\boldsymbol{p,y}) = 0$—results in market equilibrium, keeping the approximate values of $dk/dt = 0$ and $dz/dt = 0$. This solution corresponds to a conventional "general competitive market equilibrium" of the Cassel-Wald-Debreu type. In the medium term we would have an expansion of capital, implying that $s(\boldsymbol{k})dk/dt = h^{**}(\boldsymbol{k})$, where the double star indicates that z is approximately constant, and x and y are kept at their equilibrium values (*mutatis mutandis*). The solution is thus a fixed-point solution of $dk_i/dt/k_i = g$, all i, where g is the balanced rate of growth.

In the very long run the slowly changing infrastructure's rate of change cannot be assumed to be zero, as given by (8.6), and the system would then cease to be as well-behaved as in the short and medium terms. It would in the very long run have all the bifurcation properties that are typical of non-linear and interactive dynamic systems. Between periods of structural change induced by infrastructural discontinuities, there would be equilibrating periods of stable economic growth. This implies that general equilibrium theory, as conventionally formulated by Wald, Debreu and others, is not general enough to account for dynamic systems (and even less appropriate for combined spatial and dynamic systems).

Modeling spatial economic development in terms of employment, production, capital formation and interregional trade requires a clear understanding of the ways in which the infrastructure is changing—and at what rate. Sometimes the infrastructure serves as a catalyst for spatial restructuring. Changes in the infrastructure can thereby trigger sudden transformations of the location patterns of production and employment as well as transport, communication and trade flows.

INFRASTRUCTURE AS RELATED TO UNCERTAINTY-BASED THEORIES AND MODELS

Table 8.2 sums up relationships among a few different *non-deterministic* theories and models, and their relevance to phenomena classified according to rate of change and scope of effects.

Two different approaches attempt to extend general economic equilibrium theory into a world of uncertainty: *stochastic general equilibrium models (SGEM)* and *agent-based general equilibrium models (ABGEM)*.

There are currently no SGEMs on par with the Wald-Debreu deterministic theory, with a foundation in microeconomic variables and relations. Instead the current models are macroeconomic; their main purpose is to serve decision makers in governments and central banks. The European Central Bank and the Swiss Central Bank both make use of SGEM models. Such models attempt to analyze the equilibrium properties of the macroeconomy. These SGEMs formulate computable systems as a set of interactive linear stochastic difference equations. Macroeconomic variables such as GDP and employment depend on dynamic variances and co-variances of endogenous variables, predetermined capital stocks and assumed shocks in exogenous technological and political variables. Solutions allegedly show how endogenous stochastic variations, assumed political decisions and uncertain but possible changes in the economic, technological and political environment jointly determine how the economy evolves over time.

Table 8.2   *Relationships between non-deterministic economic theories and*
                the nature and speed of economics processes

Scope of effects	Rate of change	
	Fast	Slow
Individual (private)	**NON-DURABLE PRIVATE CAPITAL** *Stochastic general equilibrium models*: (Chapter 8) *Agent-based general equilibrium models:* Gintis (Chapter 8) *Entrepreneurship theory:* Schumpeter; Knight; Kirzner (Chapter 7)	**DURABLE PRIVATE CAPITAL** *Capital value theory*: Markowitz (Chapter 7) *Asset pricing theory*: Sharpe; Lintner; Mossin (Chapter 7) *Arbitrage pricing theory*: Ross (Chapter 7) *Entrepreneurship theory*: Knight (Chapter 7)
Collective (public)	**NON-DURABLE PUBLIC CAPITAL** *Information and interaction models*: Schelling; Granovetter; Arthur; Gintis (Chapter 4)	**DURABLE PUBLIC CAPITAL** *Infrastructural theories*: Pirenne; Braudel; Heckscher; Schumpeter (Chapter 9) *Institutional theories*: Veblen; Commons; Buchanan; North (Chapter 10) *Spontaneous order theories*: Smith; Menger; late Hayek; Polanyi (Chapter 10)

Gintis (2007) proposes an agent-based model of general economic equilibrium dynamics, with a much more pronounced foundation in Walras-Wald-Debreu theory. The significant change as compared with those earlier theorists is the introduction of an adaptive learning process that leads toward equilibrium. Gintis formulates *four general principles* of clear relevance to the modeling of market economies.

First, a highly decentralized Walrasian economy has—under a wide range of plausible conditions—a unique and stable steady state in which the economy is reasonably close to Pareto-efficient.

Second, the stability of a market system depends on the fact that prices are *private* information, in the sense that each agent, consumer, firm and worker possesses a set of reservation prices that they deploy in order to decide when and with whom to trade. These reservation prices are private information that each agent updates through time as a result of trial and error as well as by imitation. We call these "private prices" in contrast to the standard assumption of public prices in general equilibrium theory.

Third, when even a small fraction of agents share the same prices and update them in a coordinated manner, as suggested by the *tâtonnement* mechanism, the price system becomes highly volatile.

Fourth, a major mechanism leading to the convergence of economic behavior is imitation—whereby poorly performing agents copy the behavior of better-performing ones. Under conditions of incomplete information, it is possible to show that equilibrium always sustains a positive level of imitation (Conlisk, 1988). This follows from the fact that a single agent can gain from copying the choices of others, if all other agents engage in costly information gathering and optimization.

Gintis then specifies a certain number of trading steps, after which agents consume goods and compute utilities. Imitation then follows, implying that agents copy the private prices of successful peers. Mutations will occur with some small probability when a new price is adopted at random. These assumptions lead to an ergodic Markov chain, implying an invariant distribution.

Gintis's simulations show that this invariant distribution converges toward a configuration where every agent uses the same (public) equilibrium prices.

However, uncertainty has been of much greater importance in theories of capital markets, as we explained in Chapter 7. This is a consequence of the fundamental role of time and expectations in decisions to invest in durable capital.

The following chapters provide analyses of the formation and impact of infrastructural capital. Chapter 9 focuses on transportation and communication networks. We show how an infrastructural revolution caused Europe to transform itself from a loosely connected system of autarkic economies into the world's first integrated continental economy.

Chapter 10 addresses the importance of institutions as part of the infrastructure. Revolutionary institutional changes were key determinants of economic restructuring from the sixteenth to twentieth centuries.

9. The role of the transport infrastructure in the First Logistical Revolution

Economic development has always taken place on an arena of material and non-material infrastructure, as theorized in the preceding chapter. The material infrastructure mainly consists of networks, either for transmitting information and knowledge or for transporting goods and people among different locations. The non-material infrastructure comprises generally accessible knowledge—such as theorems, compositions and languages in the public domain—as well as the set of formal and informal institutions that provide behavioral rules for groups of people. Constitutions, legal systems and durable laws and regulations are examples of formal institutions. Informal institutions are group-specific norms and customs; these institutions may apply to civilizations, nations, regions or subcultures— they often reflect influential ancient philosophies, religions and ideologies. Members of relevant groups often comply with informal institutions while being unaware of their own compliance; applying such rules of behavior then seems like doing the normal thing, being polite or being practical. There is a good cognitive reason for this: human cultures are so complex that even people who like to be untraditional or "edgy" comply with most of the informal institutions of their respective societies most of the time.

In their different ways, economists and historians such as Adam Smith, Veblen, Commons, Heckscher, Schumpeter, Hayek, Pirenne, Braudel, Maddison and North have all shed light on different aspects of the impact of changing infrastructural conditions on the development of the world economy from medieval to modern or postmodern times. Some have focused on material infrastructures, while others have focused on the spread of knowledge or the role of institutions.

The economists Johann Heinrich von Thünen (1826/1930) and Eli F. Heckscher (1941) as well as the historians Henri Pirenne (1936) and Fernand Braudel (1979) are the most important theorists and chroniclers of the decisive role of transport networks for long-term economic development around the world. Von Thünen's analysis of the interdependencies among transport infrastructure, trade and location had a major influence on both Pirenne and Braudel. Pirenne's main research interest was the effect of the improved European transport network in the late medieval era. Braudel built on Pirenne's insights by extending the analysis to the whole world from medieval to modern times.

TRANSPORT NETWORKS AND ECONOMIC RESTRUCTURING

The slow and steady transformation of transport and other interaction networks are key factors that explain the long-run development of European production, settlement and trade. The qualitative interrelationships are as follows.

A region or nation can only develop a specialized economy when there is sufficient transport capacity for the profitable exchange of a production surplus with other regions specializing in other production. Trade in perishable goods will remain unattractive unless terminals, transport routes and vehicles have attained a critical level of technological efficiency in terms of speed and reliability. The critical efficiency is different for different goods. Profitable trade requires that the combined marginal transport and interregional transaction costs of exchanging a good between any pair of regions do not exceed the difference between the two regions in the marginal cost of producing the good (see Appendix 9.1 for a formal exposition of this reasoning).

An investment in the transport infrastructure usually results in lower transport costs between two or more regions. This means that investments in the physical infrastructure, leading to reduced transport costs, provide new opportunities for trade and increased specialization of local production, as shown already in the early nineteenth century by von Thünen. Increased trade and specialization cause greater overall efficiency and higher real incomes.

The regions that benefit most from lowered transport costs also gain most from increased specialization. Rising real incomes in such regions provide incentives for inbound migration; lagging regions may as a result lose people (see Puu, 1997, pp. 203–6).

Rich regions that have a comparative advantage in products that need relatively little land per unit of value while benefiting disproportionately from good overall accessibility will experience greater population densities and more intensive uses of land. If densities increase sufficiently much, we call this process urbanization.

The combination of limited need for land but greater need for general access on networks is at the core of von Thünen's and Braudel's analyses.

Their common concern was the long-term transformation of the European economy and their understanding of economic development is our starting point for examining the origins and future of development.

THE ROLE OF TRANSPORT NETWORKS

All trade in goods requires flows on physical networks. These networks consist of *nodes* (edges) and *links* (vertices) that connect the nodes. Nodes are also called terminals and usually have one of three main functions. One function is to be the *source* of flows, as when a factory gives rise to a node that is a source of goods. A second function is to be an importing node or *sink*, as when a residential neighborhood receives goods from factories. A third function, which has become more important over time, is to be a *saddle*. A simple example is the exporting harbor of a factory; the node then functions as a transit and reloading location for the flow of goods and services. Hong Kong and Singapore are modern examples of "saddle cities," specializing in collecting, repackaging and redirecting goods.

Transportation possibilities must always precede actual transportation and trade. Physical transport networks therefore constitute the arena for trade. A slow but steady development of links and vehicular technology influences the systems of trade, the specialization of source regions and the production and employment structures of each regional economy.

Figure 9.1 illustrates the radical consequences of a seemingly marginal investment in a link. The potential critical link (C) is different from other links because it will transform the connectivity of the system as a whole, linking A and D for the first time.

Networks grow in two ways. One is as between nodes (regions) A and B in Figure 9.1. Assume that these nodes have different resource availabilities. With the appearance of a transport link between A and B there will then be gains from trade that exceed those of the preceding no-link state. The addition of the link is advantageous as long as the cost of building the link is smaller than the gains from integrating the two nodes. It is possible to view the small-scale integration of pairs, triples and quadruples of nodes as consequences of marginal cost-benefit calculations.

Sooner or later a critical link (C in Figure 9.1) will however be built, with qualitatively different economic consequences. It will cause a jump from one equilibrium structure onto another, after a phase of instability and disequilibrium. Hence a seemingly marginal investment in a network link can sometimes—at a critical stage of a network expansion program—give rise to synergetic (system-wide) effects, causing a phase transition of the

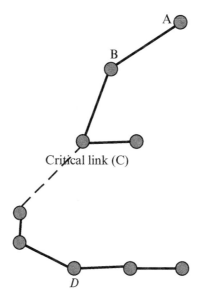

Figure 9.1   Transport and trading network with missing critical link

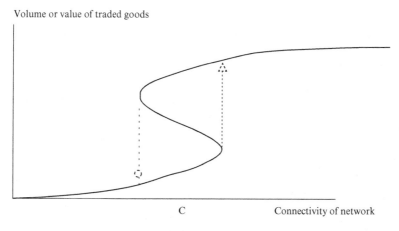

Figure 9.2   Bifurcation as a consequence of investing in a critical transport link (C)

economic system. Figure 9.2 illustrates such a phase transition after a long period of successive incremental investments.

Up to point C there are small improvements to the equilibrium state of the economy. At point C the stable equilibrium structure is lost, and the

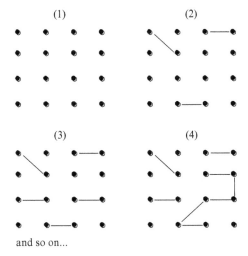

Figure 9.3   Random growth of network connections

economy starts moving toward a new equilibrium structure with a higher level of production, trade and urbanization.

There is no need for any sort of coordinated plan to guide the evolution of a network. It can emerge as the result of random connections. To illustrate this we can use Kauffman's (1995) model of a biological process. The starting point is a finite regular grid with nodes of communication at each intersection (see Figure 9.3).

Each node in the grid is initially unconnected. In the next period a transportation technology has become available, and one randomly selected node decides to invest in a link to a neighboring node. This investment gives rise to net benefits, which other nodes might observe. We then assume that two more nodes (again randomly selected) decide to connect themselves with neighboring nodes, as in Figure 9.3 (2).

This random generation of links proceeds in the same way period after period. The probability that a specific cluster of (directly or indirectly) interconnected nodes exists will increase with an increase in the total number of randomly generated links. Computer simulations of such random network generation among a large number of nodes show that this is always a non-linear process, leading to bifurcations (phase transitions). Figure 9.4 shows how the size of the largest interconnected cluster depends on the number of random links.

Such a random link-generating process may have been the trigger that caused trade between northern and southern Europe to expand in the late medieval period.

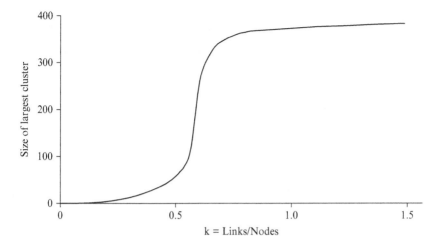

Figure 9.4   A simulated growth process involving random links

THE FIRST LOGISTICAL REVOLUTION IN EUROPE

In the late Middle Ages, Europe underwent a transition from being a stagnant system of semi-autonomous small fiefdoms into a trading network of larger regions. Rapid growth in the number of trading towns accompanied this transition.

Pirenne was the first economic historian to study the great logistical transformation of Europe around the year 1100. He claimed that the only credible cause of the transition from a stagnant equilibrium to rapid economic development must have been the slow and steady growth and integration of the transport network, permitting relatively fast and secure transport along seacoasts, navigable rivers and a sprinkling of usable roads. It was consequently this growth of linked nodes into the first integrated European transport network that provides the clearest illustration of how important the transportation infrastructure is for long-term economic development. This was the First Logistical Revolution.

The link-generating process that ultimately caused the First Logistical Revolution lowered interregional transport and transaction costs. Drastically reduced costs of trading between northern and southern nodes made long-distance trade advantageous, and a new network of trading towns came into being in northern and western Europe. This was the Hanseatic League, with Bruges and Lübeck as key nodes.

Complicated and high-risk modes of transportation, such as horse riding along natural paths and river shipping, had been the only options for trade between the north and the Mediterranean in the early medieval era. Often robber barons such as the Kuenringers controlled the main trading routes:

> Hadmar III von Kuenring is alleged to have captured ships traveling downriver with an iron chain stretched across the Danube. This became too much for Duke Friedrich, who decided to storm the castle. But the castle was known to be able to resist any direct assault, so he resorted to more devious methods. . .. There was a merchant from Vienna by the name of Rüdiger whom Hadmar had attacked too many times. Friedrich dispatched Rüdiger to Regensburg, where he outfitted a sturdy ship. Loaded with valuable cargo above and with heavily armed soldiers below, the ship traveled back down the Danube. As it passed Schönbühel on its way to Aggstein, as a ship that looked to be carrying a rich load, it was hailed and detained. The precious cargo had lured Hadmar himself to the ship. As he boarded the ship, he was overpowered by the soldiers. Just then the ship hove to and cruised towards Vienna, where the Duke was waiting. The leaderless castle was taken immediately. The Duke granted Hadmar his life and liberty on the condition that he returned all the stolen goods and atoned for the injuries he had inflicted. (wikipedia.org/wiki/Aggstein_Castle)

Formally, an increase in trade between two regions would—in the calculations of a merchant—require that the expected unit price in the consuming region minus the unit price in the producing region should exceed the unit transportation and transaction cost, including expected additional compensation for the uncertainty of the expedition (see Appendix 9.1). A general expansion of trade would only be profitable if there were simultaneous improvements to the safety of merchants and the speed of transporting their cargos. Pirenne based his study of the European medieval transformation by intuitively referring to this type of network improvement. Pirenne's analysis of the role of networks was later further developed by Braudel (1979).

Alistair Mees (1975) investigates the theoretical plausibility of explaining a qualitative restructuring and the appearance of specialized regions with only urban production—such as in Venice, Florence or Genoa—as the consequence of general improvements to the transport system or, alternatively, of technological progress. Mees's bifurcation analysis shows that Pirenne's logistical revolution hypothesis is the more plausible of the two alternatives. This theoretically deduced hypothesis forms one basis of our theory of logistical revolutions. It is the theoretical foundation that undergirds both this and the next chapter.

THE RESTRUCTURING OF MEDIEVAL EUROPE

The changes to Europe's economy, trade and culture during the First Logistical Revolution occurred along two routes. An extended route along the periphery of coasts and rivers enclosed a second overland route. The two routes were not confined to the waterways and roads of the Roman Empire. The earlier northern and western borders of the Roman Empire were traversed at an increasing number of locations, by sea as well as by land. There was a gradual integration of the entire northern European high sea trading area that consisted of the Baltic Sea, the North Sea, the English Channel and the Irish Sea. Only later would the land transport routes become secure routes for trade between the north and south of Europe.

But this was not the most spectacular part of Europe's transformation into an economically integrated entity. In the period between 1150 and 1250, there was unsurpassed growth in the number of towns. One example is that more than 3,000 new towns were founded in what would much later become Germany.

Most of the towns were small and almost resembled villages, but there were also many that evolved into real cities. These larger towns were important centers for the development of the arts, trade and market fairs. They relied on the agricultural surplus of surrounding rural areas as the basis for their existence. In return for produce, they supplied their hinterlands with locally manufactured goods—the towns acting like local monopolists. The survival of towns depended on access to the system of waterways, while the lack of long-distance roads protected the local monopolies.

How did the system of coastal waterways and navigable rivers come to support the emerging network of European towns? We must divide the answer to that question into several parts.

The European road network, which the Romans had put in place, had progressively deteriorated because of neglect. The decay of the road capacity was concurrent with institutional restructuring. Europe had been decomposed into a great number of small fiefdoms after the long period of Roman dominance. The feudal lords viewed trade as an opportunity for exploitative fiscal coercion, which they usually backed with military force. Even if mutually beneficial trade was possible in principle, it was seldom practicable.

Major changes had also taken place at sea. Islam had conquered much of Mediterranean Europe in the seventh and eighth centuries. The repeated conflicts and invasions made most of the Mediterranean too dangerous for trade. It was not until the ninth century that Mediterranean trade began to expand again. This was the period when well-situated ports on the coasts of Sicily and southern Italy became centers of the emerging trading networks. Amalfi, with its sheltered but small natural harbor, secured one of these important positions.

The importance of trade to Amalfi made the development of a maritime legal system a necessity, which came to serve as the foundation for the maritime laws of all Christian areas around the Mediterranean. Venice followed Amalfi's lead. Hills protected Amalfi, while some seventy-odd islands near the northern end of the Adriatic protected Venice. But Venice had even fewer natural resources than Amalfi. It did not even have its own drinking water. This lack of natural resources forced it to develop within the confines of the specialized urban functions of the time, that is to say, in trade and in primitive manufacturing.

The starting point was similar for Genoa. Along with Pisa and Florence, Genoa and Venice became the centers of the system of trade that developed in the course of a few centuries from the eleventh century onwards. Venice assumed an especially important role in the trade of southern Europe. By continuously expanding its territory to reach a commanding position over the lagoons, the rivers and the Brenner Pass to the north, the city state attained a position of power that proved to be highly beneficial, especially to its relations with Byzantium. Venice was also unparalleled in taking advantage of the Crusades, with their unprecedented transport needs. The rulers of Venice seized the opportunity and grew into a great maritime nation. The Sack of Constantinople (1204) finally enabled the city to take control of Byzantium. The Mongol invasion and the opening of the Silk Road to China strengthened its position even further. Trade in spices and other valuable goods enabled northern Italy to emerge as the center of an expanding trading system, which by then also included parts of northern Europe.

New ideas that spawned demands for new consumption and production patterns contributed to the growth of trade and urbanization. The dissemination of ideas is an important secondary factor that shaped late medieval European trade growth as well as the associated increase in the number of trading towns.

New transport links between previously isolated trading systems and cultures were the main cause of the establishment and later growth of towns. Technological or ideological changes were secondary, or reinforcing, factors. Improved access decides the general growth of trade, while technological factors shape its composition.

A second regional economic system existed in northern Europe. This system was known as the Hanseatic League, comprising between 70 and 170 towns in the Low Countries, northern Germany and around the Baltic Sea. Lübeck, Bruges, Danzig (Gdansk), Visby and Riga were some of the major centers. The Hanseatic network controlled trade on both the Baltic Sea and the North Sea. The success of the Hanseatic League rested on its shipping technology, in particular a thirteenth-century type of ship known as the *cog*, whose loading capacity was vastly superior to earlier types. But the *cog* was not the only determinant of Hanseatic power. It is more likely that the interplay between shipping technology and two maritime networks was what ultimately secured Hanseatic domination of Europe's north. The sea routes between a number of fortified towns—each with its own guilds, warehouses and patricians—amounted to one such network. The other network was a new and slowly emerging institutional economic network (*Lex mercatoria*), which developed commercial codes of conduct, mutual privileges, threats and counter-threats. Standard cargo documents codified and Italian bookkeeping practices controlled and regulated the commercial flows of the trading system. This institutional network made it possible for goods to be transported without accompanying owners or merchants.

Europe thus had two major maritime trading systems: The Mediterranean system and the Hanseatic League. Both systems were connected to towns in the Low Countries and both stimulated the growth of trade in coastal towns and along navigable rivers. Between these two maritime trading systems, there was a weaker overland link centered on the Champagne fairs.

The changes to the European structure of trade, location and culture during the First Logistical Revolution followed two related patterns. The first involved the periphery with its seacoasts and rivers, while the second was an interior pattern of overland roads connecting the river towns and coastal ports to their hinterlands. In the south, trading towns such as Amalfi, Venice, Florence and Genoa served as coordination centers for the Mediterranean trading network. In the north the Hanseatic network grew in general economic importance by allowing towns such as Bruges and Lübeck to host new economic and political powerbrokers. The *cog* was especially important to the northern network, since it was a small but effective vessel for transporting goods between maritime towns in different parts of the Hanseatic area and along rivers to interior hinterlands that were rural but rich in natural resources.

Continent-wide integration became a reality with the formation of the critical links between the southern and northern trading systems. First, a weak link was established with the Champagne fairs. Second, a new bridge over the river Reuss opened up trade opportunities across the St Gotthard Pass. That investment made the abundant natural resources of southern Germany accessible to the rest of Europe. Third, Genoa managed to develop a regular seaway between the Mediterranean Sea and the North Sea—via Gibraltar—by the end of the thirteenth century.

Table 9.1   *Population size (in thousands); leading European cities, 1050 to 1500*

c. 1050		c. 1200		C. 1330		C. 1500	
Cordova*	450	Palermo	150	Granada	150	Paris	225
Palermo*	350	Paris	110	Paris	150	Naples	125
Seville	90	Seville	80	Venice	110	Milan	100
Salerno	50	Venice	70	Genoa	100	Venice	100
Venice	45	Florence	60	Milan	100	Granada	70
Regensberg	40	Granada	60	Florence	95	Prague	70
Toledo	37	Cordova	60	Seville	90	Lisbon	65
Rome	35	Cologne	50	Cordova	60	Tours	60
Barbastro	35	Leon	40	Naples	60	Genoa	58
Cartagena	33	Ypres	40	Cologne	54	Ghent	55
Naples	30	Rome	35	Palermo	51	Florence	55
Mainz	30	Bologna	35	Siena	50	Palermo	55
Merida	30	Toledo	35	Barcelona	48	Roma	55
Almeria	27	Verona	33	Valencia	44	Bordeaux	50
Granada	26	Narbonne	31	Toledo	42	Lyon	50
Speyer	25	Salerno	30	Bruges	40	Orleans	50
Palma	25	Pavia	30	Malaga	40	London	50
Laon	25	Messina	30	Aquila	40	Bologna	50
London	25	Naples	30	Bologna	40	Verona	50
Elvira	22	Genoa	30	Cremona	40	Brescia	49
Cologne	21	Angers	30	Pisa	38	Cologne	45
Trier	20	Palma	30	Ferrara	36	Seville	45
Caen	20/	Speyer	30	London	35	Marseille	45
Lyon	20	Worms	28	Montpelier	35	Malaga	42
Paris	20	Ferrara	27	Rouen	35	Valencia	42
Tours	20	Orleans	27	St.-Omer	35	Ferrara	42
Verona	20	Metz	27	Lisbon	35	Rouen	40
Worms	20	Valencia	26	Angers	33	Cremona	40
Lisbon	15	Cremona	25	Marseille	31	Nuremburg	38
Florence	15	London	25	Toulouse	30	Bruges	35

Source: De Long and Shleifer (1993).

The slow and steady development of the European network infrastructure in terms of harbors, sea routes, roads, bridges and alpine mountain passes had integrated northern and southern Europe into a first "world economy" based on division of labor, trade, transport of goods and people, and, notably, *rapid urbanization*, as illustrated by Table 9.1. The cities of northern Italy grew to become important centers of finance, trade and creativity in the sciences and arts until the early sixteenth century;

they were subsequently surpassed by Lisbon, Antwerp, Amsterdam and London.

During the period 1150 to 1250 Europe saw extreme growth in the number of cities and towns. Although most of these were quite small by modern standards, they developed new kinds of urban culture, trading activities and markets—with a typical inner structure along the lines of the Von Thünen Model.

These towns developed a division of labor based on trade with their agricultural hinterland, and to facilitate local transport they built roads into and out of the town gates. Their rulers enforced monopolies for their artisans and the frictions of long-distance transport reinforced local protectionism. The early Swedish liberal economist Anders Chydenius complained about local town monopolies as late as in the eighteenth century; these were still a fact of life in Finland and Sweden at that time.

Nonetheless, growing trade volumes and increasing numbers of trading towns implied increasing dissemination of ideas among the cities and towns of the European trading system, including new ideas in the arts. The selective nature of gains from growth in the period following the First Logistical Revolution led to the rise of the great families of trading and banking capitalists, such as the Fuggers and Medicis. The greatest fortunes were amassed and put on display in the coordination centers of the European system, such as in Bruges, Florence and Venice. Ultimately, the wealth accumulation opportunities arose because of the earlier establishment of network-expanding critical links in the transportation network.

The economic history of the First Logistical Revolution is a clear illustration of how infrastructural changes may affect the course of history in a non-incremental way. Eight points sum up the lessons learned from these changes:

1. A slow but persistent expansion of the transport and institutional infrastructures caused the First Logistical Revolution. The consequence was a drastic reduction of general transport and transaction costs, affecting trade between towns in different parts of Europe.
2. Centrally located regions such as the cities of Flanders and northern Italy expanded their trade and manufacturing activities faster than the rest of the network of towns, provided that their institutions accommodated entrepreneurial market entry.
3. Transport and financial innovations improved opportunities for the economic integration of towns with their respective rural hinterlands.
4. An expanding trading system increased the advantages of regional specialization, in accordance with relative supplies of immobile production factors, information and technological know-how.

5. The First Logistical Revolution entailed a discontinuous increase in specialization opportunities, causing thousands of market towns to arise as part of Europe's first wave of urbanization.
6. The new system of urban nodes facilitated discoveries of previously untapped resources and entrepreneurial innovation and diffusion of new technologies, designs and fashions. Some entrepreneurs and their families thereby amassed great wealth, and these leading entrepreneurs (in the Knightian sense) lived in the great cities of the period, such as Bruges, Lübeck and Venice.
7. Some affluent entrepreneurial families used their newfound wealth to act as philanthropic supporters of creativity in the arts and sciences. A major motivation seems to have been social recognition among fellow members of the new class of merchants.
8. Forces of creative destruction placed previously protected organizations and established institutions in jeopardy. This early example of the dislocations accompanying development created conflicts and tensions among the new merchants, the old feudal lords and the Roman Catholic Church.

APPENDIX 9.1: TRADE AND LOGISTICAL COST

The following model shows the relation between trade and combined transport and transaction costs as perceived by medieval traders. Assume $\sum_{j=1}^{N} x_{ij} = Q_i$; where x_{ij} = flow of good from location i to location j; Q_i = production of the good in location i. The total costs of production, transport and transactions is to be minimized subject to the constraint that total demand in each location j, D_j, is satisfied:

$$H = \sum_{ij=1}^{N}(c_i(Q_i) + \tau_{ij}x_{ij}) - \sum_{j=1}^{N} p_j(\sum_{j=1}^{N} x_{ij} - Q_i);$$ Necessary conditions are:

$\frac{\delta c_i}{\delta Q_i} + \tau_{ij} - p_j = 0$ for any positive trade flow; $\sum_{j=1}^{N} x_{ij} - Q_i = 0$; (i=1,. . .,N); and $\frac{\delta c_i}{\delta Q_i} = \frac{\delta c_i}{\delta x_{ij}}$.

If the price p_j is greater than the sum of the unit transport and transaction costs (from i to j) plus the marginal cost of production in the source location then trade will expand until a new equilibrium is reached. Thus, other things being equal, a network investment that reduces transport and/or transaction costs increases trade flows.

10. Institutional infrastructure and economic games

The rapidly changing games of both markets and politics take place on a slowly changing infrastructural arena. The arena facilitates certain types of actions and decisions, while at the same time discouraging others. Here we would like to present two complementary arguments. One is strictly methodological. The methodological argument is that the possibility to *predict* what will occur in markets and in short-term political decision making depends on our ability to identify long-term changes to the arena. The other point of view concerns *controllability*, which refers to the ability of governments and other policymakers to influence socio-economic development processes.

We believe that political attempts to regulate short-term fluctuations are futile. Political decision making is often for tactical reasons oriented toward addressing conflicts as reported and perhaps exaggerated in the mass media. This frequently leads to decisions that mainly concern individual firms or specific industries or perhaps classes of households. Such decisions are not in the general interest of society as a whole, and often have unintended consequences, such as when one group of households demands preferential treatment in response to what some other group received as a governmental response to some real or imagined need.

Strategic political decision making in a limitedly predictable world requires a focus on the long run. What matters in the long run are the slowly changing factors that impact all households and firms in a spatially delimited jurisdiction. This slowly changing *public capital* constitutes the infrastructure of society. As we have stressed repeatedly in earlier chapters, the infrastructure does not only comprise roads, railroads and public utilities, but also the soft (non-material) infrastructure of legal systems, shared values and shared knowledge. The general theory of infrastructure as presented in Chapter 8 applies to *all* the different types of infrastructure.

Economic equilibria as well as growth and development processes thus always take place on an arena of hard and soft infrastructures. The soft infrastructure is made up of generally accessible knowledge (shared spoken languages and writing systems, technological know-how, organizational practices, political and legal systems and informal rules of behavior).

The hard, physical infrastructure—the focus of Chapter 9—mainly consists of transport and communication networks, which link producers and consumers in different locations to one another.

Run-of-the-mill macroeconomists tend to treat the infrastructure as a constant factor for the relevant forecasting or planning period. This is invariably an implicit treatment, and it is doubtful whether they are even aware of the potential relevance of most infrastructural factors. This treatment seems self-evident to an empirical economist fixated on short-term fluctuations, in the same way that an actor considers the arena of the theater to be a fixed, unchanging environment. And such an arena perspective may be appropriate for short-term and possibly sometimes for medium-term economic forecasts. Whether such forecasts have any intrinsic interest to other people than their makers is another matter.

In longer-term contexts, however, infrastructural changes become decisive. The empirical economist—and, also, one might add, the empirical political scientist, sociologist or historian—must include them in any meaningful analysis of policy or socio-economic change. The cumulative growth or decay of the infrastructure over the course of a century may be substantial or even revolutionary. Such positive or negative change may completely transform the conditions for production and exchange.

HOW SLOW INFRASTRUCTURAL CHANGES LEAD TO LOGISTICAL REVOLUTIONS

In the economic history of Europe, there have been three logistical revolutions: we encountered the first one in Chapter 9, and its onset was in the early twelfth century. The second one started in the fifteenth century. The third one is the most noted one and is often called the Industrial Revolution. It started in England in the late eighteenth century and then gradually spread to the rest of Europe and to North America during the nineteenth century. But that is not all. Similar but faster industrial revolutions occurred repeatedly in initially less connected and more peripheral regions of the world throughout the twentieth century, including in large swathes of China and India.

These logistical revolutions were consequences of a slow, but persistent, extension of transport and communication networks, which eventually reached critical points. After the establishment of critical links there is a period of dramatic restructuring. This restructuring involves thoroughgoing economic, cultural and political transformations and temporary imbalances such as structural unemployment and accelerated urbanization.

It is instructive to use the same type of bifurcation or phase transition analysis to understand the collapse of the Soviet empire. If the maintenance of transport and other networks is systematically neglected or politically constrained, then the resulting gradual reduction of the network capacity will eventually lead to a catastrophic collapse. The decay of the Soviet infrastructure in the end reached a downward phase transition through the successive elimination of critical links, which precipitated the disintegration of both the economic and political systems.

THE ROLE OF INSTITUTIONS

The soft infrastructure of shared institutions is the foundation for all economic exchange and cooperation. Institutions are socially enforced rules of the game that reduce both the transaction costs of using markets and the governance costs of organizations such as firms (North, 1990; Kasper et al., 2012). They also structure human decision making and knowledge acquisition (Clark, 1997), thereby influencing transformation and transport costs as well as transaction and governance costs. Institutions even have an influence on the importance of luck (pure unpredictable chance), in that luck plays a smaller role in "institution-thick" communities (Rescher, 1995).

Transaction and governance costs would be prohibitive in a hypothetical institution-free environment. An institution-free society would for example entail that murder could be freely engaged in, unrestrained by formal punishments, stigmatization or even a bad conscience. Such an institution-free environment, which may be pictured as some sort of Hobbesian struggle of all against all, has never existed in the history of humankind. But the shared institutions have differed greatly between communities at various points in time or space, with some institutional sets being more conducive to the division of labor and growth than others.

Although institutions are indispensable for understanding economic development and systematic differences in economic performance between cultures or jurisdictions, most economists neglected them for a very long time. This was because the dominant twentieth century paradigm in economic theory builds on the assumption of substantive rationality, which means that individuals are assumed to maximize utility with perfect knowledge. This assumption makes it relatively straightforward to model relationships between price, supply and demand, but it also results in neglect of other relevant economic variables, such as transaction costs, the inner organization of firms and entrepreneurship.

Psychologists have widely criticized the substantive rationality assumption; they contend that real human beings arrive at decisions in ways that bear little resemblance to the perfect utility maximizers of neo-classical economics. Individuals often act on hunches, and even when they gather information to make more structured decisions, it would be far too time-consuming to evaluate all available options. Moreover, individual decision makers do not usually construct a complete ordering of their preferences.

Herbert Simon (1982) contends that economists should rely on an alternative rationality assumption, which has become known as *bounded rationality*. This type of rationality assumes that human reasoning is constrained by a number of environmental and practical factors. The rational individual, according to this assumption, *satisfices* rather than optimizes, especially when making long-term decisions that rely on expectations that are unavoidably uncertain. Since individuals have limited knowledge and time at their disposal, they will choose courses of action that they judge to be good enough, rather than the utility-maximizing ones. Still, bounded rationality is similar to substantive rationality in that it involves systematic evaluations of alternatives according to explicit rules.

The philosopher Andy Clark (1997) criticizes the satisficing principle for being too reliant on explicit reasoning. He argues for a connectionist approach to rationality, which places a much greater emphasis on pattern recognition. Clark describes it as follows:

> In place of explicit rules operating on language-like data structures, connectionists posit an intermingling of data and processing supported by a dense parallel architecture of idealized "neurons." Such systems are often trained on examples of a desired input-output mapping and learn (by a process of gradient descent learning) to assign weights (positive and negative numeric values) to the interconnections between the idealized neurons. These weights cause the network to behave as an interpolating associative memory: they enable it to re-create patterns of designed output given fragments of the original inputs and to generalize its knowledge so as to deal with novel cases on the basis of partial similarity to the training cases. (Clark, 1997, p. 277)

What is particularly interesting about Clark's approach is that he argues that the cultural environment of the individuals—including institutions and shared knowledge—to a large extent determines the "training cases." The cultural environment both reduces individual cognitive loads and expands problem-solving abilities. It expands problem-solving abilities by allowing attained knowledge (including new knowledge) to be transmitted among individuals, which over time also may change the cultural environment, although on a slower timescale. A competitive market is one of Clark's examples that have the effect of reducing individuals' cognitive loads. The rules of the market induce strategies that approximate profit maximization, regardless of individual motivations. Simulation experiments with so-called "zero-intelligence traders" support this argument. The experiments show that non-thinking agents achieve market outcomes that are only slightly inferior to real humans, but that the institutional setting can result in much greater efficiency improvements (Gode and Sunder, 1992).

While institutions both restrict and expand individuals' reasoning and scope for action, there are enormous institutional quality differences among communities. The institutions of one community may for example be limited to proscribing certain actions that raise transaction costs, whereas another community may proscribe any action that is perceived as a threat to the ideology or economic position of the political establishment. In the latter case, we should expect much less room for experimentation, entrepreneurship and the open exchange of ideas. Institutions are thus crucial both for individuals' acquisition and use of knowledge and for the economic outcomes of a society.

INFORMAL AND FORMAL INSTITUTIONS

It is customary and indeed useful to divide institutions into informal and formal ones (North, 1990; 1994). Informal institutions are rules or constraints that evolve spontaneously in a society and which change only slowly. They are a subset of what is often referred to as culture, where culture denotes widely shared values, symbols and traditions.

An institution is distinct from other cultural factors in that there is some sort of enforcement method that is both decentralized in application and spontaneous in origin. If most members of a culturally defined group consider an unusual action a legitimate personal choice, even though it contravenes a widely held value or generally practiced tradition, we may consider such an action as being culturally atypical. It is not, however, a violation of an informal institution. Displaying openly gay behavior is untraditional and not a majority personal preference in any society, but it is nowadays a tolerated action in most Western cities. Hence there is no informal constraint that discourages this type of action, unlike in the same cities a generation or so ago.

Kasper et al. (2012) divide the enforcement of informal institutions into conventions, internalized rules and informal sanctions. Conventions are the most unproblematic of these, because individual self-interest leads to spontaneous self-enforcement. Examples are grammatical rules and systems of measurement such as the metric system.

Internalized rules are also self-enforcing, but are conditioned by inculcation and education within a shared culture. While a member of a culturally distinct minority interacting with a member of the majority will have an incentive to self-enforce conventions, this is not always the case for internalized rules, which exhibit substantial cross-cultural variation. The deeply held moral beliefs of an individual are reflected in internalized rules, as are personal rules as to what constitutes acceptable behavior. The violator himself sanctions the violations of these rules in the form of a bad conscience.

The internalized rules are, of course, in part specific to each individual. For example, a vegan in a modern Western society has a stricter internalized rule regarding animal rights than the cultural norm, whereas a thief has a weaker internalized rule regarding property rights. But there are still rules that are sufficiently widely shared for them to be considered culturally determined. Frequently, these widely shared rules have their roots in religious or religion-like precepts. A member of a community with Christian roots can therefore be expected to adhere to a certain set of internalized rules. But many precepts were also adapted to accommodate previously existing rules, and were gradually adjusted over time in accordance with local development trajectories. We therefore find that the exact interpretation of an internalized rule may differ between communities (for example, in the delimitation of a "white lie"), and also that societies with different religious or philosophical rules may gradually converge because of spontaneous imitation of rules that have proved to reduce the costs of transactions and governance in economically successful communities.

Even if most individuals self-enforce the informal institutions of their community, there will always be a minority who impose weaker constraints on themselves. In all human societies, there are socially deviant individuals, such as inveterate liars and opportunists. This is where collective informal sanctions become important. These can have a powerful inhibitory effect on potential transgressors. Common informal sanctions include censure, shaming and ostracism. Potentially dishonest business people may for example choose to be honest in order not to lose repeat business. Typically, community-wide informal sanctions apply to certain minimal standards of behavior. In a typical Western community, a thief will be shunned but a carnivore will not be, although pork-eaters may be shunned in some Muslim communities.

Sometimes, however, the violation of an informal institution may be committed because an individual believes that the institution is detrimental to society or simply because it seems pointless. And there are certainly examples of when the abolition of an informal institution reduces coordination costs, thereby facilitating attempts to capture potential gains from trade. Examples of such unproductive institutions include the medieval proscription against lending money at interest or the various restrictions against exchange relationships with "outsiders," however defined, in many communities throughout history. Breaches of such inefficient institutions often attract imitators, with the effect that they may lead to a social adaptation of inherited informal institutions. There may also be examples of an adaptive "thickening" of the informal institutions, such as spontaneously emerging sanctions against tardiness or reckless driving.

Although more generally associated with governmental institutions, there are also cases where the enforcement of non-state institutions relies on formal sanctions, and thus belong to the set of formal institutions. This is for example the case when private trading networks voluntarily submit to third-party adjudication or arbitration. Formal enforcement of privately initiated institutions is especially common in interjurisdictional transactions and in exchanges involving financial traders, academics and athletes.

Most formal institutions are imposed by governments and are normally backed by the use of force. They tend to be codified in written laws, statutes and regulations; their violations incur formal sanctions, such as fines or imprisonment. Typical of such institutions is that they have a hierarchical structure, where higher-ranking institutions override lower-ranking ones. In the United States, the higher-ordered institutions include the Bill of Rights, the Constitution and the Anglo-Saxon tradition of common law. At a lower level, there are legislated statutes, which in their turn override by-laws and regulations. Organizations such as courts, the police, the Internal Revenue Service and prisons enforce the state-sanctioned formal institutions of the United States.

THE RELATIONSHIP BETWEEN INFORMAL AND FORMAL INSTITUTIONS

All societies throughout history have had informal institutions, but only relatively developed societies have developed formal institutions to reinforce (or, in some cases, suppress) the informal institutions. The informal institutions of small tribal communities were built upon principles of communal property, sharing and honesty toward other members of the community. These communities were small and personalized and had neither governments, nor subdivided property rights, nor any systematic division of labor.

The most profound early institutional change occurred as a result of the Neolithic Revolution, which began in the Middle East and northern Thailand about 10,000 years ago (Kasper et al., 2012). This signifies the introduction of agricultural society, which coincided with the emergence of private property rights. The first formal system of laws was created by Hammurabi almost two millennia BC. Much of that system was concerned with the protection and exchange of property rights. Nearly one-half of the Hammurabi code dealt with matters of contract.

Agriculture and exclusive property rights made larger settlements and a (limited) division of labor possible. And it is the size of human settlements that decides whether formal institutions are needed. Even though informal institutions are more important for most people in all societies, it is formal institutions that become increasingly valuable with the growth of settlements, as some people will engage in opportunistic behavior when they interact with strangers.

The normal early process of institution building was that established informal institutions were codified and that the spontaneous informal enforcement of an institution was backed up by a formal enforcement mechanism. Although the great majority of the population adhered to the institution spontaneously or because of informal sanctions, there was an additional need for formal punishments to dissuade breaches of institutions by the most recalcitrant individuals. Conversely, when formal institutions are imposed that are not derived from established informal rules—which has also been common in many societies—there will either be widespread non-compliance or, alternatively, enforcement will be much more costly. (Note, however, that if a new state-imposed formal institution is enacted according to institutional procedures that are regarded as legitimate and binding by most individuals, this may lead them to spontaneously adhere to a new formal institution even if it does not amount to a codification of an internal rule.)

The emergence and development of informal institutions is an elusive subject. There seems to be no inevitable trend toward increasingly efficient institutions. This is demonstrated by the lack of any worldwide convergence of informal institutions toward high levels of honesty and non-aggression; institutions that are associated with impersonal trust and low transaction costs. Rather, the development trajectory has been described as path-dependent (Putnam, 1993). On the other hand, there are many individual instances of societies that have become increasingly well served by their (spontaneously evolving) informal institutions over time, in the sense that individuals have become increasingly adept at capturing potential gains from trade or cooperation. One example is northern Italy, which throughout the post-war period has exhibited high and rising levels of impersonal trust. This has facilitated entrepreneurship, trade and social cooperation (Putnam, 1993; Inglehart, 1997).

Informal institutions evolve spontaneously and are not designed by any one in particular. This makes it impossible for any one individual or organization to control or plan the set of such institutions that apply to a specific society. The only institutions that can be imposed are formal ones. The Communist Party of the Soviet Union could create new formal institutions, but they could not create a new Soviet man. In fact, the Soviet Union is an illustrative example of how the informal and formal institutions of a society can be thoroughly contradictory, which, as we noted earlier, causes enforcement problems. The Soviet Union solved this by creating a police state with draconian punishments, which has historically been a common strategy when authoritarian rulers have sought to impose their personally preferred rules on reluctant subjects.

Formal institutions that combine constitutional democracy with the rule of law are widely regarded as especially conducive to freedom, prosperity and peace. But there are limits to what such institutions can accomplish. The formal institutions are only as good as the inherited informal institutions allow them to be. Robert Putnam's study of Italian regions provides a striking illustration of this. While all Italian regions have identical (higher-level) political and legal institutions, they remain dissimilar in many cultural, economic and political respects. According to interview surveys, residents of the Emilia Romagna region have much higher levels of impersonal trust than those in Italy's south. The generally accepted internalized rule of honesty in Emilia Romagna has had profound implications for transaction and governance costs: Emilians are much more likely to join civil associations, to start businesses and to join informal business networks. Differences in informal institutions even affect the implementation of government programs. One example out of many is that a nationally funded program for day-care centers resulted in one center per 400 children in Emilia Romagna as compared with one center per 12,560 children in Campania, even though the allocation of funds was proportional to the regional population (Putnam, 1993).

INSTITUTIONS AND INTERJURISDICTIONAL COMPETITION

So far we have only considered societies in isolation. But there are fundamental differences between institutional development paths that are caused by the relative openness and degree of centralization of a jurisdiction. In this context, openness refers to the ease with which human and physical capital can move between jurisdictions (geographical units with different formal institutions), while centralization refers to the degree of central political control within a jurisdiction. Heckscher (1935) makes the case that the ideology of mercantilism, which favors centralization and a closed economy, is particularly inimical to economic development.

Societies that have always been rather centralized and closed have historically tended to develop informal institutions based on hierarchical relationships and personalized (constrained) trust. Such societies have had to rely on personalized exchange rather than on anonymous market exchange. In addition, organized cooperation typically takes place within families or in coercive organizations with strictly hierarchical chains of command.

Open societies engender processes that make them adopt increasingly efficient institutions over time. This is because individuals have the option to vote with their feet (migration) or wallets (imports, investments) for other jurisdictions, which is a powerful discipline on political decision makers, regardless of whether they are autocrats or elected representatives. Openness triggers a process of *interjurisdictional competition*, which provides the incentives for rulers to search for policies that create rather than redistribute wealth. This is because their power depends on their ability to retain and attract production factors such as mobile human and physical capital. An open society exposes people to other communities through trade or migration, which over time habituates people to higher levels of cross-cultural impersonal trust, which by itself is a necessary condition for the functioning of impersonal markets. Political decentralization (democratic federalism) within an open society can enhance the adaptive capacity of institutions, since it improves the opportunities for institutional experimentation and benchmarking within jurisdictions. Decentralization thus partially extends the efficiency-inducing traits of higher-level competition to also encompass lower-level interjurisdictional competition.

INSTITUTIONAL INFRASTRUCTURE CHANGE AND THE LOGISTICAL REVOLUTIONS

The first historical instances of open communities emerged because of the fragmentation of the feudal system in medieval Europe. The first examples are trading places that arose in the jurisdictional vacuum between fiefdoms for the purpose of conducting interjurisdictional trade. In this setting, traders could for the first time interact without feudal hierarchical considerations. This gave rise to the gradual strengthening of impersonal trust and horizontal market relationships (contracts and legal equality). The productivity of these interactions eventually caused these trading places to grow, and the spontaneously evolving system of trading relationships eventually resulted in the Custom of Merchants, a non-state institution with formal sanctions (Rosenberg and Birdzell, 1986). Formal institutions based on the same principle, equality before the law, were first adopted by the small and open city states of northern and central Italy in the twelfth century (Putnam, 1993).

In many cases, the same geographical area has alternated between closed and open political systems over the centuries. The medieval city states in Lombardy and Piedmont, for example, later came under the political domination of absolutist monarchies for several centuries. While this may seem to contradict the assumed greater efficiency of open jurisdictions, it should be remembered that military power rests on total rather than per capita income (Mokyr, 1995). The city states of Emilia Romagna and Venice proved more durable, but the limitation of interjurisdictional competitive pressures probably made the rulers more complacent. The guilds, which originally had been facilitators of economic exchange (Putnam, 1993), responded to their less competitive environment by becoming rent-seeking interest groups of the sort that has been analyzed extensively by public choice economists (c.f. Olson, 1982; Tullock, 1993).

While the relative openness of jurisdiction-specific institutions may change substantially between two points in time, many observations and a limited number of empirical studies indicate that informal institutions operate on a slower timescale. While openness is conducive to impersonal trust and thereby extends the market, the societal adoption of what may be termed the institutions of capitalism seems to be an extremely slow and protracted development. Robert Putnam (1993) notes that the cultural disparities between northern and southern Italy can be traced to the 300 or 400 years of civic republicanism (that is, decentralization and openness) that was only experienced in northern and central parts of the country. But these 300 or 400 years ended more than 500 years ago! In China, it is noteworthy that treaty ports and former colonies such as Shanghai, Xiamen, Guangzhou and Hong Kong have experienced openness and interjurisdictional competition for at least a century longer than most inland and northern cities.

In this chapter, we present the argument that economic restructurings are the result of critical links that extend the market and increase opportunities for the division of labor. While these logistical revolutions are accompanied by institutional changes, it seems that the original impetus for the changes originate in the expansion of trade, which is partly determined by improved transport and communication networks. Archaeological research has shown that trade preceded the Neolithic Revolution and agricultural society (Leakey, 1981). And as we noted earlier, long-distance trade between fiefdoms preceded the emergence of capitalist institutions. Still, there are probably also interdependencies. For example, the existence of a reliable system of contract enforcement may have accelerated investments in shipbuilding during the late Middle Ages. One can conceptualize the logistical revolutions as having openness and interjurisdictional competition as a necessary but insufficient condition and the appearance of a critical link as both a necessary and a sufficient condition.

Another illustration of the sequencing of an economic restructuring is the communications revolution of the twentieth century. Although it is still much too early for us to comprehend many aspects of this ongoing economic transformation, it seems as if the critical technological link preceded the associated institutional transformation. In any case, "Postmaterialist values" (Inglehart, 1997), which are quite suitable for supporting new and more flexible and cosmopolitan rule systems, only emerged as community-wide standards in the early twenty-first century, and only in the most post-industrial and globalized regions of the world.

THE SECOND LOGISTICAL REVOLUTION: LINKING THE CONTINENTS BY COMBINING NEW SHIPPING TECHNOLOGY AND LOWERED TRANSACTION COSTS

Trade is conditioned on credit. Trade with distant regions requires access to long-term credit. Already in the twelfth century, it became common to use bills of exchange rather than direct monetary transfers in Italy, which led to the creation of the first banks. Florence became a leading center of early banking. But these early private banks, which were created by the Medicis, Fugger and other merchants, were often regarded as unreliable because of their part in bankrolling the Church and the nobility. There were attempts to create banks with public guarantees in northern Italy, but these attempts were insignificant in quantitative terms.

The types of ship that were common during the First Logistical Revolution were appropriate for relatively short voyages. The *Cog* and its Mediterranean counterparts were designed for coastal shipping. Transatlantic voyages remained impossible. But a new type of ocean-going sailing ship, the *Caravel*, was developed during the second half of the fifteenth century. This was an Iberian ship with two to four masts, and it was this type of ship that Christopher Columbus used for his transatlantic voyages. The *Caravel* opened up the high seas, and shifted the European trading system's center of gravity toward the Atlantic coast. Lisbon became the center of European trade flows for a short period, but its centrality was soon obscured by the rise of the competing northern Atlantic cities of Antwerp and Amsterdam.

The Dutch had meanwhile developed a ship that was highly suitable for long distance trade, the *Fluyt*. The *Fluyt* was voluminous and yet slender, and could be sailed by a relatively small crew. With this innovation, the Dutch had created one of the conditions for Amsterdam's emergence as the center of world trade.

The steadily increasing distances over which goods were exchanged led to an increasing need for credit. It became necessary to find a reliable method for funding trading projects that were both risky and protracted. The demand for secure and predictable instruments of credit mounted.

The rulers and merchants of the city of Amsterdam seized the opportunity to meet the needs of traders with a number of financial inventions and innovations at the beginning of the seventeenth century. The establishment of a stock exchange was followed by the first publicly guaranteed bank. Merchants could deposit silver coins for which they received guaranteed banknotes, which could then be used in international trade. The transaction costs associated with trade were thereby reduced and Amsterdam's head start in effecting this reduction enabled it to become a temporary center of the world economy. At the end of the seventeenth century, the bank in Amsterdam was however joined by a larger bank with public guarantees, the Bank of England, which was allowed to conduct business in both money and bills of exchange. It could thus both provide credit and print banknotes. The Bank of England later became the prototype for central banks all over the world. The City of London had thereby secured its lasting position as an international financial center.

New transportation technology, which made transoceanic trade possible, set the stage for the Second Logistical Revolution. The resulting expansion of trade caused severe shortages of credit. These shortages were redressed by the introduction of publicly guaranteed banks, first in Amsterdam and later in London. The center of gravity of the European and world economy therefore moved from the Mediterranean and the Baltic to the North Atlantic coast. Antwerp, Amsterdam, London and Paris expanded, while the Hanseatic and Mediterranean cities stagnated. The wealth of the new North Atlantic cities also caused them to become the most important centers of science and culture. It was in these cities, with London as the outstanding center, that philosophers and mathematicians laid the foundations for modern science.

THE THIRD LOGISTICAL REVOLUTION: THE INDUSTRIAL REVOLUTION

The first and second logistical revolutions extended the arena of trading capitalism. For every decision about a new trade link it sufficed to compare the price difference of a good between the importing and exporting node with the transport and transaction costs associated with trade. The merchants were as a rule not concerned with the production conditions in the exporting region.

The Third Logistical Revolution was based on entirely different considerations. The mercantilist policy of France had encouraged a strong interest in production technology. Although Colbert's and other politicians' interest in production technology rarely led to any profitable economic ventures, it had become possible to envision capitalist development through other means than trade.

The Scottish philosopher and economist, Adam Smith, became the most influential critic of mercantilism. But his critique was not aimed at the mercantilist preoccupation with manufacturing technology. Smith's aim was rather to attack the misconception that politicians could achieve greater production and welfare through central planning than what was achievable by competition between a multitude of independent producers and consumers. He was also entirely opposed to the view that a trade surplus and the attendant accumulation of reserves of gold and silver would be conducive to the welfare of a country. For Smith, there was an intimate connection between the exchange of goods and specialization. The general welfare could only be secured by a thoroughgoing division of labor, where each country, region, firm and individual should seek an appropriate economic specialization. Smith (1776/2012) liked to use metaphors in his writings and his pin-making example has become especially famous:

> To take an example, therefore, from a very trifling manufacture; but one in which the division of labour has been very often taken notice of, the trade of the pin-maker; a workman not educated to this business (which the division of labour has rendered a distinct trade), nor acquainted with the use of the machinery employed in it (to the invention of which the same division of labour has probably given occasion), could scarce, perhaps, with his utmost industry, make one pin in a day, and certainly could not make twenty. But in the way in which this business is now carried on, not only the whole work is a peculiar trade, but it is divided into a number of branches, of which the greater part are likewise peculiar trades. One man draws out the wire, another straights it, a third cuts it, a fourth points it, a fifth grinds it at the top for receiving the head; to make the head requires two or three distinct operations; to put it on is a peculiar business, to whiten the pins is another; it is even a trade by itself

to put them into the paper; and the important business of making a pin is, in this manner, divided into about eighteen distinct operations, which, in some manufactories, are all performed by distinct hands, though in others the same man will sometimes perform two or three of them. I have seen a small manufactory of this kind where ten men only were employed, and where some of them consequently performed two or three distinct operations. But though they were very poor, and therefore but indifferently accommodated with the necessary machinery, they could, when they exerted themselves, make among them about twelve pounds of pins in a day. There are in a pound upwards of four thousand pins of a middling size. Those ten persons, therefore, could make among them upwards of forty-eight thousand pins in a day. Each person, therefore, making a tenth part of forty-eight thousand pins, might be considered as making four thousand eight hundred pins in a day. But if they had all wrought separately and independently, and without any of them having been educated to this peculiar business, they certainly could not each of them have made twenty, perhaps not one pin in a day; that is, certainly, not the two hundred and fortieth, perhaps not the four thousand eight hundredth part of what they are at present capable of producing, in consequence of a proper division and combination of their different operations. (Smith, 1776/2012, pp. 9–10)

The English economist David Ricardo (1817/1996) later developed Adam Smith's insights further with his law of comparative advantage. The Ricardian law shows that it is not the absolute advantages of an individual that determine the benefits of specialization. A person can be superior to others at producing several goods. It would nevertheless be advantageous for him to concentrate on producing the good where he has the greatest relative superiority. It is thus sufficient to know one's best ability relative to others. The law can be generalized to hold for firms, regions and nations as well as for individuals. Production in excess of what is locally demanded can be exchanged with products from regions with generally inferior productivity levels in an absolute sense, but which can have comparative advantages in the production of some goods (that is, they should trade their least inferior products).

The Swedish economists Eli Heckscher and Bertil Ohlin would later refine the theory of specialized production and trade (Ohlin, 1933/1967). They reformulated it as a theory of factor proportions, which implies that each region should specialize in production that makes use of the relatively most plentiful regional resources. This means that a region with a relative abundance of labor, but with a shortage of technological know-how or physical capital, should specialize in labor-intensive products in exchange for capital-intensive goods and services. Trade then becomes a way of harnessing asymmetric resource endowments. In contrast, Johann Heinrich von Thünen (1826/1930) and later Martin Beckmann (1952; 1953) developed a theory of trade in which transport and transaction cost are the most important drivers of trade and specialization of regions (see Chapter 3).

The Third Logistical Revolution was only possible because of the combined effects of improved transport networks and improved institutions that supported free trade, specialization and production. Trade was no longer limited to the exploitation of given price differences between regions. The new focus was on the difference between the price of a good in the importing region and the lowest possible total cost of supplying the good. Importers therefore became interested in influencing the entire chain of costs of bringing a good to the market, including the costs of organizing production, of trading and of transporting the product to the market. Every cost came to be seen as variable and amenable to potential cost-cutting measures.

This implies that a new general equilibrium requires $p_j(\mathbf{x}) - p_i(\mathbf{x}) \leq C_{ij} + T_{ij}$, for all i and j, where:

p_j = price received in import region j for the good
p_i = price charged in export region
C_{ij} = unit transport cost when imported to region i from region j
T_{ij} = unit transaction cost

Transport and transaction costs can also be functions of the vector of trade flows $\mathbf{x}$.

These cost-cutting measures were not always benign. Slavery became a way of reducing the production cost of North American cotton. The lure of distant regions with abundant natural resources also encouraged a colonial foreign policy, which was made possible by the rise of the nation state and was justified by the emerging ideology of imperialism.

Britain became the unrivalled center of the world economy in this period. There were many reasons for Britain's economic power. Ocean shipping was still technologically more advanced than other modes of transportation. Britain's location in the North Atlantic and the superior strength of its navy made it possible to keep sea transport costs at a lower level than in other countries, especially since most of the population lived on the coast or near navigable rivers or canals. This general proximity to waterways greatly facilitated factory production. Moreover, the efficiency-inducing restructuring of British agricultural production had made most agricultural workers economically redundant. That group was consequently available for employment in the new factories at very low cost.

The Third Logistical Revolution had an enormous impact on the cities of Europe. At the beginning of the Industrial Revolution, there were four cities with a population of more than 50,000 in England and Scotland. In the span of a lifetime, the number of British towns of this size grew tenfold. One of the most important new urban centers was Manchester, which grew from a population of 20,000 in 1770 to almost half a million by the middle of the nineteenth century. There was no way in which cities such as Manchester could provide an adequate infrastructure for a population that was growing at a rate of nearly 4 percent per year. The lack of adequate sanitation and water provision compounded the problems of overcrowding, pollution and crime.

The concentration of the workforce in large factories made it profitable to make use of wood- or coal-fueled machines. The garment industry was the first to be organized in large-scale industrial and logistical complexes, which was occasioned by the invention of the steam-powered spinning wheel and the power loom in the second half of the eighteenth century. The contemporaneous invention of the cotton gin lowered production costs on the American plantations, which enabled the British to quintuple their annual imports of cotton in 30 years. The imported cotton was ever more efficiently woven in British factories, which allowed British textile manufacturing to become the world's largest export industry. The successful innovation of steam power in the textile industry provided an incentive for further inventions and innovations. Important innovations in nineteenth-century Britain included the industrial exploitation of iron and coal and improvements to the organization of the British merchant marine.

The new industrialists formed an aspiring elite in much the same way that a bourgeoisie of merchants had arisen as a class opposed to the privileges of the aristocracy in Europe's early city states. Like the elites of earlier eras, they were looking for ways to obtain public approval. One way of achieving respectability was by supporting scientific research and the arts. For this reason, England became the creative center of Europe in the nineteenth century.

Another notable development was that the class structure became increasingly polarized in the nineteenth century, since a working class with its own political and intellectual leaders took shape for the first time. The rapid growth of a new proletariat in the cities made the emerging class structure not only possible but above all conspicuous.

The transportation infrastructure of the industrializing Western world was essentially based on two dominant networks. The sea transport network became increasingly interlinked and reliable, with the North Atlantic connection between Europe and North America at its core. On the west coast of Europe and the east coast of North America (which topologically includes the Great Lakes), a number of large industrial cities and seaports became the nodes of the shipping network. The national railway networks, which mainly aimed at accessing inland natural resources, also converged on the harbors and factories of the great coastal cities. Together, the sea and rail networks were the logistical foundations of early industrialism. The typical industrial metropolises of early industrial Europe and North America, with gigantic factories, wharves and railway junctions, became the palpable symbols of industrialism. The literature, films and songs of industrialism were well served by harbors, ships, trains and railway stations as appropriate settings.

The dominance of the railways as a mode of transportation reached its peak in the 1870s in America and about ten years later in Europe. At the peak, railway tracks accounted for about 80 percent of all built transport infrastructure, with roads and canals accounting for the remaining 20 percent (Grübler, 1990). Roads mainly functioned as local complements to railways and sea transportation. The tremendous concentration of production and industrial employment in new urban centers such as Liverpool, Hamburg, Glasgow and Baltimore, to give a few examples, was the joint consequence of scale economies in the production nodes and nodal linkages to the sea and rail networks. Harbors, railroads and shipbuilding are activities with substantial indivisibilities and other economies of scale. The transport networks therefore also favored the spatial concentration of large-scale production of industrial goods, which combined a thorough division of labor with mass production of standardized goods.

COMMON FEATURES

The purpose of the brief survey of the logistical revolutions in Europe's history is to draw attention to a number of commonalities that unite all three revolutions that we have discussed so far, as well as the ongoing fourth logistical revolution. Each restructuring has had similar causes and consequences:

- They have been caused by a slow but persistent expansion of the infrastructure. Usually it involves improved opportunities for transport, knowledge and information search, contracting and other economic transactions. The restructuring is triggered by a phase transition of the general transport and transaction cost level toward a new, much lower, level.
- The major expansions of trade have occurred when the transport and transaction costs have been reduced on centrally located and therefore critical links. Such improvements to the transport and transaction systems even cause peripheral regions to achieve improved opportunities for trading, both with the center and with other peripheral regions.
- The expansion of an integrated trading system to encompass new regions increases the advantages of specialization in accordance with

the relative local supply of immobile production factors, including technological know-how.

- Some regions have their greatest comparative advantages in producing goods that primarily require good general accessibility and only to a limited extent need land and other natural resources. This means that production, employment and housing can locate jointly in cities. Other regions have their greatest comparative advantages in producing goods that need greater inputs of land and natural resources, thereby retaining a sparsely inhabited rural character.
- Since every logistical revolution has entailed increased specialization, there has always been a concomitant growth in the number and sizes of cities and the total urban population.
- Every logistical revolution has entailed the discovery of new resources, new technologies and new products. This has given rise to unusually protracted periods of monopolization and unusually high profits. These temporary monopolies have enabled entrepreneurs to amass great fortunes.
- The *nouveaux riches* have been viewed contemptuously by the privileged group of the preceding era. This contempt encourages attempts to legitimize the new-found wealth. A common strategy has been to support science and art. There are striking similarities between Lorenzo de' Medici of the First Logistical Revolution, Alfred Nobel of the Third Logistical Revolution and Bill Gates of the Fourth Logistical Revolution. All have used their wealth to achieve social recognition.

CREATIVE DESTRUCTION

Industrial society sowed the seeds of its own demise. The combination of railways, new steam-powered ships and big enterprises with factory production amounted to a recipe for success. The profits could be used to further extend industrialization by means of ports, ships, railways and trains. But it was frequently more advantageous to search for previously inaccessible natural resources, which could only with great difficulty be reached with canals or new railway lines. Roads, and the newly developed motor vehicles, were much more suitable for reaching natural resources in mountainous or remote areas. Beginning in the 1920s, it became more profitable to make cars and roads rather than to extend the railway network any farther. The long-term effect of this shift, although imperceptible at first, would be that a new arena would supersede the arena of industrialism. The benefits associated with large-scale manufacturing and large-scale shipping gradually dwindled and society became increasingly decentralized.

The arena of industrial society was also reshaped by changes to the infrastructure for transmitting knowledge and information. During the Industrial Revolution, messages were transported in the same way as regular goods. News was disseminated by mail, newspapers and journals transported by rail or sea and distributed by mail carriers. More advanced knowledge entailed personal trips by train or passenger ship at great cost and sacrifice of time and comfort. The information flows coincided with the nodes and links of the rail and sea networks. The spatial organization of firms was therefore also constrained by the shape of the networks. For the sake of efficiency, it became necessary to coordinate knowledge and information in the same location that hosted the production of goods. Large corporate headquarters adjoined large manufacturing plants with chains of command that were typically hierarchical, unidirectional and slow.

The benefits from a more flexible transmission of information were obvious. Rothschild had already used pigeons for transmitting information about the outcome of the Battle of Waterloo. But pigeons were nonetheless unwieldy and unreliable information carriers. An important breakthrough in the technology of disembodied information transmission was the invention of telegraphy, which led to the construction of the first telegraph line in Britain in 1837. But simultaneous information exchange was only possible with the establishment of a telephone network in the last decades of the nineteenth century. And it was a new way of using the telephone network that became one of the constituent causes of the Fourth Logistical Revolution almost a century later.

THE FOURTH LOGISTICAL REVOLUTION AND THE EMERGING CREATIVE SOCIETY

The real economy of the world is currently in a process of two structural transformations, both of which have been caused by the improvement of logistical networks, implying greater global competition. Competitive industrialization is one of these two major transformations influencing all the newly industrializing countries as well as the formerly Soviet-dominated economies.

Conversely, the advanced Western economies, and especially their main urban centers, are undergoing a process of transformation—*a Fourth Logistical Revolution*—away from the industrial system into a globally extended post-industrial system of creative regions. In these creative regions, the production system is increasingly being based upon the exploitation of modern communication systems and the cognitive capacities of the population. These regions specialize in the production of goods and services that tend to be more complex and creative than those that are produced in other regions.

This transformation is leading the advanced economies away from the simple old growth paradigm, within which the quantities of goods and services are increasing at constant or declining world market prices. The main consequence of increasing product complexity is increasing product value rather than increasing product quantity. High regional and industry-specific research intensity engenders more complex products, greater willingness to pay among consumers and globalization of markets. In the same way that investment in physical capital requires a marginal efficiency that at least corresponds to the risk-compensating rate of interest as set in the global financial market, there is an analogous requirement that guides investments in research, development and design. An implication of the efficiency requirement is that the real rate of interest determines the general rate at which products become more complex or what we may term "the complexity growth rate."

The level of complexity that is efficient in a region depends on the education level of its workforce and on its scientific and industrial research strategies. Policies affecting universities and research institutes are thus becoming more important for the dynamic comparative advantages of a region than in previous eras. We shall return to these knowledge-related issues in Chapter 13.

Infrastructural investment strategies are also essential for industrializing regions, but for them the relevant infrastructure mainly consists of railroads, roads, ports and other transportation links. In creative regions, the infrastructural focus shifts to scientific research, international airports and global communication systems.

11. Real estate capital

WHAT IS REAL ESTATE CAPITAL?

Economists often postulate that the output of production is a function of three types of input—land, labor and capital. This is misleading. The most obvious way in which this conventional formulation leads us astray is the idea of labor as a homogeneous and undifferentiated resource, which is at odds with real-world markets, where an individual's specific skill set is more important than the quantity (time) of the work effort. But this is not the only misleading aspect of conventional production functions. Land is somehow also seen as a homogeneous resource. Nothing could be further from the truth. The value of a piece of land—a lot—varies enormously, and depends on where it is located. To be more specific, the value of land depends on its accessibility to various resources and amenities that allows its owner to save time relative to less accessible locations. All land that offers accessibility benefits relative to the least accessible land—perhaps a lot somewhere in Antarctica—is thus capital in the sense of providing a valuable input into production processes over a non-negligible period of time.

While labor should be reclassified as differentiated bundles of capital attributes, almost all "land" is actually a mixture of two types of capital: physical capital such as the various scarce natural resources that a specific lot provides to its owner, as well as the social capital that is associated with accessibility to other people and the spatial impacts of their actions.[1] Hence the relevant inputs in any production process are not land, labor and capital, but physical capital, human capital and social capital, with land combining physical and social capital attributes, in the same way that "labor" combines valuable attributes of both human and social capital.

So "land" is actually capital. Usually, a lot includes not only "land" but also one or more structures, which most people usually call "real estate." But this does not denote a qualitative change from undeveloped "land." Such "land" is already a combination of physical and social capital, which implies that the construction of buildings only adds additional physical capital attributes to a bundle of location-specific attributes that is already quite complex even before the builders start digging. We therefore refer to lots with or without building as "real estate capital," keeping in mind that such capital virtually always combines physical capital with social capital attributes.

What is then the value—that is, the market price— of a specific unit of real estate capital? The answer to that question is analogous to a question about capital in general. It is the value of the sum of the expected discounted future (direct and indirect) utility of all attributes associated with the specific unit. And these attributes are either physical capital or social capital attributes. The value of the physical capital comprises the utility of site-specific buildings and natural resources and also the value of differentiated access to other buildings and natural resources. The social capital part of the value is similar: it is the expected discounted future utility of location-specific accessibility to other people, as well as the spatio-temporally differentiated social effects of their actions. Unlike other types of capital, accessibility to other people can yield negative utility and thus a price discount rather than a price premium. This happens whenever buyers of property wish to avoid certain people, such as those with a criminal record. Usually, however, access to other people is valued, and—as always—it is the valuation of the highest bidder that determines the price.

There are obviously different categories of real estate, such as housing, commercial properties and industrial sites. While at first sight it may appear as if only commercial and industrial real estate are capital, this is mistaken. Dwellings are also bundles of attributes that serve as capital, since households engage in unpriced production of a great variety of services, for example home-cooked meals and home entertainment (Becker, 1976).

THE IMPORTANCE OF REAL ESTATE CAPITAL

It is easy to underestimate the importance of real estate among the different types of capital when in fact it is the most important source of household wealth. Statistics from both the United States and the European Union show that direct ownership of real estate account for about half of all household assets. In the Eurozone, the value of households' direct real estate ownership amounted to more than €15 trillion in 2015 (ING Economic and Financial Analysis, 2016), while the total value of the commercial property market was about US$11 trillion in the United States in 2009 (Florance et al., 2010). Households are the ultimate owners of equity in firms, and a sizable portion of firms' assets consists of real estate. While it is difficult to calculate the exact amount of households' direct and indirect holdings of real estate, it is clear that it outweighs all other types of material capital in value terms.

We can therefore draw the conclusion that the physical and social capital embodied in immobile real estate capital is a more important source of the productive potential of an economy than mobile physical capital such as machine tools and other types of production equipment. This should come as no surprise, since location and space for working is arguably a more important complement to the human capital of a firm's workers than production machinery. This is especially true of the most valuable types of human capital, which typically do not involve the operation of machinery. Human-machine complementarities typify manufacturing and extraction work rather than work involving people with the highest marginal human-capital products, for example management and research.

RENT AND CAPITAL VALUE

People can either own or rent real estate. There are established methods for deriving capital values from market rents. The simplest method assumes that the market is in deterministic equilibrium. If we ignore the durability of capital, $K = R/r$, where K is the capital value, R is the market rent or, equivalently, the annual returns and r is the real rate of interest. This is not a particularly realistic view of real estate, especially since land and buildings tend to have unusually high durability, which implies that uncertainty is a more severe problem than for shorter-lived goods.

If we do not correct for the durability of the good, which is anyway a minor effect for highly durable assets, we can use a modified version of the deterministic formula for calculating capital values. When facing an uncertain future, an investor in real estate should calculate the capital value as $K = (R - M - VC)/(r + r_{uc} + E(NRG))$, where M are annual maintenance costs, VC are annual variable costs, r_{uc} is a subjective uncertainty compensation that differs among individuals and $E(NRG)$ is the subjective expectation of the growth rate of net rents (gross rents minus maintenance costs and variable costs) that may also differ among individuals with different expectations of the future. The formula that accounts for the uncertainty of the future shows that—other things being equal—individual investors who are less uncertainty-averse (commonly referred to as "less risk-averse") will have a higher willingness to pay for a specific unit of real estate than more uncertainty-averse investors. It also shows that investors who expect rents to increase at a fast pace will have a higher willingness to pay than investors expecting low, zero or negative growth of net rents.

An example can show how these different factors can influence the decisions of forward-looking investors. Let us assume that there is a single-family home on the market in a large city. A property developer acquired land and built the house at a now irrelevant cost of $1,000,000. A buyer expects annual maintenance costs and variable costs of $10,000 each and she additionally expects an annual growth rate of net rents of 2 percent and her level of subjective uncertainty aversion is such that she demands a 2-percentage point premium above the real interest rate, which we assume to be 5 percent per year. How much should the buyer be willing to pay for this house?

Given this combination of subjective and objective factors, it is easy to use the uncertainty-adjusted formula to calculate a rational maximum willingness to pay, which in this case amounts to $1,600,000. Indeed, this example shows why sales prices of real estate are often much higher than what current property rents would seem to imply. The main reason is an expectation of higher rents in the future, although there may also be an additional ownership premium for the uncertainty reduction associated with owning rather than renting an individual property. An oft-noted seeming discrepancy is that between high sales prices—or, to be more exact, high 70-year lease prices—and moderate market rents in most Chinese cities. But Chinese market rents have nevertheless been increasing for decades, and the present "ownership premium" over and above what current rents imply is an indication that the highest bidders in Chinese real estate markets expect net rents to continue rising at a relatively high rate.

Note that in our example we assume that the potential buyer receives indirect utility from the house. That is to say that she expects utility from the rental stream that she can command by offering her house for rent to the highest bidder. In contrast, the renter receives *direct* utility from the various valuable consumption attributes that the use of the house entails. Such attributes make up a "bundle" that influences the willingness to pay of both buyers and renters. Since real estate is immobile, each unit will be associated with a unique bundle, even when two houses seem identical. This is due to the location specificity of each house, and the impossibility of keeping accessibility levels constant when changing the exact location of a house with constant structural (that is, non-location-specific) attributes.

There is an entire subfield in economics—hedonic price estimation—that deals with estimating attribute prices. These prices are called *implicit*, since sellers never list the price of each attribute. Instead they list the price of the entire bundle of attributes.

ATTRIBUTES OF REAL ESTATE CAPITAL

We have noted that real estate capital consists of capital attributes that are either physical or social, where "physical" relates to structures and natural resources and "social" refers to differentiated and valued access to other people and their social impacts. That is however not the way that hedonic studies of real estate classify attributes.

The normal classification is to distinguish between "structural" and "location" attributes. It is also common to subdivide the location attributes further by distinguishing between accessibility and neighborhood attributes. There is a good reason for this subdivision. Accessibility attributes give rise to so-called "price-distance gradients," which means that there is a continuous decrease (increase) in the implicit price of an attribute with increasing distance to the relevant amenity (disamenity). Neighborhood attributes, on the other hand, are as a rule specified as a uniform effect within spatially delimited subareas of the analyzed area.

Table 11.1 gives examples of structural, accessibility and neighborhood attributes that are commonly included in empirical studies of real estate markets, together with an alternative classification of the same attributes as physical or social capital. Most hedonic studies of multi-attribute goods have analyzed housing markets, but there are also a smaller number of studies of other segments of the real estate market, such as hotels, industrial sites and offices. Other hedonic studies deal with heterogeneous mobile capital, such as automobiles and human capital.

Some of the attributes that make up real estate capital are relatively easy to interpret, and it is then also often easy to estimate implicit attribute prices. This is particularly true of some structural variables, such as floor area and lot size. Other attributes are trickier to isolate from one another. For example, many desirable neighborhood traits are often highly correlated, such as education levels, income levels, crime rates and measures of school quality. There is also the related problem that different participants in the same market may interpret attributes in different ways, and this—again—is a problem that primarily affects neighborhood attributes. For example, different people may delimit the spatial extent of a neighborhood in different ways and often rely on broad categories of neighborhood reputation rather than on exact statistical information when deciding on their willingness to pay for a particular property.

Nonetheless, there are broad empirical regularities that can be gleaned from thousands of hedonic price studies of real estate. There are of course strong theoretical reasons why larger lots and larger and newer buildings are associated with higher prices; land and building materials are scarce resources and buildings must be maintained or they depreciate in value in

Table 11.1   Examples of real estate attributes by category

Attribute category		Examples	Type of capital	Examples
Structural		Lot size; floor area; age of structure; bathrooms; garage	Physical	Lot size; floor area; age of structure; bathrooms; garage; parks; landscaping; sports facilities in neighborhood
Location	Neighborhood	Parks; landscaping; sports facilities in neighborhood; neighborhood school quality; crime rate; income level; education level; municipal tax	Social	Neighborhood school quality; crime rate; income level; education level; municipal tax; distance to employers, co-workers, specialists, service workers
	Accessibility .	Distance to employers, co-workers, specialists, service workers; distance to major infrastructure, such as airports, seaports, transit networks, highways and convention centers	Physical	Distance to major infrastructure, such as airports, seaports, transit networks, highways and convention centers

predictable ways. There is also a well-developed theory of how real estate prices reflect relative accessibility, as we have discussed in earlier chapters with the Von Thünen Model as a starting point. Indeed, using only one distance as in the monocentric model often captures a substantial part of the overall variability in households' accessibility. This leads some urban economists to argue that cities have a natural tendency to stabilize as monocentric functional urban regions (Cheshire and Sheppard, 1995).

It is much more difficult to provide theoretical reasons for why people should prefer certain types of neighbors, and most such explanations are sociological rather than economic. The sole exception is the crime rate, since home insurance premiums may vary with neighborhood-specific historical risks of burglary. Even so, there are strong empirical grounds for the argument that people are willing to pay for having rich and educated neighbors rather than poor and/or poorly educated ones. Studies of commercial and industrial property markets show that such neighborhood attributes are much less important than in housing markets, and also that overall accessibility is—if anything—an even more important considera-tion than among people seeking a home.

AN ILLUSTRATIVE EXAMPLE: HOTEL ROOMS IN SHANGHAI

An example of a well-designed hedonic price study will clarify how such studies are better at getting a general understanding about what type of attributes influence bundle prices than at getting exact estimates of implicit attribute prices. Andersson and Jia (2016) estimate several differ-ent (but similar) hedonic price functions for the market for hotel rooms in Shanghai. Most such studies report several functions, for the purpose of checking the robustness of the various estimated implicit prices. We shall however only present the hedonic price function with the best distribution of residuals in this chapter.

From the 1980s onward, better computer software has made it pos-sible to estimate more advanced hedonic functions than ordinary least squares. The Box-Cox-transformed function (Box and Cox, 1964), which maximizes the log-likelihood of the chosen function from a set of possible functions, has proven particularly suitable for hedonic price estimation. According to Tukey (1957), a transformed function has one or more of the following objectives: stabilization of the error variance, attainment of a more symmetric distribution of residuals and selection of a function that is in some sense linear. Among other functional forms, Andersson and Jia (2016) use the "each-side Box-Cox function" with separate trans-formations for the dependent and the set of independent variables. This transformation simultaneously yields a preferred functional form and a distribution of residuals that is approximately homoscedastic and nor-mally distributed. Formally,

$$Y^{(\lambda)} = \alpha + \beta_1 X_1^{(\theta)} + \beta_2 X_2^{(\theta)} + \ldots + \beta_i X_i^{(\theta)} + \ldots + \beta_k X_k^{(\theta)} + \varepsilon; \qquad (11.1)$$

where:

$Y^{(\lambda)} = (Y^\lambda - 1)/\lambda$ for $\lambda \neq 0$; $X_i^{(\theta)} = (X_i^\theta - 1)/\theta$ for $\theta \neq 0$;
and $Y^{(\lambda)} = \ln Y$ for $\lambda = 0$; $X_i^{(\theta)} = \ln X_i$ for $\theta = 0$.

This is one of the most widely used functional forms for estimating attribute prices in real estate markets.

Our illustrative example is the online market for hotel rooms in Shanghai during a specific week in May 2016.The study includes 622 hotels with two stars or more—and with at least five consumer reviews each—that could be booked through agoda.com. Despite being a city with some of the highest housing prices in the world, Shanghai offers unusually affordable hotel rates, reflecting a dramatic increase in the supply of hotel rooms in recent years. Three-star international chain hotels such as Ibis and Holiday Inn Express offer online double-room rates that are surprisingly affordable, ranging from US\$60 to US\$80 in most downtown locations at the time of the study.

The hedonic study used information from the agoda.com website, as well as a monocentric accessibility attribute that measured the distance in minutes by car (with a correction for average congestion levels) between each individual hotel and People's Square (*Renmin Guangchang*) in the heart of the *Puxi* area of Shanghai. There are hotels in all of Shanghai's districts, but the greatest concentration is to be found in the old downtown area (The Bund; Nanjing East Road, *Xujiahui*). The new business district in *Pudong* (*Lujiazui*) offers another cluster of hotels, with an overrepresentation of newly built five-star chain hotels. There are also smaller clusters in the vicinities of Shanghai's two international airports.

Among the hotels, the most common category is two-star hotels, accounting for 38 percent of the total. This is followed, in order, by three-star (20 percent), four-star (19 percent) and five-star (13 percent) hotels. The least common category consists of one-star and "unrated" hotels, which jointly comprise less than 10 percent. The sample of hotels that accounted for the observations that were used for estimating the hedonic price functions did not include unrated and one-star hotels. The latter category was excluded because it tends to attract a segment of consumers who consider cost more important than almost all other possible choice criteria. This segment mostly comprises low-income Chinese and backpackers. Table 11.2 presents descriptive statistics for all included hotel attributes.

All hotel guests booking their rooms through the Agoda website receive emails that invite them to provide feedback some days after their stay at a hotel. The invitees may provide a written description of their experience and they are also offered the opportunity to rate the quality of five different hotel attributes that reflect different types of real estate capital: cleanliness (physical capital); room comfort/standard (physical capital); location (social and physical capital as well as a subjective combination of accessibility and neighborhood attributes); staff performance (social capital) and food/dining (physical and social capital). Respondents rate hotel attributes according to a five-point Likert scale. The five-point scale is rescaled to a scale with a range of eight when attribute and overall averages are reported (that is, a unanimous minimum score of 1 out of 5 points for each attribute yields an "overall quality rating" of 2.0 out of 10.0 possible points).

Table 11.2   Descriptive statistics, Shanghai hotel market (May 2016)

Hotel attributes	Mean	Standard deviation	Minimum	Maximum
Price (CNY)	505.98	464.57	78	5374
Accessibility attribute (mix of social and physical capital)				
Distance to center (minutes)	23.06	15.68	2	110
Objective structural attributes (physical capital)				
Number of rooms	200.40	155.12	4	1162
Swimming pool (dummy)	0.22	0.42	0	1
Wi-Fi (dummy)	0.49	0.50	0	1
Free cancelation (dummy)	0.82	0.38	0	1
Official rating attributes (structural attribute combination/physical capital)				
3,4 or 5 stars	0.79	0.41	0	1
4 or 5 stars	0.54	0.50	0	1
5 stars	0.25	0.43	0	1
Online feedback attribute (mix of all attribute types and both types of capital)				
Overall score	7.21	0.81	2.9	9.3

Source: Andersson and Jia (2016).

The mean value of all five attributes—the overall score—is a conspicuous feature of Agoda's webpage for each individual hotel, along with the online rate. Agoda also "translates" the overall score into a word that describes the overall evaluation (for example "excellent" if the average score is between 8.0 and 9.0). The number of reviews for an individual hotel ranged from zero to over 3,000, with most hotels receiving between ten and 1,000 reviews (hotels with zero to four reviews were excluded from the sample). The overall score, which was the only rating that was consistently significant across all functions in which it was included, reflects a combination of subjectively evaluated structural, neighborhood and accessibility attributes, and therefore also a subjective assessment of the quality of a given hotel's combination of physical and social capital. A detailed examination of the impact of each feedback attribute showed that "location" contributed most to hotels' price variability (*ceteris paribus*), and we may interpret this as the impact of neighborhood attributes and of small-area accessibility that are not captured by the objective accessibility measure, which is the distance in minutes to People's Square. In this context, it is important to keep in mind that accessibility and neighborhood attributes reflect both social capital (relative access to other people) and physical capital (relative access to material infrastructure).

Time, space and capital

Table 11.3 *Each-side Box-Cox-transformed hedonic price functions for*
            standard double rooms in Shanghai, 2016

Attribute	Estimated coefficient	Chi-squared
Constant	2.748	
Official rating attributes (structural attributes; physical capital)		
3, 4, 5 stars	0.065	55.48***
4, 5 stars	0.084	96.65***
5 stars	0.063	45.20***
Online feedback attribute (mix of attributes; physical and social capital)		
Overall score	0.077	16.23***
Other structural and accessibility attributes; physical and social capital		
Distance to center	–0.014	22.85***
Number of rooms	–0.001	0.62
Swimming pool (dummy)	0.044	20.72***
Wi-Fi (dummy)	0.012	4.03**
Free cancelation (dummy)	–0.037	18.95^^^
Regression statistics		
Number of observations	622	
Lambda (λ)	0.256	
Theta (θ)	–0.268	

Note: **: p<.05; ***:p<.01 (one-tailed test; expected sign); ^^^:p<.01 (two-tailed test;
unexpected sign).

Table 11.3 presents the best model in terms of both explanatory power and distribution of residuals, using Box-Cox-transformed prices and attribute values. The set of observations includes hotels with online ratings that have two or more official stars, which means that the star effects imply the price difference between a hotel with a specific number of stars and a two-star hotel. Since the star ratings include a specific minimum number of stars, we may interpret the star effect as the effect of moving one level higher in the star hierarchy. Adding an additional star is associated with economically and statistically significant price effects, controlling for various objective features of the hotel, overall accessibility and the consumers' overall quality assessment.

The estimated hedonic price function makes it possible to compare the impacts of the official star rating and the overall consumer feedback. The consumer feedback attribute is statistically significant even when controlling for the star attributes. This implies that consumer feedback is a complement to the star rating; it accounts for quality variability given the number of stars. Andersson and Jia (2016) show that this is mostly the effect of the relative attractiveness of a hotel's location, since stars are never awarded based on amenities *outside* the area that is under the direct control of the hotel. It is also clear that general accessibility within the city of Shanghai is an important influence on the willingness to pay and therefore also on the combination of real prices and vacancy rates. Hotel rates are theoretically speaking short-term rents and the results show that these rents reflect the utility of using combinations of physical and social capital for a specific time period.

THE ENTREPRENEURIAL CREATION OF REAL ESTATE ATTRIBUTES

Real estate may often take the shape of buildings that are made of stone, but the capital attributes that such buildings embody are not set in stone. Entrepreneurs continually introduce new valuable attributes to pre-existing material resources, including buildings and lots. Andersson (2008) gives an illustrative example of entrepreneurial attribute combination in the hotel market, which is a particularly suitable example for this chapter.

The example shows how Accor Hotels added value to pre-existing resources by acquiring a building in central Hong Kong. The building had previously been used as an underperforming independent hotel. Accor rebranded the hotel as Ibis North Point, and the interesting aspect of this is how an existing unit of real estate came to embody a new set of valuable attributes. For example, Ibis offers its guests a so-called "fifteen-minute satisfaction guarantee," which means that the hotel promises not to charge for the use of a hotel room if hotel staff are unable to solve practical problems such as a defective air conditioner or a broken television set within 15 minutes of a complaint being lodged. This is an example of how an existing (physical) structure can evolve into a new bundle of attributes through the addition of valuable service attributes within an unchanged physical manifestation of the product. Other examples in this particular case include connections to global reservation and feedback networks and a requirement that receptionists be fluent in both Chinese and English.

Given the high durability of most real estate, it is easy to observe how specific lots and buildings are adapted to new uses—an example of the effects of entrepreneurial judgment—as economic conditions change. Entrepreneurs may change the economic function of a waterfront warehouse repeatedly, perhaps transforming its use from storing furniture to providing office space and then again into upscale apartments with a view. The location and structure may seem identical, but the same location does not have constant accessibility over time, nor does the type of accessibility with the highest value necessarily remain the same.

All goods are to greater or lesser extent multi-attribute goods, but real estate provides an especially conspicuous instance of attribute heterogeneity. Producers have a strong incentive to create (or discover) new resource attributes, since by doing so they are able to reap time-limited entrepreneurial profits. Lancaster (1966) provides a model of multi-attribute goods as rays of product characteristics that consumers combine in a utility-maximizing fashion. But the model obscures certain features while illuminating others. Like most mainstream economists, Lancaster did not take people's cognitive limitations and knowledge imperfections seriously. Thus, his product characteristics model describes each attribute as consisting of *objective* rather than *subjective* quantities. For example, a specific type of coffee is associated with objective levels of chemical compounds rather than subjective perceptions of flavors such as "spiciness," "chocolate" or "campfire." But it is consumers' imperfect perceptions that determine their willingness to pay, not the results of laboratory tests.

THE ROLE OF SYSTEM CONSTRAINTS

Subjective perceptions and imperfect knowledge imply that the set of attributes that make up a bundle is intrinsically open-ended, with an equally open-ended opportunity set of future entrepreneurial attribute creation. Indeed, the open-endedness of the list of future attributes associated with a given resource imply that entrepreneurs shoulder Knightian uncertainty when they judge that it is worthwhile (that is, potentially profitable) to create new resource attributes that they believe will be attractive to buyers.

More than anything else, the entrepreneurial creation of attributes is an attempt to escape a tight system constraint (see Langlois and Koppl, 1991; Koppl, 2002; Andersson, 2014). Koppl (2002) argues that markets with atomistic competition and stable institutions give rise to a system constraint that is tight and where producers act in ways that resemble the price-taking behavior in models of perfect competition. Moreover, they cannot escape the logic of "acognitive expectations." Koppl explains:

> The "expectations" of economic theory are often acognitive expectations. We say that creditors "expect" zero inflation if they do not insist on an inflation premium. This "expectation" may be nothing more that the conformity to old habits and ways of doing business. Conceivably, some creditors might even have expectations of inflation. If they don't understand the effect of inflation on purchasing power, they won't ask for an inflation premium. The case imagined is not

purely hypothetical. In 1997, an important Italian labor leader expressed concern over the government's low inflation target. Such low inflation, he objected, would reduce the purchasing power of workers' wages. (Koppl, 2002, p. 15).

What Koppl is trying to say here is that "rational expectations" in mainstream neoclassical models do make sense if it is the case that markets enforce conformity with "best" expectations, in the sense that behavior that reflects deviant expectations causes market exit. Cognitive expectations, on the other hand, are real human expectations that reflect the subjectivity and cognitive limitations of individuals. These do play a role in economic life, but only if the system constraint is loose. According to Koppl (ibid.), the system constraint may be loose because institutions are unstable and/ or competition is non-atomistic.

Entrepreneurs seek to escape atomistic competition by becoming temporary monopolists. Not so often noted side effects of successful entrepreneurial monopolies are loose system constraints and the freedom to let behavior reflect cognitive expectations. A loose system constraint implies that there is slack in the system. The theoretical implication is that even though atomistic competition forces producers to behave as if they were profit maximizers, monopolies do not necessarily choose the profit-maximizing price-quantity combination. Monopolists will survive in the market as long as they at least break even in the long run. Thus, any place between the break-even point (as would occur if a monopolist does not reduce output to increase profits) and the profit-maximizing point is a choice that the market sustains.

Profit-seeking producers are always looking for opportunities to create new valuable attributes. These attributes may be purely subjective and seemingly superficial, such as when "endorsed by Kobe Bryant" is an attribute of Nike basketball shoes. But they may be much more ambitious, as in the following example, which involves the transformation of real estate attributes through the creation of new social capital.

Sørensen and Jensen (2015) describe how a boutique hotel in Copenhagen transformed the bundle of attributes on offer by introducing a more interactive type of service provision. The idea was to increase consumers' willingness to pay by personalizing the encounters guests had with the hotel staff. Rather than providing general-purpose information about popular tourist attractions in Copenhagen, the hotel manager encouraged frontline employees to collect information prior to a specific guest's visit about *individual* preferences and interests. For example, a receptionist would sit down with a hotel guest and discuss the best possible use of her time, given an expressed interest in, say, modern art and Scandinavian design. The hotel would also attempt to assign guests to rooms that best corresponded to their aesthetic preferences. In this way, hotel employees became a type of localized social capital and—at the same time—reduced the transaction costs that guests faced when attempting to access social *and* physical capital in the Copenhagen region. What we see in this case is an unusually clear-cut example of the entrepreneurial creation of new real estate attributes as an attempt to create "attribute monopolies," with an associated loosening of the system constraint.

SPACE AND THE ENTREPRENEURIAL CREATION OF PUBLIC GOODS

Entrepreneurship in real estate markets also shed light on the understanding of public goods in non-spatial economics, which is often unnecessarily confused. Public goods, according to the conventional line of reasoning, are goods that are non-rival and non-excludable. But this is only true of widely disseminated knowledge, such as human languages and mathematical formulas. Most public goods are in fact *territorial* rather than pure, and have spatial delimitations. The key difference is that exclusion costs are positive, and not infinite or zero as in the textbook definitions of public or private goods. Moreover, non-rivalry in consumption only applies to territorial public goods as long as they remain uncongested.

There are several studies that show how profit-seeking entrepreneurs supply territorial public goods to paying users (Foldvary, 1994; Andersson and Moroni, 2014). Entrepreneurs can do this since the value of such goods becomes capitalized in the price of land and thus also in the sales price and rent of affected real estate. Hotel corridors are territorial public goods, as are gardens within condominium developments, atriums in shopping malls and streets in the private American neighborhoods known as "homeowner associations." The key criterion for successful private provision of territorial public goods is that public-good producers own most of the land that is affected by the benefits of such goods, so that they—as a minimal requirement—can recoup the costs as rental or sales price premiums.

The entrepreneurial process of successive introductions of novel attributes works in exactly the same way for territorial public goods as it does for those that are closer to pure private goods. A property developer will attempt to develop unique and therefore initially monopolized public-good attributes, for example new types of (publicly visible) architectural designs or new sports facilities that all members of a gated neighborhood can use at their discretion. If such goods become popular enough to generate congestion problems, a common strategy is to privatize them by imposing user charges. This is an efficiency-inducing strategy in all those cases where the sum of the transaction and exclusion costs are smaller than the gains from avoiding overuse of the resource (for example, bundle of attributes) in question (Andersson, 2008).

It is noteworthy that typical territorial public goods such as roads and parks are an important subset of physical capital; they benefit almost all types of production, ranging from manufacturing over knowledge-intensive services all the way to the unpriced production of households.

THE IMPACT OF LAND-USE REGULATIONS

In most cities, real estate capital markets are more regulated than other markets, except for markets for education services and health care. Pennington (2002) contends that land-use planning is the part of the economy that most resembles central planning. Britain is an example of a country with unusually restrictive land-use regulations. While labor and financial markets are less regulated than in France, the opposite relation pertains to real estate markets. Evans (1991) shows that the main reason that consumer goods are more expensive in Britain than in France is that it is much more difficult to obtain approval for new retail developments in Britain. In England, there is even a requirement that applicants who wish to establish a new shop demonstrate that the local population base is sufficiently large so that there is a "local need" for the shop. It is difficult to find a closer analogy to Soviet-style central planning in Western Europe.

A relevant question concerns the causes of the unusual degree of interventionism in real estate markets. We believe that one of the main reasons is that university urban and regional planning departments have attracted scholars that are critical of the functioning of markets as well as skeptical of the appropriateness of market prices as the main signals that guide the land-use decisions of residents, firms and property developers. Influential tracts on urban planning such as Friedmann (1987) and Harvey (1973) make explicit use of Marxian theories. Such approaches fail to note that a reliance on governmental allocation of resources as a replacement for decentralized markets is associated with various knowledge and incentive problems.

Another problem with the "critique-of-markets approach" that is common among urban and regional planners is that its understanding of markets focuses on the most atomistic type. This implies that ownership of land is subdivided into a large number of tiny units. In fact, there are numerous examples of how private developers reduce negative externalities and supply territorial public goods that affect relatively large land areas. Large-scale examples include privately funded streets, squares and utility networks that benefit the residents of privately planned towns such as Reston, Virginia or Discovery Bay, Hong Kong, both of which have tens of thousands of residents. In China and India, there are even larger privately planned "neighborhoods" with population sizes of up to 200,000 (Andersson and Moroni, 2014). But in many of the world's cities, such decentralized entrepreneurial creation of territorial public goods has been outlawed.

We shall look at one influential but extreme example, which is how land-use planning has distorted the prices, quantities and location patterns of real estate capital in Britain. Similar planning systems govern the determination of land-use patterns in Australia, New Zealand and the Nordic countries, and to a lesser extent in the so-called "New Commonwealth" countries.

THE BRITISH PLANNING DISEASE

The Town and Country Planning Act of 1947 represents the starting point of interventionist planning in Britain. In the nineteenth and early twentieth centuries, Britain in fact had much less regulated markets for real estate capital. But in 1947 the situation changed. From that point on, land-use planning has been the responsibility of cooperating national and local planning authorities. Each local planning authority (LPA) must design a local development plan that conforms to national guidelines. Each parcel of land within the total land area of Britain must belong to a "use class" such as land for residential or commercial use. The use classes are often much less inclusive than, say, commercial use in general. Each land-use conversion requires LPA permission. These conversions may be minor ones, such as converting a home to a bed and breakfast or a clothing store to a restaurant. The LPA must take the local development plan into consideration when deciding whether to authorize a specific conversion, but may deviate from the plan if they deem it to be in the public interest. Most deviations have been refusals to approve land-use conversions or land developments that are in fact in line with the local development plan.

It is in practice impossible to develop land outside of areas classified as "urban" in the 1950s. The supply of land within each use class has also been fixed for more than half a century. This means that public-sector planners decide the supply of land for each type of production and for housing, which means that explicit price information about the opportunity cost of land—its highest valued use—is unavailable. The allocation of land to different uses proceeds entirely according to principles of socialist planning as interpreted in the late 1940s.

Britain's funding system makes the situation worse, since 80 percent of local government spending is funded by central government revenue, while at the same time there is substantial national tax equalization of local property taxes. The property tax of commercial properties was nationalized in 1990, except for the City of London (London's financial district). According to Cheshire et al. (2014), local authorities therefore must pay what is in effect a fine for permitting commercial development of land, since they have to spend more on infrastructure and maintenance without any corresponding increase in revenues. The system is also made worse because LPAs plan at the lowest feasible level of spatial aggregation, which causes a serious so-called "insider problem."

In England, even more restrictive land-use regulations were introduced in two stages in 1988 and 1996 through a policy known as Town Centre First (TCF). TCF stipulates that the LPA should make a detailed allocation of land to commercial uses in downtown areas, while making it even more difficult than previously to obtain planning permission for commercial development in other areas. Within the framework of TCF, regulators introduced a "needs test" and a "sequential test" for each proposed commercial development. An example of what the "needs test" means is that the owner of a firm who wants to open a new grocery store must show that an area "needs" more such stores and, additionally, that the proposed new store will not undermine the competitiveness of similar stores in the same city. The "sequential test" means that the firm's owner also must show that there is no available downtown site before she can apply for a site in another urban neighborhood. A site outside the urban area is only possible if the firm can show that there is *neither* any available downtown site, nor any sites in other urban neighborhoods. A site near one of England's motorways is therefore no longer a viable option for commercial property developers.

Cheshire et al. (2015) show that TCF has caused a decline of about 20 percent in the total factor productivity of English supermarkets, as compared with the expected level in the absence of that particular policy. This reduced productivity is primarily the effect of new supermarkets having undersized premises in logistically difficult locations. The estimate is based on the productivity growth of English supermarkets between 1966 and 1988, which was the year when the first TCF regulations came into effect. Newer supermarkets had higher productivity before 1988, but lower productivity after that year, with the newest supermarkets being least productive of all. The reduced productivity did not affect Scotland, Wales or Northern Ireland, which all had less restrictive land-use regulations than England and did not require a "needs test" or "sequential test."

However, it seems likely that the British planning system has caused

Table 11.4   Regulations quantified as an implicit tax on office space as a percentage of the price in 12 urban business districts, 1999– 2005 (average)

City (district)	Country	Implicit regulatory tax (%)
London (West End)	United Kingdom	800
London (City)	United Kingdom	449
Frankfurt (downtown)	Germany	437
Stockholm (downtown)	Sweden	379
London (Canary Wharf)	United Kingdom	327
Milan (downtown)	Italy	309
Paris (downtown)	France	305
Barcelona (downtown)	Spain	269
Amsterdam (downtown)	Netherlands	202
Paris (La Défense)	France	167
Brussels (downtown)	Belgium	68
New York (Manhattan)	United States	25

Source: Cheshire (2011); Glaeser et al. (2005).

productivity losses that are substantially greater than 20 percent. The productivity of supermarkets has always been higher in the United States than in Britain; the productivity of American supermarkets increased at an especially high rate in the 1990s (Haskel and Sadun, 2009), while British supermarkets were becoming less productive.

The British planning system also affects housing and offices, primarily through much higher prices than less restrictive land-use regulations would imply. Cheshire and Hilber (2008) measured the extra cost of land-use regulations as the difference between real estate prices and marginal construction costs. They call the difference a "regulatory tax." Table 11.4 shows that London has Europe's highest regulatory tax. It amounts to 800 percent in the West End, 449 percent in the City and 327 percent in Canary Wharf. The reason that it is so much higher in the West End than in the City or in Canary Wharf is that there are almost no high-rise buildings in the West End, since almost all permits for high-rise construction have been granted to projects in the other two business districts.

Table 11.4 also shows that Manhattan has a much lower regulatory tax than any large European city. This is because it is generally possible to construct office buildings up to a height that is in the proximity of the building-specific optimum. The optimal height is given by the equality of the market price per square meter of floor area and its marginal construction cost. The optimal height is unique, since the square-meter price is a diminishing or constant function of size, while the square-meter construction cost is an increasing function of building height. European countries all have regulations that mandate inefficiently low buildings in their downtown areas. Hence all major European cities have a higher regulatory tax on offices than does New York City.

PLANNING AND HOUSING COSTS

Housing is also unnecessarily costly in Britain, but there are several other countries that use similarly restrictive regulations. It is mainly restrictions on urban size— "urban containment"—that drive up housing prices. A noted British example is London's Metropolitan Green Belt, which ensures that large areas around London are off limits for housing construction. The only permitted economic activity is agriculture, which has had the consequence that the land price is about £7,500 per hectare within the Green Belt, while its use for housing would—according to econometric estimates—result in a land price of about £7,000,000 per hectare (Cheshire et al., 2014). The most valuable land use is thus on the order of 1,000 times greater than the most valuable *legal* land use. Several other metropolitan areas around the world have similar restriction on the supply of housing, with predictable discrepancies between potential and legal land values.

Local governments in the United States intervene much less in markets for offices and commercial activities than their British counterparts. American zoning regulations involve less micromanagement of land than British local development plans. In addition, there is greater political acceptance of downtown skyscrapers and suburban shopping malls. American local politicians tolerate a great deal more market-led spatial allocation of production on account of strong incentives to attract inward investment by firms. The property taxes that owners of real estate pay generate local rather than federal tax revenue and property taxes paid by owners of new non-residential real estate usually exceed the local government spending increments associated with these new land uses.

Conversely, many local politicians in the United States have similar attitudes to housing development as their British counterparts. They want to avoid new residents that contribute less in property taxes than they take out of the public coffers. Many local governments—especially of suburbs with large tracts of single-family housing—have outlawed multi-family housing and small residential lot sizes. It has also become popular to introduce "urban growth boundaries," especially in those parts of America where there are strong "ecological" or "green" interest groups. The combined result of these tendencies is especially noticeable in California,

Table 11.5   *20 least affordable metropolitan housing markets in Canada,*
                the United Kingdom and the United States; median house
                price/median household income, 3rd quarter 2015

Metropolitan market	Nation	Median multiple
Vancouver, BC	Canada	10.8
San Jose, CA	United States	9.7
Santa Cruz, CA	United States	9.6
Bournemouth & Dorset	England, UK	9.6
San Francisco, CA	United States	9.4
Honolulu, HI	United States	9.2
London	England, UK	8.5
Kahului, HI	United States	8.3
Kapaa, HI	United States	8.2
San Diego, CA	United States	8.1
Los Angeles, CA	United States	8.1
Napa, CA	United States	7.6
Salinas, CA	United States	7.4
San Luis Obispo, CA	United States	7.2
Swindon & Wiltshire	England, UK	7.2
Plymouth & Devon	England, UK	7.2
London Exurbs	England, UK	7.1
Santa Rosa, CA	United States	7.0
Santa Barbara, CA	United States	7.0
Victoria, BC	Canada	6.9

Source: Cox and Pavletich (2016).

where many homeowners simultaneously want to avoid in-migration of
low-income households, preserve open space and keep property taxes low.
Table 11.5 shows that many cities in California and England are among the
least affordable in the English-speaking world.

REGULATIONS, EXPECTATIONS AND THE VALUE OF REAL ESTATE CAPITAL

Excessive land-use regulations, as in Britain or California, do not only
make real estate more expensive than in less regulated areas. It also makes
it more difficult to predict future price trajectories, with the consequence
that the subjective expectations of individuals become more important for
the determination of market prices. The most important consequence of
all types of land-use regulations is that they make the supply of new real

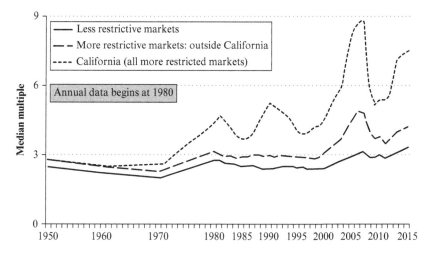

Source: Cox and Pavletich (2016).

Figure 11.1 Housing affordability in US metropolitan areas, 1950–2015

estate less elastic. In the most extreme cases, the supply is approximately constant, even during periods of rapidly rising demand. Figure 11.1 shows the development of housing affordability in American housing markets, with a division of markets into three types: very restrictive markets (all in California), non-Californian restrictive markets and less restrictive markets.

In the most regulated markets, the only effect of a change in demand is a change in price, which means that price levels—and therefore also affordability—change more or less in tandem with (regionally distinct) phases of the business cycle. Thus, there was a surge in Californian property prices between 2000 and 2008, followed by an equally dramatic fall after the onset of the financial crisis; then there was a renewed surge after 2011. The affordability time series for California looks rather like a roller coaster with a progression of increasingly steep inclines and drops.

Hence an investor in real estate must be able to forecast future phases of the business cycle, as well as the effects of booms and busts on the demand for various specific types of real estate. In highly regulated markets, it tends to be difficult to change land uses, and thus a plot is sold to the highest bidder within a specific user category rather than the highest bidder regardless of intended use. Market segmentation therefore increases with increases in regulation.

Regulation-derived transaction costs also increase with increasing regulation, which makes it more difficult for small developers to enter markets. Evidence from Sweden, which has highly restrictive land-use regulations, shows that there are only a handful of large property developers that have sufficient resources and political connections to build apartment houses. Despite rather modest levels of product innovation, these firms have been more profitable than the Swedish stock market index for decades (Andersson and Andersson, 2014). Similar big-player phenomena have occurred whenever individual urban planners have wielded considerable discretionary powers, as Robert Moses did in New York City after World War II (see Jacobs, 1961, for an influential attack on Moses's type of top-down planning).

This means that over-regulated real estate markets are likely to be subject to big-player effects, which means that it becomes worthwhile to base one's expectations on the perceived personal characteristics of named individuals rather than on atomistic market processes (Koppl, 2002). So not only is it necessary to predict the timing and submarket-specific effects of future business cycles; it also becomes necessary to interpret the motives, behaviors and effectiveness of influential actors such as politicians, urban planners and the owners and managers of large real-estate firms. There is thus much leeway for behaviors—among the buyers and sellers of real estate—that reflect subjective cognitive expectations rather than market selection of behaviors that correspond to rational decision making, given correct assessments of market conditions.

An additional way in which property values become erratic in highly regulated markets is the so-called "slippery slope effect." Once planners and politicians get used to intervening in a specific market, they tend to do it over and over again. This implies that both the value and the composition of a bundle of property rights that is traded in a market with habitual government intervention become more uncertain relative to markets with stable and known rules. If a planning authority decides that the allowable use of a specific lot will change from "commercial use" to "convenience store use," this represents a transfer of property rights from the owner to the authority as well as a potentially dramatic reduction in the market price of the lot (Andersson, 2008). So, real estate owners must base their expectations not only on subjectively predicted cyclical effects and big-player-initiated future development plans, but also on the combined impact of artificially reduced future supply and political transfers of property rights (over real estate attributes) on the price of a unit of real estate. This is not an easy task.

In the United States it is however becoming increasingly evident that the competitiveness of metropolitan areas with less regulated real estate markets is improving at the expense of more regulated ones. A striking example consists of the contrasts between the major metropolitan areas in two states, Texas and California (Andersson and Taylor, 2012). The agglomeration economies that developed at an early stage in California had the effect of giving local and state politicians the opportunity to increase the regulatory burden. This was brought about by using up some of the capital-derived surplus—relative to other states and metropolitan areas—that had been created by means of the higher productivity that characterizes a knowledge-intensive and urbanized regional economy.

A contributing cause of California's extreme supply restrictions, apart from the possibility of introducing them, was the ideological makeup of the state's politicians and voters. On the American West Coast, the highly educated elite of the dominant Democratic Party has become increasingly environmentalist. At the same time, the inherited land-use regulations from the 1970s provide compelling incentives to make housing construction more difficult among those who are more interested in defending the property values of homeowners than in environmental issues, such as most Republican voters and politicians. Republican politicians in California thereby resemble Conservative politicians in Britain, who are also known to favor prohibitions against housing construction as the most effective way of defending the interests of homeowners (Cheshire et al., 2014). Not-in-my-backyard-conservatives have joined left-wing environmentalists in an unlikely alliance of change-averse residents.

In Texas, the situation is entirely different. It is only recently that the state has joined the post-industrial knowledge economy. The regulatory framework is less restrictive, which has made homeowners protect home values through private covenants rather than through the political process. Environmentalism is less prevalent: Republicans dominate at the state level and many Democrat-controlled local governments are in areas with a high proportion of low-income minority voters. A reasonable hypothesis is that poor households give priority to housing affordability over nature reserves.

Table 11.6 gives comparative price and income information for the two main metropolitan areas in each state. The table also shows that Texas has gained population during the same period that there has been net domestic outmigration from California. This redistribution of the population is in no small part due to housing being more affordable in Texas than in California, endowing Texans with higher real incomes at given wage rates. It is also much easier for homebuyers to form reliable expectations in Texas, since house prices have tended to stay almost constant in both Dallas and Houston during booms and busts (O'Toole, 2014). We believe that this is a particularly striking illustration of how simple and stable rules govern complex capital markets more effectively than complicated and unstable ones (Epstein, 1995).

Table 11.6   Texas versus California, 2000–2012

Metropolitan area	House price (2012)	Household income (2012)	Price/income (2000–2012)	Population (2012)	Net domestic in-migration (2000–2012)
Texas: Dallas-Fort Worth and Houston					
Dallas-Fort Worth	$127,000	$43,300	2.7	6,500,000	+6.9%
Houston	$128,000	$42,700	2.8	6,100,000	+5.6%
California: Los Angeles and San Francisco-Oakland					
Los Angeles	$272,400	$44,200	6.8	12,900,000	−11.4%
San Francisco-Oakland	$436,000	$56,200	7.7	4,400,000	−8.3%
State-level comparisons					
	Taxes/ regulations	Per capita income	Annual income growth	Population	Net domestic in-migration
Texas	14/50	$30,400	+2.6%	25,700,000	+4.2%
California	49/50	$34,100	−0.4%	37,700,000	−4.5%

Sources: Cox and Pavletich (2016); Ruger and Sorens (2013); US Census Bureau (2014).

NOTE

1. The phrase "social capital" has been used in almost as many ways as the word "capital." Perhaps the most common use is as the economically useful networks that connect people to one another. We define social capital in a more inclusive way. It includes the existing interpersonal networks of individuals, their accessibility to *potential* interpersonal networks and the spatially delimited domain of the effects of others' actions on the spatio-temporally specific productivity of physical or human capital. This means that institutions—or "institutional capital"—become a subset of social capital. Institutions often have spatial effects that resemble neighborhood attributes in property markets; they have clearly defined borders and a uniform effect within those borders. For example, a municipal income tax is an institution that influences the value of land (see, for example, Andersson et al., 2013). Likewise, we often see discontinuities in land values at interjurisdictional border crossings, for example between the New Territories in Hong Kong and Shenzhen or between Woodlands (Singapore) and Johor Bahru (Malaysia). It is important to remember that institutions—both laws and cultural norms—are non-material effects of peoples' behavioral rules. Analogously, a worker is actually a bundle of human and social capital attributes. We shall come back to this theme in Chapter 12.

12. Re-conceptualizing social capital

We have been arguing in this book that the idea that production involves inputs of labor, land and capital is misleading. Instead, we subscribe to the Knightian view that all production inputs are more or less durable capital. There are three main categories of capital: physical, human and social. How do these categories relate to the traditional three factors of production? It is our contention that labor is best described as a heterogeneous bundle of production attributes that are partly embodied in the individual worker— thus we refer to this part as "human capital"— and partly in his or her connection to other individuals and collectivities—thus "social capital."

Land is similarly multifaceted. It may consist of scarce natural resources such as gold or oil and it then takes on all the characteristics of physical capital. Access to natural resources—including land formations that are valuable because of their beauty—is yet another physical capital attribute. But land is also valuable for the access it provides to other people, in which case land should be conceptualized as a bundle of social capital attributes. Thus, the traditional definition of capital corresponds to a bundle of physical capital attributes, "land" is a bundle of physical and social capital attributes and labor similarly consists of a bundle of human and social capital attributes.

Unfortunately, the uses to which economists, sociologists and other social scientists have put the term "social capital" have often tended to be rather vague and inconsistent. Jacobs (1961/1992) contains the first use of the term "social capital" in its modern sense, when she writes that:

> a good city neighborhood can absorb newcomers into itself, both newcomers by choice and immigrants settling by expediency, and it can protect a reasonable amount of transient population too. But these increments or displacements have to be gradual. If self-government in the place is to work, underlying any float of population must be a continuity of people who have forged neighborhood networks. These networks are a city's irreplaceable *social capital*. Whenever the capital is lost, from whatever cause, the income from it disappears, never to return until and unless new capital is slowly and chancily accumulated. (Jacobs, 1961/1992, pp. 137–8, italics added)

While this passage does not provide a clear definition of the term, it does point to the importance of interpersonal networks in generating social capital. The network perspective has also been the dominant socio-logical approach to social capital (Granovetter, 1974; Coleman, 1988). Granovetter (1974) is an especially influential contribution, which demonstrates that the presence of so-called "weak links" is especially important for the matching of people to jobs.

Aldrich and Martinez (2001) offer a broad—but again somewhat vague— definition that is like ours, when they describe social capital as resources that individuals or collectivities can access because of their social relations. This definition is broader than that which defines social capital as the networks that link individuals. It also includes Putnam's (2000) conception of social capital as the institutionalization of norms and values among members of a social network or group.

If we think of capital (in general) as first and foremost an input that adds value to production processes, the logical next step is to conceive of *social* capital as all those productive attributes that derive from *relation-ships* linking an individual human being—or indeed an individual plot of land—to *external* individuals, groups and polities. This implies that we will have to treat other concepts in use in the social sciences such as "institutional capital," "cultural capital" and "religious capital" as no more than subsets that are wholly contained within the social capital concept that we make use of here.

In practice, this means that all social aspects that add value to—or subtract value from—the value of the human capital attributes of an individual worker make up her social capital bundle. This is in addition to the complementarities that involve human and physical capital, to which economists have traditionally paid more attention. It also means that all social aspects that affect the value of land are social capital, which is to say that "location attributes" are also—for the most part—a bundle of social capital attributes.

We have on several occasions stressed the importance of subdividing phenomena according to timescale and scope. Certain phenomena change at a very slow rate and affect large numbers of people—we call these phe-nomena the infrastructure of the group being investigated. Most of the time the infrastructure remains stable, but occasionally there are phase transitions when the addition of some kind of "missing link" causes a transformation of the collectivity being investigated. The collectivity that we have mostly focused on is the population of a functional urban region, but this concept is in actuality scalable all the way from the level of the organization over the nation state to the global economy as a whole. We can make use of a similar subdivision for our analysis of social capital, but we think a division into *three* levels of aggregation is more useful in this context.

Table 12.1   Typology of social capital

Scope of effects	Speed of change	
	Fast	Slow
Individual (micro)	"Fleeting" personal network of temporary acquaintances	Personal network of durable strong and weak ties
Group (meso)	Fashions (temporary group preferences); Meetings and information dissemination within group Groups that fail to bond	Social values of group/ subculture; Informal institutions of group/subculture (primarily prescriptive institutions)
Society (macro)	Mass media; propaganda	Stable and shared values within a polity; Informal institutions (primarily proscriptive institutions); The formal institutions of a jurisdiction

Table 12.1 shows that we have added a *meso*-level between the micro-level of the individual and the macro-level of the polity, with the latter usually understood as an unusually influential polity such as a nation state. The *meso*-level consists of all those associations, organizations and communities that are intermediate between the individual and the polity, ranging from families and kinship networks over firms to ethnic, ideological, religious and other subcultural communities that constitute sources of social capital to subsets of individuals within the same overarching polity.

The social networks that have been the main concern of economic sociologists from Granovetter onward are represented as durable or slowly changing social capital with individual impact. Such interpersonal networks are an important differentiating factor in many labor markets, particularly those for which it is important to continually draw upon a great many types of task-specific expertise beyond what can be expected from any one worker. There are also shorter-term links that come into being during informal socializing in unexpected surroundings (non-durable, micro-level social capital); the most promising of these temporary links may move into the durable, slowly changing category, which would then amount to the dynamic process of network-building.

The *meso* level represents all those social groups that fall between individuals (including networks among individuals whose group affiliations are of subordinate importance) and a relevant macro-level polity. Here we find all the various subsets of a population that are defined by one or more pertinent differentiating attributes. The most effective groups are those that constitute a population *minority* and have developed shared world views and rules of behavior. It is no coincidence that ethnic or religious minorities have often monopolized certain economic functions, particularly in societies with underdeveloped legal institutions. Such minorities often develop informal institutions that increase the level of interpersonal trust *within* the group. They often rely on effective threats of exclusion against those who are unable to live up to group-specific norms of honesty, reciprocity and frequently also seemingly irrelevant behaviors such as adherence to a group-specific diet or religious practice. Examples of such groups and their economic functions include the roles of Hasidic Jews in the international diamond trade, ethnic Indians as the money lenders of South East Asia and even immigrant ethnic Poles as the proprietors of many of Scandinavia's cafes.

Putnam (2000) argues that one should distinguish between "bridging" and "bonding" social capital and that the bridging variety is the "good" type that expands networks and makes an economy more productive. But this is a bit simplistic. Clearly, the bonding component has to be present for there to be a group in an economically meaningful sense and—additionally—bonding becomes more difficult as membership in the group approaches membership in the greater polity of which it is a subset. Bonds will be stronger between Roman Catholics in Hong Kong than in Italy and "gayness" is a more likely source of group formation than is heterosexuality.

Table 12.2 is an attempt to subdivide the *meso*-level by the strength of both types of ties: bonding and bridging. One of Putnam's examples of a group with strong bonds is the Ku Klux Klan, which he correctly describes as being rather resistant to bonding with more mainstream groups. But it is also possible to describe many traditional corporations as networks of individuals who bond internally but are wary of interpersonal ties with other—competing—firms. Many of the most successful religious organizations in terms of growth are also better at bonding than bridging, such as the Jehovah's Witnesses, the Church of Latter Day Saints and Orthodox Judaism. Stark and Finke (2000) offer a compelling reason as to why communities that exhibit a high level of tension with mainstream society are better at attracting new members: one way to raise the quality of a service is to make membership costlier so as to exclude potential free-riders who would make the experience less meaningful for those who desire a high level of bonding.

This does however not mean that groups with strong bridging char-

Table 12.2   Bridging and bonding

Bonding	Bridging	
	Strong	Weak
Strong	Silicon Valley start-up	IBM
	Small centrist political party	Ku Klux Klan
	Mainline church	Jehovah's Witnesses
	Cohesive ethnic minority with high intermarriage rate	Cohesive ethnic minority with low intermarriage rate
Weak	Open source software project	Autarkic farm
	Extroverted unattached individual	Introverted unattached individual
	"Groups" that are no more than coalitions of individuals → intrinsically unstable	

acteristics are necessarily less successful in all contexts. Saxenian (1996) shows that Silicon Valley's relatively open and accessible software firms were able to out-compete more closed and secretive firms along Boston's Route 128 by virtue of providing greater opportunities for creative inter-actions among employees of competing firms. And small but "bridg-ing" political parties in parliamentary democracies with proportional representation—such as *Democraten 66* in the Netherlands and *Radikale Venstre* in Denmark—have often achieved real and sustained political influence, unlike extremist parties that pursue bonding at the expense of bridging.

Indeed, while successful organizations are invariably successful at bonding, there are successful business firms, political parties and religious organizations of both the bridge-building and "bridge-averse" variety, although bridge building is obviously more important for those groups that are small relative to the economy or polity as a whole. Although groups that cannot bond tend to be short-lived, many successful (micro-level) interpersonal networks involve individuals that are better at bridging than bonding.

At the macro-level, we find not only the formal and informal institu-tions that have been the main concern of institutional economists such as North (1990), but also widely shared social values (cf. Inglehart, 1997). While such phenomena, unlike those of the *meso* level, at first sight seem rather distant from a network perspective, they are in fact the mostly unin-tended results of ideas that interpersonal networks have disseminated in the past. Sometimes this past is very distant; some of the most widespread and influential sets of proscriptive institutions—the Decalogue comes to mind—are thousands of years old.

Many institutional economists make a sharp distinction between prescriptive and proscriptive institutions (cf. Kasper et al., 2012). Prescriptive institutions are rules of the "do X" rather than the "don't do Y" type, which means that they are particularly demanding of those who are subjected to them. Such rules become increasingly controversial as one increases the size of the groups that are governed by them, owing to the unavoidable increase in population heterogeneity.

Hayek (1988) makes a distinction between the small non-market communities of the distant past and later market-based societies. In small communities, people share most goals and the means of attaining those goals. In the "Great Society," by contrast, people rely on anonymous markets, which bring people with different cultures and preferences into contact and economic dependence on one another. Hayek's argument is that one of the most common—but also the most serious—mistake of political reformers is to believe that the type of prescriptive institutions that are well-adapted to the interests of self-sufficient and isolated groups of 100 or 200 people can be adopted by "the Great Society." Indeed, this has been one of the main bones of contention between classical liberalism and other influential political ideologies such as socialism, conservatism and fascism. Beginning with Adam Smith, classical liberals have come to believe that a modern mass society should have *no* substantive aim other than the facilitation of the multitude of aims that animate the individuals and groups that jointly constitute a polity. They note that a limitation of the formal institutions of the nation state to proscriptive institutions would make them conform to what is already the quintessential feature of the informal institutions of all multicultural polities.

This tension between tribal pre-market society and its successor type points to the salience of *development stages* and the institutional conflicts that may arise during periods of transition. Hayek did not adopt a development-stage perspective in his analysis of institutional change, but even those who have done so offer no compelling explanation as to *why* a society transitions from one stage to the next. Inglehart (1997) and Florida (2002) assert that we are transitioning from a modern or industrial society to a postmodern or creative one, and that this new society involves new priorities, values and lifestyles. But they offer only ad hoc or fragmented explanations of what caused this transition to occur in the first place.

In this book, we believe that we do offer a compelling explanation of the process that propels a region or society from one stage to the next. The explanation requires the basic tools of synergetic theory as it has been developed in natural science. In particular, it requires that we distinguish between processes of change that evolve according to different timescales (see Chapter 8).

In the most economically developed regions of the world, this protracted logistical revolution (or phase transition) has affected the economic decisions of large numbers of people since the 1970s. The new emerging creative society does not only entail new occupational and industrial structures; it also entails a new value structure and new formal institutions that support the new economy. Not surprisingly, the transition from one value structure to the next, which is really also a transition between world views, has caused conflicts between those who have internalized the new society and those who cling to past ways of viewing the world. It is to this change and conflict that we now turn.

PROCESSES OF VALUE CHANGE AT THE MACRO LEVEL

Andersson et al. (1997) contend that the conflicts that characterized North American and Western European politics in the first three decades after World War II concealed an underlying value system to which almost all people subscribed. The conflicts were about the distribution of the gains from economic progress; the political left and right shared a world view that affirmed economic growth, law and order and national self-determination as the overriding priorities of a polity. This is no longer true.

Based on tens of thousands of interviews in 43 countries, Inglehart (1997) similarly asserts that the West is in the midst of a transformative value shift, leading away from economic growth towards self-expression as the top societal priority. As part of this shift, people shift from "materialist" to "post-materialist" values, along with related changes in the direction of greater acceptance of minorities (however defined) and individual lifestyle choices that do not conform to the predominant norms of industrial society.

Andersson (1985) in the case of Sweden and later Florida (2002), in the case of the United States, survey the parallel transformation of the occupational structure, whereby knowledge-handling or creative jobs grew at a fast pace in both absolute and relative terms from the 1970s until the end of the twentieth century. This was at the expense of the manual or working-class jobs that were predominant wherever the industrial assembly of standardized components was the main type of production. As had happened during the Industrial Revolution, there was also a parallel increase in various measures of income inequality, so that creative and knowledge-intensive workers saw their real earnings rise at the same time as the real wages of poorly educated blue-collar workers declined (Andersson and Andersson, 2015).

This shift in the occupational structure and the relative and absolute remuneration of various jobs has a strong relationship to what kind of values are most supportive of continued economic development (Andersson, 2011). If the bulk of the workforce is occupied with routine tasks, it is traits such as honesty, obedience and conscientiousness that are most important for making the economy more productive: widespread honesty and discipline raise interpersonal trust and lower average (static) transaction costs. But if most workers are paid to come up with new ideas and designs, other personality traits and environmental conditions come to the fore as development accelerators, including openness to experience, a high migration propensity and population diversity (Rentfrow, 2011; Simonton, 2011). New and profitable ideas result from combining existing ideas in unexpected ways, and such combinations are more likely to come about as the result of a fortunate combination of skill, curiosity and diversifying experiences.

It is becoming increasingly evident that it takes time for a new value system to establish itself. Many in the older cohorts of a restructuring society will tend to have learned their marketable skills and adopted their value structure during adolescence, at a time when the new economic structure was nowhere in evidence. It is then not surprising that they are resistant to change: what was once a well-adapted bundle of human and social capital has become a maladaptation with a low or non-existent market return. Table 12.3 is one illustration of this. It shows how Americans' evaluation of the past depends on their level of formal education as well as birth cohort, and how it was the conflict between the old and the new economy rather than between the left and the right that was the hallmark of the 2016 presidential election campaign. Table 12.4 uses the same demographic categories to show the contrast in value systems; while most Americans have a positive valuation of ethnic and racial diversity, the dissenting minority conforms to the expected demographic pattern.

It is clear that the main political fault line in the early twenty-first century is not between larger versus smaller government, as it was for most of the post-war era, but rather between those who feel at ease in the new creative society and those who would have preferred a continuation of a more homogeneous industrial society. The political reaction against the new society is not limited to the United States. Similar movements have become more important in several Western European countries, including Britain, France, Germany and Sweden. The typical adherent to the view that the past was better than the present is everywhere the same: it is a poorly educated elderly man with the same ethnic, linguistic, religious

Table 12.3   *Views of whether life for people like the respondent is better now than 50 years ago, US-registered voters in 2016, percentages*

Category	Worse	Same	Better
All voters	47	13	36
Educational attainment			
High school or less	56	12	30
Some college	50	14	34
College graduate	41	14	41
Postgraduate	29	14	51
Age group			
18–29	34	20	43
30–49	45	14	37
50–64	54	10	33
65 or older	50	12	36
Race/ethnicity			
White	52	12	33
Black	20	23	51
Hispanic	39	17	40
Voting intention			
Clinton	19	18	59
Trump	81	6	11

Source: Pew Research Center (2016); N=2,010.

and sexual affiliation as the majority of the population (Andersson et al., 1997).

Florida (2002) argues that social tolerance is one of the distinguishing features of the most creative cities in the United States and uses three indicators to measure a city's relative tolerance: percentage of same-sex households, percentage of residents born abroad and percentage of the workforce in "Bohemian" (art and entertainment) occupations. This is similar to Inglehart's (1997) earlier discussion of postmodern societies, although Inglehart considers "tolerance of out-groups" as just one of several attributes of what he describes as the "well-being values" that characterize postmodern society.

Andersson et al. (2013) attempt to measure the statistical association between various indicators of a post-industrial value structure as measured by the World Values Survey and other—more objective—indicators of socio-economic development or post-industrialization. Comparing the

*Table 12.4   Views of whether an increasing number of people of different
             races and ethnicities make the US a better or worse place to
             live, US-registered voters in 2016, percentages*

Category	Worse place	No difference	Better place
All voters	8	34	57
Educational attainment			
High school or less	14	43	42
Some college	6	34	59
College graduate	4	28	66
Postgraduate	4	20	76
Age group			
18–29	4	36	60
30–49	5	31	63
50–64	9	37	53
65 or older	12	32	54
Race/ethnicity			
White	9	32	58
Black	5	44	51
Hispanic	3	36	59
Voting intention			
Clinton	2	26	72
Trump	16	43	40

Source: Pew Research Center (2016); N=2,010.

predictive performance of eight different post-materialism or tolerance
questions (that is, Inglehart's four-item and 12-item post-materialism
index; acceptance of gay, immigrant or other-race neighbors and justification of divorce, homosexuality and prostitution) show that all nine questions are statistically significant correlates of seven common measures of
socio-economic development at the level of the nation state. However, two
measures stand out as being especially strongly correlated with development: the average justification of homosexuality (measured on a ten-point
Likert scale) followed by the percentage of people who would rather avoid
having gay neighbors.

The best-performing two-variable index is a weighted combination of
justification of homosexuality and the percentage who can accept other-
race neighbors (these two indicators of a "postmodern value system" had
the lowest bivariate correlation coefficient among the eight investigated
variables, although all pairwise combinations exhibited statistically signifi-

Table 12.5   *Correlation coefficient between a two-variable tolerance index and each of seven socio-economic and institutional indicators of development, 1999–2009*

Indicator that is correlated with the two-variable tolerance index	Correlation coefficient
Corruption Perceptions Index (Transparency International)	0.765***
Global Innovation Index (INSEAD)	0.735***
Press Freedom Index (Freedom House)	0.731***
Political Rights and Civil Liberties (Freedom House)	0.723***
Human Development Index (UNDP)	0.681***
Economic Freedom Index (Heritage Foundation/*Wall Street Journal*)	0.548***
Economic Freedom Index (Fraser Institute)	0.501***

Source: Andersson et al. (2013); ***: $p<.01$; N=83.

cant correlation coefficients). Table 12.5 shows the correlation between this index and each of seven indicators of development.

The reason that acceptance or tolerance of gay people is such a good indicator of post-industrial development is not that gays are especially important for development. They are not. Rather, it is that gays constitute a non-conforming minority whose lifestyle or actions are difficult to misinterpret as a threat to the job prospects of the population majority. It is in other words a "recession-proof" variable. Other minorities, ranging from Jews in Nazi Germany to immigrants and guest workers in post-war America and Europe have often been portrayed as "stealing" the jobs from native populations. Thus, opposition to work-related immigration as well as disparagement of entrepreneurial minorities tend to peak during economic depressions, despite the lack of sound economic arguments in favor of such sentiments. Gays, on the other hand, are mostly natives of the country in which they live and are neither numerous enough nor sufficiently homogeneous in their economic role to be perceived as jeopardizing the jobs of others. Attitudes to gays and other members of the LGBT community has therefore—empirically speaking—become the best measure of the general level of tolerance in society.

TRUST, TOLERANCE AND DEVELOPMENT

In Schumpeter's (1934) theory of development, entrepreneurs are portrayed as constituting a tiny minority of innovative heroes. These innovators are the only ones brave enough to challenge the norms of society; Schumpeter describes the bulk of the population as rather dull practitioners of unchanging conventions. Much of mainstream economic theory subscribes to this view, albeit in less explicit terms. In textbook models, labor is a homogeneous production factor with a uniform marginal product that equals the wage rate. In more refined models, there is differentiated human capital, but the underlying assumption of static skills and well-known production functions remain. It is a theory that may be good at describing the non-entrepreneurial majority of an industrial economy, but it is singularly unsuitable for a society where most people are paid to come up with new compositions, designs and ideas.

Coase (1937) offers a first concession to realism when transaction costs enter the picture. If we allow for transaction costs, institutions must matter. And institutions are a major component of macro-level social capital. The normal argument is that "good" institutions—for example norms of honesty and a level playing field—serve to increase trust in other people and in the institutions of society, thereby reducing the general transaction cost level, making more potential transactions profitable and thus viable. There is but a small leap to the proposition that whatever increases the level of trust will reduce transaction costs. Since low transaction costs are good for development it is efficient to embark on any policy that raises the level of trust. This may seem reasonable, but it is nevertheless erroneous. And the error has much more serious consequences in a post-industrial society than in an industrial one.

The proposition that greater trust is always better is only tenable with a *ceteris-paribus* qualifier. But this is no trivial addition. The reason is twofold. First, with given formal institutions, it is an oft-observed empirical fact that rural areas and small towns have higher levels of trust than large cities. Second, it is also well known that a more homogeneous population tends to be associated with higher levels of trust than a more diverse one, other things being equal. Hence a simple application of the "trust maximization principle" would lead to policies that promote culturally homogeneous villages, in other words places where a handshake can replace complex contractual provisions.

On the other hand, it is reasonable to suggest that high levels of honesty and discipline, leading to a high level of interpersonal trust, are desirable characteristics of workers performing well-defined and unchanging tasks. And these are exactly the traits of the most prevalent type of work in a society where most people work in large factories or bureaucracies. So, those who desire more homogeneity and less urbanity are in a sense correct, but only if it had been possible to revert to an earlier development stage. And even in industrial society, there is a need for diverse urban environments that provide sufficient stimulation for the "captains of industry" who according to Schumpeter (1934) were responsible for the avoidance of economic stagnation. The Austro-Hungarian Empire was in most places a rather conventional and conservative milieu, but its capital city was a world center of creativity in both the arts and sciences.

What matters most for the small entrepreneurial minority in an industrial society is the same thing that matters most for most workers in the emerging creative one. It is the factor that reduces the *dynamic* transaction costs associated with invention and innovation rather than the *static* transaction costs that predominate in mature industries. It is a form of generalized tolerance that is not only accepting of well-defined minorities, but also tolerant of ideas and experiments that at first sight may seem unusual, eccentric or even ridiculous.

Table 12.6 is an attempt to represent how different nation states are associated with two macro-level types of social capital: the level of trust and the level of tolerance. We regard a high level of interpersonal trust as a factor that supports economic development since it lowers static transaction costs, but it is a factor that is *less* important in post-industrial than in industrial societies. Conversely, a high level of social tolerance is always important for creativity and innovation, but it is a *key* factor influencing the general competitiveness of post-industrial societies. In the table, tolerance is measured as the mean Likert score on whether respondents think homosexuality is justifiable, with a score of ten indicating that homosexuality is "always justified."

One of the main differences between trust and tolerance as measured by the World Values Survey concerns intertemporal stability. Countries with high measured levels of trust have tended to stay that way since the inception of the survey in the early 1980s. Measures of tolerance involving gays have tended to increase in most of the rich world: the percentage of people stating that homosexuality is never justified as well as the percentage of people seeking to avoid gay neighbors has been declining since the 1980s or 1990s in countries as different as Brazil, China, Spain, Sweden and the United States. More detailed region-level data indicate that younger cohorts and residents of the most cosmopolitan cities drive this change. By way of example, Hong Kong has a more diverse population and a more knowledge-intensive economy than any mainland Chinese city; it also combines a lower level of interpersonal trust and a higher level of social tolerance as compared with the mainland Chinese averages.

Table 12.6 also includes several countries' relative rankings on a publication-based measure of science intensity. Countries are only ranked if they count among the 36 countries with the greatest total science output, which means that large countries tend to have a ranking even if their per

Table 12.6   *Percentage reporting that most people can be trusted (trust)*
and mean Likert score on "justification of homosexuality"
(tolerance) in 78 nation states, 2005–2014* (in parentheses:
ranking of science intensity** among the 36 nations with the
greatest science output, 2008–2010)

	High trust (50–100%)	Medium trust (25–49%)	Low trust (10–24%)	Very distrustful (0–9%)
High tolerance (5.5–10.0)	Australia (8) Denmark (2) Finland (6) Netherlands (4) New Zealand (15) Norway (7) Sweden (3) Switzerland (1)	Canada (10) Germany (17)	Andorra Argentina (31) Chile France (18) Spain (20) Uruguay	–
Medium tolerance (3.0–5.4)	–	Estonia Great Britain (13) Hong Kong (N/A) Hungary (27) Italy (22) Japan (26) Singapore (9) South Korea (25) Taiwan (21) Thailand United States (16)	Bulgaria Guatemala Israel (12) Mexico (35) Poland (28) Slovenia South Africa (33)	Brazil (32) Colombia Cyprus Lebanon Malaysia Peru Philippines
Low tolerance (2.0–2.9)	China (34)	Bahrain Belarus Kazakhstan Russia (30)	Algeria India (36) Mali Moldova Ukraine Zambia	Ecuador Romania
Very intolerant (1.0–1.9)	Vietnam	Indonesia Iraq Kyrgyzstan Yemen	Armenia Azerbaijan Burkina Faso Ethiopia Iran Jordan Libya Morocco Nigeria Pakistan Qatar Rwanda	Georgia Ghana Trinidad Zimbabwe

Table 12.6   (continued)

High trust (50–100%)	Medium trust (25–49%)	Low trust (10–24%)	Very distrustful (0–9%)
		Tunisia Turkey (29) Uzbekistan	

Notes:
* Great Britain: 1998; Denmark: 1999; Israel: 2001;
** science intensity is number of SCI-indexed articles per head in the 2008–2010 period (Hong Kong is included in the figure for China); countries ranked by science intensity but not surveyed by the World Values Survey are Ireland (5), Belgium (11), Austria (14), Greece (19), Czech Republic (23) and Portugal (24).

Sources: World Values Survey (2005–2014); Andersson et al. (2013).

capita output is very low (India is the most extreme example of this). Interestingly, out of the nine top-ranked nation states included in the table, seven combine a high level of trust with a high level of tolerance, and all nine have at least medium tolerance *and* medium trust.

Interpersonal trust seems to be a feature that is rather stable, and is perhaps at least partly influenced by a nation's dominant cultural tradition (all high-trust countries are historically Protestant or Confucian). Conversely, it seems reasonable to hypothesize that attitudes toward gays is transitioning in tandem with the Fourth Logistical Revolution, with intermediate levels—such as in Britain and the United States—being an unstable intermediate step between marginalization and universal acceptance. This hypothesis is supported by several recent American opinion polls. A 2015 poll of a random sample of more than 2,000 US residents aged 18 and above showed that while 73 percent of respondents born in 1986 or later were in favor of same-sex marriage, this was only true of 39 percent of those born in 1945 or earlier (Pew Research Center, 2015).

It seems likely that it is those cities, regions and nations that are tolerant—not only in terms of accepting sexual minorities, but also ethnic, linguistic, religious and other lifestyle minorities—that will be most conducive to the creative endeavors that are becoming an increasingly important source of economic competitiveness in the creative age. Sometimes this tolerance will refer to well-defined groups of people, but it will also sometimes refer to tolerance of eccentric individuals.

So far, we have referred to the following forms of social capital as being conducive to economic development: interpersonal connectivity within informal networks; membership in organizations and other groups whose members bond with one another, some of which are also good at building bridges to other groups and membership of or residence in polities with high levels of interpersonal trust and/or tolerance. The final type of social capital consists of those formal institutions—mainly political and legal systems with associated laws and regulations—that decide whether new ideas or new forms of cooperation can be transformed into profitable ventures within local or global markets.

FORMAL INSTITUTIONS AS SOCIAL CAPITAL

There have been numerous attempts to measure the quality of jurisdiction-specific formal institutions. As noted in Chapter 8, Heckscher (1935) contends that English common law is particularly conducive to the development of dynamic markets. More generally, many institutional economists stress the importance of the rule of law, including a level playing field where individuals and organizations compete on equal terms.

All eight of the nation-state jurisdictions in the cell furthest to the northwest in Table 12.6 are known as countries that uphold the rule of law and provide a more-or-less level playing field for entrepreneurs and other market actors. But we can be a bit more specific regarding which institutions are likely to increase in relative importance.

A creative society implies that entrepreneurship will become a more important feature of economic life (Holcombe, 2011). This implies that those institutions that impact entrepreneurial activity more than routine production will have a greater impact on jurisdictional competitiveness than during earlier stages of development. The aim of market entrepreneurship is economic profit, which equals the difference between revenue and opportunity cost. Profits result in dividends, reinvestment and/or capital gains. Thus, high taxes on profits, dividends or capital gains are likely to diminish the incentives for market entrepreneurship, which is the most direct link between creativity and economic development.

Another facet of entrepreneurship is experimentation in attribute space (Andersson, 2008). Product innovation often involves the creation of new bundles of pre-existing attributes, such as a hotel-and-golf-course bundle (a golf resort) or a telephone-internet-music-and-GPS bundle (a smartphone). Sometimes the legal system is supportive of such creative re-bundling efforts, but sometimes it is not. Examples of how legal institutions and regulations impede creative market entrepreneurship are plentiful. These include the effects of the Food and Drug Administration on entrepreneurship in the American pharmaceutical industry, the effects of the Town and Country Planning Act on land-use entrepreneurship in the United Kingdom and the effects of the widespread practice of raising market entry costs through costly and inflexible licensing requirements in industries such as education, health care and transportation services. All in all, we can expect jurisdictions that offer below-average taxes on the returns to entrepreneurship as well as having low levels of product regulation to gain more from these institutional social-capital features in the new than in the old economy.

13. Creative knowledge capital

Knowledge as a subset of both human and social capital was rarely analyzed by economists before the 1980s. If at all mentioned it was in some disguised form such as (general) human capital or technology. The recent interest in the role of knowledge in the structure and growth of economies is related to the consequences of the protracted expansion of education in both the industrial and post-industrial economies, the rapid growth of knowledge-based occupations and industries and the increasing focus of manufacturing industries on knowledge investments in the form of industrial research and development (R&D).

In contrast to economics, knowledge has been a focus of philosophical inquiry for many centuries, ultimately paving the way for more recent contributions in cognitive science and computer science. Of some importance for our analysis are theories proposed by the philosopher Bertrand Russell and the philosopher and economist Frank Ramsey, as combined and reformulated by Nils-Eric Sahlin (1990). In *The Problems of Philosophy*, Bertrand Russell states that:

> [w]hat we firmly believe, if it is true, is called knowledge, provided it is either intuitive or inferred (logically or psychologically) from intuitive knowledge from which it follows logically. What we firmly believe, if it is not true, is called error. What we firmly believe, if it is neither knowledge nor error, and also what we believe hesitatingly, because it is, or is derived from, something which has not the highest degree of self-evidence, may be called probable opinion (Russell, 1912, p. 81).

Building upon Russell, Ramsey concludes—in Sahlin's (1990, p. 93) interpretation—that "[k]nowledge is not true justified belief but rather a belief is knowledge if it is obtained by a reliable process and if it always leads to success" (cf. Andersson and Beckmann, 2009, p. 6). The *creative* potential of knowledge, formulated as a proposition, model or theory is central to Ramsey and to his follower Braithwaite:

> It is only in theories which are not intended to have any function except that of systematizing empirical generalizations already known that the theoretical terms can harmlessly be defined. A theory which is hoped may be expanded in the future to explain more generalizations than it was originally designed to

explain must allow more freedom to its theoretical terms than would be given them were they to be logical constructions out of observable entities. A scientific theory which, like all good scientific theories, is capable of growth must be more than an alternative way of describing the generalizations upon which it is based, which is all it would be if its theoretical terms were limited by being explicitly defined (Braithwaite, 1955/1968, p. 76).

It is obvious that any serious analysis of the concept of knowledge—as defined by Russel, Ramsey or Braithwaite—is closely related to hypotheses and theories that have been scientifically scrutinized and shown to be successful in terms of being useful for decisions to invest, innovate and create in its most general sense.

Knowledge should not be confused with information, data, news or other related concepts. Knowledge is the *output* of a reliable process that makes use of information (bits), data or concepts (see Figure 13.1).

Figure 13.1 illustrates the hierarchical relation between the entities in the build-up of knowledge from information to skills. Information in the sense of information theory is the initial primitive building block, consisting of strings of zeros and ones. By an encoding process, these strings are

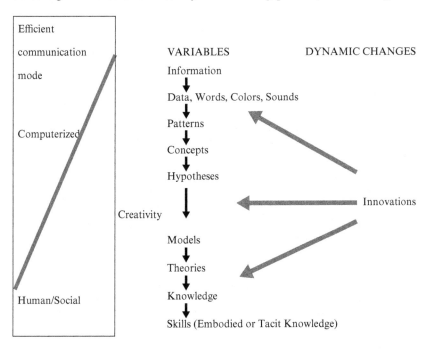

Figure 13.1   Efficient communication modes—from information to embodied knowledge

transformed into meaningful data, words, colors or shapes. These entities can then be arranged into semantically meaningful patterns (for instance melodic lines, equations or sentences). A set of such patterns can be conceptually structured so as to be part of some hypothesis about the real world (or in the arts about some imagined world).

For the scientist it is then quite common to shape a set of hypotheses into a mathematical, mechanical or computerized model. At some level of complexity, the model may be transformed into a realistic theory, to be tested with logical or empirical methods. After scientists have subjected a theory to sufficient testing and scrutiny, it may be transformed into *disembodied* and thus public knowledge.

The final step is practitioners' application of the disembodied knowledge in real life. The practitioners thereby add the individual ideas that are necessary for the efficient application of the theory to real life situations. There will then be a transformation of the disembodied knowledge into skills, embodied knowledge or, in Polanyi's (1958; 1967), personal or tacit knowledge.

There have been attempts to bridge the gap between tacit and disembodied scientific knowledge. These have involved artificial intelligence and robotized solutions to complex human tasks. One example is "Autoland," as regularly used at Heathrow Airport to land large commercial aircraft in foggy weather. Most of us would agree that the landing of an Airbus at Heathrow Airport is an activity that requires a lot of skills (or tacit knowledge). Recently, scientists at MIT have attempted to develop systems for much more complicated substitutes of human landing capacity:

> Since loss of power can occur at any point during the flight and the pilot can become incapacitated at any point in time, the autoland system to be developed needs to have a larger scope than the typical autoland systems on commercial aircraft, which only take over once the aircraft is aligned with the runway centerline on final approach. For the case of partial or complete pilot incapacitation, the pilot needs to be able to rely on autoland to automatically select a suitable landing site, guide the aircraft to the landing site and perform the approach and landing. For complete pilot incapacitation, autoland may not require any input from the pilot. However, there is the possibility of a passenger being present, which autoland aims to draw on, in order to provide control inputs to enhance autoland performance in the event of complete pilot incapacitation. This passenger is assumed to be untrained in piloting the aircraft, so that any interaction with the passenger should be kept as simple as possible. The same applies to any interaction [with] partially incapacitated pilot. (Siegel and Hansman, 2011)

In 2015, the firm Diamond Aircraft reported:

Table 13.1   Knowledge and information divided into four categories

Scope of effects	Rate of change	
	Fast	Slow
Individual	Information (influence on consumer choice)	Scientific tacit knowledge Artistic tacit knowledge Industrial tacit knowledge
Collective	Widely disseminated information: News Fashion Propaganda Advertising	Widely available (published) ideas, models, theories and compositions (infrastructural knowledge)

that it has successfully demonstrated a fly-by-wire autoland system in its DA42 four-seat twin. The system, which Diamond once dubbed an "electronic parachute," is designed as an emergency backup in situations such as pilot incapacitation or engine failure. The system can be activated by either the pilot or the airplane. For example, if the airplane's software detects that the airplane is nearing its destination but there have been no pilot inputs, the autoland kicks in. (Diamond Aircraft, 2015)

Similarly, in the automobile industry, where cars are being developed that would not need any driver even if used in heavy road traffic.

These examples illustrate knowledge that has traditionally been associated with direct rather than indirect human action. But no matter what type of knowledge we are discussing, its formation constitutes an important part of investments in the infrastructure of society. Table 13.1 illustrates the relationship between knowledge, domain of effects and speed of change. While information exhibits a fast rate of change, knowledge evolves at a much slower pace.

Education-based skills or tacit knowledge are obviously a part of each individual's property rights and individuals therefore capture most of the returns to scarce tacit knowledge as wages or salaries. However, exclusion is never perfect, and therefore tacit knowledge also generates positive external effects that benefit others, especially those who are co-located with the source of these spillovers within the same cluster or conurbation. There are also individual property rights to patented scientific knowledge, which sometimes cause monopoly profits to accrue to the patentee.

As mentioned earlier, Artificial Intelligence (AI) has increasingly been applied to the process of transferring skills from humans to robots and computerized production systems. These new forms of non-human

embodiment have—after expiration of the relevant patents—become disembodied stable knowledge with collective effect; they have thus become
parts of the knowledge infrastructure.

THE KNOWLEDGE-BASED INDUSTRIES

The number of workers specializing in the use of manual skills has declined
since the 1950s in most advanced Western economies. Machlup (1980)
is an early account of the rise of the knowledge industry, which shows
that this industry accounted for almost 30 percent of US gross domestic
product in the 1970s. Machlup's classification includes occupations that
are likely to produce new knowledge as well as those involved in the transfer of knowledge and information; people in those occupations are called
"knowledge workers." Using American labor statistics, Machlup (ibid.)
shows that this group of workers had grown faster than other groups in the
decades leading up to the 1970s.

Subsequently, Andersson (1985a; 1985b) provides a broad historical
overview of creativity, infrastructural changes and economic growth,
suggesting that an assessment of the relative knowledge orientation of
an economy should exclude occupations that focus on information transmission. Andersson's definition of "knowledge-handling occupations" is
thus a subset of Machlup's occupations and mainly consists of workers
involved in education, research and the arts. Andersson et al. (1993) have
shown that the number of workers in this occupational category is growing
faster than other categories in Sweden and other advanced economies.

Anderstig and Hårsman (1986) show that the percentage of
"knowledge-handlers" is increasing in manufacturing as well as in services
and that this expansion is fastest in large metropolitan regions. Florida
(2002) and Glaeser and Mare (2001; see also Glaeser et al., 2004) elaborate
upon these early findings in an American context, with the conclusion that
US metropolitan areas increasingly depend on highly educated workers
or—in the words of the quasi-Marxist Richard Florida—host an increasingly dominant "creative class."

In the 1970s and 1980s, producers in the electronic, pharmaceutical,
optical and transport industries were becoming increasingly aware of the
need for R&D; this was to secure dynamic comparative advantages in their
location and trading decisions. Figure 13.2 is an attempt to visualize the
relationships among the different aspects of knowledge capital, creative
research, innovation and production.

Figure 13.2 makes it easy to avoid the common mistake of *not* separating creativity from innovation (or diffusion) in a systematic way. In early

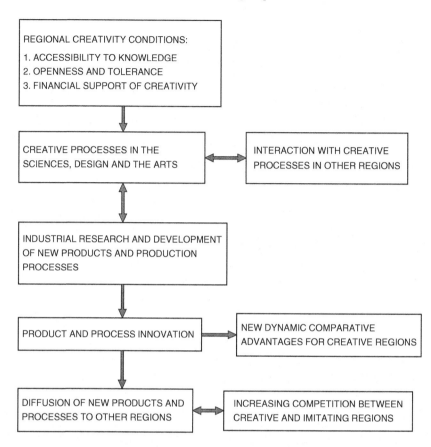

Figure 13.2   Knowledge capital, research and production

industrial society, there were clear "stages of innovative production," whereby the lone inventor (often with some engineering education) provided the industrial entrepreneur with the key input for a successful innovation. The infrastructure of scientific knowledge, as provided by Newton and other theorists in mathematics and physics, was for the most part a prerequisite that enabled such innovation processes to occur.

Even today there are some managers who fail to perceive the links between production and scientific creativity. Instead they try to internalize scientific research into their production systems to privatize scientific knowledge. Such strategies misallocate knowledge resources. The increasing complexity of products and production systems necessitates a stronger, almost permanent, interaction between the creativity of basic science in the public domain and proprietary technological R&D within firms.

Our contention is that scientific creativity is becoming increasingly important for industrial research and innovation. This will not only affect the location of industries and their knowledge capital. It will also change the location of scientists. Lööf and Nabavi (2013) provide empirical evidence that locations with high levels of basic science output benefit knowledge-intensive industries. Analyzing 10,000 Swedish export firms over a 12-year period, they conclude that both persistent and non-persistent innovators benefit from a science-based local environment. Moreover, this type of firm-external knowledge exerts a positive influence on the productivity growth of firms classified as persistent innovators.

THE LONG DURATION OF THE PROCESS OF TRANSFORMING SCIENTIFIC CREATIVITY INTO INDUSTRIAL R&D AND PRODUCT INNOVATION

Fundamental creativity in the sciences is shaping the dynamic comparative advantages of regional and national industries. The intermediate factor is industrial R&D, with product and process innovations as direct outputs. Surprisingly, scientific research accounts for only a modest part of overall spending, even in those economies that are most "science-intensive." Spending on industrial R&D—which tends to be more incremental and short-sighted—is more than three times greater than spending on scientific research in the nations that produce most of the world's scientific research (see Table 13.2).

The public sector—which is the main source of research funding in the higher education sector—attaches much less importance to science than the private sector attaches to applied industrial research. There are at least three reasons for this. First, scientific research tends to be associated with a much longer time horizon than industrial R&D. There is consequently greater uncertainty of success in the sense of Ramsey (1927, pp.153–70; Sahlin, pp.88–94). Second, scientists tend to focus less on financial or private returns than most others, and this unusual attribute makes it difficult for politicians and other relevant policymakers to assess the success of projects. Third, scientific returns are by their very nature intended to be public in their effects because of the academic institution of disseminating scientific results without access restrictions. Scientific research thus creates a type of infrastructure that is unusually similar to the economic definition of a pure public good.

Politicians and bureaucrats often wrongly assume that innovation policies that happen to be fashionable at the moment are the best policies for promoting the comparative advantages of the future. The implication is

Table 13.2   *Scientists/R&D workers per 1,000 workers (2014–2015);*
percentage of GDP allocated to R&D (2008–2011);
percentage of GDP allocated to scientific research (2008–
2011); 13 advanced economies

Country	Scientists/R&D workers per 1,000 workers	Percentage of GDP allocated to science and R&D	Percentage of GDP allocated to science
Sweden	14.1	3.43	0.90
Denmark	14.7	3.06	0.90
Finland	15.3	3.89	0.79
Netherlands	8.7	1.83	0.75
Switzerland	7.5	2.97	0.72
Germany	8.2	2.79	0.51
France	9.9	2.12	0.48
United Kingdom	8.9	1.70	0.48
Japan	10.5	3.33	0.45
South Korea	13.5	3.58	0.40
United States	8.9	2.28	0.39
Italy	4.9	1.25	0.36
Greece	7.5	0.60	0.30
OECD average	**8.0**	**2.17**	**0.44**

Sources: OECD Science and Technology Indicators (2012); OECD (2016).

that they tend to support industrial R&D rather than scientific research, in spite of the (potentially) much greater and more widespread social returns that scientific creativity brings about. Politicians seem to believe in the continued relevance of the industrial structure of the nineteenth century, when independent inventors/innovators such as Edison or Nobel could almost single-handedly initiate industrial miracles.

The increasing complexity of biomedicine and computer science as well as the communications-based industries implies that large and multidisciplinary science teams are becoming increasingly important for scientific research (Hollingsworth, 2007); such teams have been responsible for the most revolutionary creative breakthroughs in both science and industry. A not very daring prediction is that the increasing complexity of scientific research will cause the demise of the independent inventor of the type that works alone in some minimally equipped lab.

DEFINING AND MEASURING COMPLEXITY

Economies, and as a consequence their research organizations, are becoming increasingly complex. We therefore need a better understanding of what the increasing complexity of products and processes implies for the organization of economic life. Several definitions of complexity have been proposed. Most of these are somewhat intuitive. In contrast, Solomonoff (1964a; 1964b), Kolmogorov (1965) and Chaitin (1966) provide a mathematically precise definition of complexity. These mathematicians claim that complexity is defined as the minimal length of a program or algorithm that yields a measurable and exact solution to a pre-formulated problem. This can be clarified with two simple examples.

Example 1: Generate the series 00200030000400000500000006 . . .
Example 2: Generate the number 121543699821345798709812699994333.

A formula or algorithm that is shorter than the series of Example 1 yields the same unique number series. Such an algorithm of minimal length is short and thus of low relative complexity. In contrast, no formula shorter than the series itself can identify Example 2, which is a random series of numbers. Example 2 is thus more relatively complex than Example 1.

It is possible to generalize the complexity of mathematical expressions and computer algorithms to phenomena such as blueprints and production process instructions (Solomonoff, 1964a; 1964b; Casti and DePauli, 2000). Standardized goods must follow strict and stepwise (that is, algorithmic) rules of composition. A simple example is a cooking recipe. For example, the recipe for a standard clam chowder is less complex than the recipe for bouillabaisse soup served in a three-star French restaurant. But despite the clarity of this example, it also alludes to limitations of the computational complexity measure.

The first limitation arises from the difference between numbers in an algorithm and ingredients in a soup. The ingredients of different fish and spices have much greater *scope* than numbers; they are heterogeneous rather than uniform in having an open-ended set of underlying attributes. A second limitation is that foods, unlike numbers, are sensitive to the skills of the individual using the recipe. Tacit knowledge is important. A recipe-using individual is not as algorithmically rule-based as a computer program. A skillful worker can adjust the recipe if the delivery of an ingredient is delayed or if an ingredient is of superior or inferior quality (in one or more of its intrinsic attributes). The structure of inputs in the production process is thus a function of the algorithmic complexity of the recipe (c_A) and the skills of the workers. Baumol captures the skill change that accompanies changes in algorithmic complexity when he writes that:

> incremental improvement of complex products may require mastery of far more demanding technical information and techniques than was needed for the original ideas that resulted in the invention of those products. The technology needed to improve the design of a Boeing-777 passenger airplane is obviously enormously more complex than that underlying the Wright brothers' first vehicle. (Baumol, 2004, p. 8)

The *cost* of production will thus depend on (at least) three factors:

1. the algorithmic complexity of the recipe (composition or design);
2. the quality attributes of the ingredients (physical capital); and
3. the skills of the worker (tacit knowledge/human capital).

Besides the complexity of production there is also the complexity of consumption. These two types of economic complexity do not coincide. More complex production is often required in order to provide *less* complex consumption. An example is computer-assisted automatic transmission systems in cars. The production complexity is substantial, whereas the user derives utility from this *high* production complexity to the extent that she values *low* consumption complexity (c_U). This implies that revenues as well as costs depend on both production *and* consumption (or user) complexity.

We can assume that consumption complexity is a function of production complexity, as specified earlier. This means that we can now formulate a profit function, *Y*, for a given good as follows:

$$Y = R(\mathbf{q}, c_U(c_A, \mathbf{v}), s) - C(\mathbf{q}, \mathbf{v}, c_A, s); \qquad (13.1)$$

where:
R = the revenue function
C = the cost function
$\mathbf{v}$ = a vector of ordinary inputs (dependent on the prevailing complexity levels), and $\mathbf{q}$ = a vector of scales of production of the given set of goods.
c_U = user complexity,
c_A = algorithmic production complexity
s = skill (tacit knowledge) of labor

In the short term, we treat the complexities of the good as given by *earlier investments in knowledge*. In the long term, algorithmic complexity, input structure and skills can all change as a result of creativity in science, in applied research and by the accumulated length of the production time. Such changes are possible only on much slower timescales than the typical timescale of ordinary business decisions about R&D-induced incremental improvements.

The accumulation of scientific knowledge thus occurs through a slow creative process that changes the algorithmic complexity of a given good:

$$\Delta C/\Delta \tau = F(C, S_r)$$
$$\Delta c_A/\Delta \tau = G(c_A, C); \tag{13.2}$$

where:
C = scientific creative capital;
S_r = funds allocated to scientific research;
τ = a long time period.

We assume the functions to be concave with respect to C, S_r and c_A, ranging from R^+ to R^+. In addition, $\tau = kt$, where k is a constant transforming ordinary time (say years) into the much longer time periods that a new scientific breakthrough needs in order to mature and gain acceptance in the community of scientists. By adiabatic approximation (G, F) ≈ 0, implying that firms will treat the current stock of established scientific knowledge as a fixed constraint on their opportunity set. We may therefore treat the algorithmic complexity of a specific time period as the knowledge infrastructure. Firms treat this science infrastructure as a stable basic input into the much more rapid applied and incremental research processes that transform scientific results into product and process innovations.

A slow but persistent long-term accumulation of knowledge in the sciences— effected through technological experiments and innovations of supporting capital equipment—can lead to an entrepreneurial expansion of investment long after the initial scientific discovery. There are numerous examples of such slow knowledge growth processes that eventually result in a massive economic impact. For example, we can trace the development of biotechnology from the early explorations by Mendel—via Hugo de Vries, Carl Correns and Erich von Tschermak in the early twentieth century and the discovery of the double helix by Crick and Watson in the mid-twentieth century—until the breakthrough of gene technology and other parts of modern biotech. Figure 13.3 illustrates such a synergetic process.

Figure 13.3 illustrates the slow and steady growth from a scientific discovery via smaller complementary findings, experiments, innovations towards the critical level (λ^*), which leads to a massive expansion of demand. Before λ^* there are only small demand responses. After λ^*, there is clustered entrepreneurial activity and an explosive increase of demand.

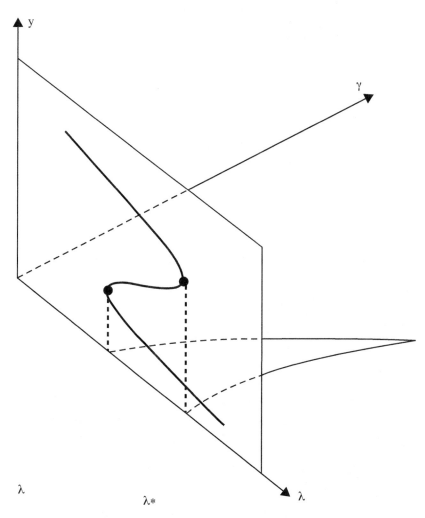

Notes:
λ = relative accumulated knowledge capital.
y = total demand or global market share.
γ = severity of institutional constraint.

Figure 13.3   Phase transition process after a long period of knowledge capital accumulation and the potential drop in demand after a process of competitive knowledge investments

The figure illustrates a manifold with an upper and a lower stable equilibrium surface as well as unstable disequilibria between the two surfaces.

CREATIVITY AND COMPLEXITY

There are numerous examples of how the creativity of scientists, designers and engineers has increased product complexity over the past five decades. Computers have been decreasing in size and their internal product complexity has increased. Much of the increasing internal complexity has served to reduce users' perceived consumption complexity. One should keep in mind, however, that recent rapid increases in the product complexity of computers would not have been possible without the scientific creativity of Alan Turing and John von Neumann in the 1930s and 1940s.

The transport equipment industry is another example of this process. A modern airplane is more energy efficient and easier to fly than vintage airplanes from the 1920s. But it was only through a massive and protracted accumulation of novel electronic and hydro-mechanical components that this increasing product complexity and decreasing consumption complexity was made possible. It is also noteworthy that workers in contemporary airplane manufacturing plants have more advanced technical skills than their counterparts in the 1920s. Likewise, improved lightweight materials have become available and contributed to the creative redesign process. One example of the close link between industrial R&D and scientific research is the development by Clemens and his associates at Montana University of lightweight structural intermetallic titanium aluminides, so-called ɤ-TiAl based alloys. These alloys are now seen as key structural materials for high-temperature application in the advanced jet and automotive engines of the next generation of Airbus models.

The trend toward increasing levels of complexity, which is now evident in most industries, has caused a restructuring of both scientific and industrial research. It has also given rise to the current political popularity of national and regional innovation strategies. Two industries have since the 1960s been at the forefront of the integration of science, industrial research and technological innovation.

The computer industry is one of these industries. It emerged from the rather simple office equipment industry. The British mathematician Alan Turing supplied the key scientific input. Turing had been analyzing the mathematical properties of digital mathematics in a seemingly simple but very general algorithm (Turing, 1936), which was later to be known as UTMs (Universal Turing Machines). Two other mathematicians, John von Neumann and Herman Goldstine, provided the original computer engineering input in the 1940s, which led to the first prototype of a programmable computer in the early 1950s. The increase in the product complexity of computers since the 1950s has been staggering. Algorithmic complexity has been increasing at an unrivaled pace from the 1950s onward. It was not just Turing, von Neumann and Goldstine who made the resulting "information revolution" possible. One determining factor was the invention of the point contact transistor in 1947 by William Shockley, John Bardeen and Walter Houser Brattain. These three scientists were jointly awarded the 1956 Nobel Prize in Physics.

However, we must go even further back in history to trace some fundamental discoveries that were prerequisites both for Turing and for the subsequent computer and information revolution. Examples include Sir Isaac Newton (the Newton technique for solving non-linear equations), Euler, Ada Lovelace (the first computer programmer) and other algorithmically oriented mathematicians.

Information technology is but one example of this type of process that connects scientific breakthroughs with increasingly complex products. Computer science and communication technology have caused increasing downstream product complexity in a wide variety of industries that includes aerospace engineering, architecture, astrophysics, biochemistry, electrical engineering, film and television, financial operations, geophysics, molecular biology, pattern cognition, robotics and transport and logistical systems engineering.

The algorithmic complexity of computer programs has relied on the increasing hardware capacity of computers as well as on decreasing consumption complexity. The user-friendly laptop computer is one outcome of this parallel development. Perhaps the most important aspect of the dynamics of hardware complexity is ever-increasing storage capacity.

These examples illustrate how scientific breakthroughs cause new inventions and how subsequent product innovations depend on interactions between parallel increases in algorithmic complexity, (physical) input complexity and skill complexity.

Another example of an industry that had an early start in the integration of scientific and industrial creativity is the pharmaceutical industry. Decision makers in that industry early on identified and acted on the need for an integration of the medical, chemical and biological sciences with firms' research and innovation strategies. Yet another example is the medical equipment industry, whose constituent firms have developed elaborate strategies for using relevant results from physics, computer science and cognitive science.

This raises the question of what type of organization is best able to cultivate the scientific breakthroughs that firms subsequently use in their product development efforts. Hollingsworth (2007) connects scientific complexity to the frequency of creative breakthroughs and the internal organization of universities, research institutes and laboratories. His focus is on biomedical science, which is unusually concerned with understanding and predicting highly complex systems. Hollingsworth (ibid, p.129) notes that "high cognitive complexity is the capacity to observe and understand in novel ways the relationships among complex phenomena, the capacity to see relationships among disparate fields of knowledge. And it is that capacity which greatly increases the potential for making a major discovery."

Hollingsworth's empirical analysis distinguishes between two different types of labs (A and B). He starts by asking (ibid, p.131) the following question: "What were the characteristics of the culture and the structure of the laboratory where the [breakthrough] research occurred?" The initial finding was that most labs never made any major discoveries, while there was a small subset that did in fact produce revolutionary scientific results. Hollingsworth labels the creative type of lab "Type A," while he calls the relatively uncreative lab "Type B." As it turns out, labs that produced creative breakthroughs had similar Type A organizational attributes, although a majority of Type A labs were unsuccessful. More significantly, *none* of the conventionally structured Type B labs ever produces a truly revolutionary biomedical finding. Table 13.3 illustrates the organizational attributes of Type A and Type B labs.

Hollingsworth's results are striking. He writes (ibid., p.132) that "almost all of the 291 discoveries in our project were made in Type A laboratories. . ..

Table 13.3   Organizational Attributes of Type A and Type B Laboratories

Attribute	Type A Lab	Type B Lab
Cognitive	High scientific diversity	Low or moderate scientific diversity
Social	High and diversified network connectivity	High network connectivity within a single discipline
Material	Access to funding for high-risk research	Limited funding for high-risk research
Personality of the Lab Head	High cognitive complexity; high confidence; high motivation	Low cognitive complexity; risk-averse
Leadership	Excellent grasp of how different fields may be integrated	Not concerned with integrating distinct scientific disciplines

Source: Hollingsworth (2007).

Type B laboratories are at the opposite end of the continuum on virtually all the lab characteristics. Significantly, none of the 291 discoveries in our research occurred in Type B labs."

On the basis of these results, we conclude that the development of science toward increasingly complex theories, models and products causes a need for more complex cognitive capacity among individual scientists as well as within laboratories and other research organizations at the micro level. Moreover, the increase in expected (but uncertain) individual creativity that accompanies good access to new and diversified knowledge (cf. Andersson, 1985a; Florida, 2002; Hollingsworth, 2007; Simonton, 2011) provides strong arguments for locating such micro research organizations in large, open and diverse cities.

THE GLOBAL AND REGIONAL DISTRIBUTION OF CREATIVE SCIENTIFIC CAPACITY

The most systematic studies of the global distribution of scientific creative capacity are all based on Thomson Reuter's Science Citation Index, which records publishing and citations in peer-reviewed scientific journals. Admittedly, only a very low percentage of published papers are truly creative. This is quite obvious. Scientific research oriented to new theory or exploring the borders of science is highly uncertain and the probability of success is low. This leads to a rank-size ordering of reading and citation within each scientific field.

The world's highest-ranked universities and successful departments and institutes are mostly located in a few American and British regions, according to popular league tables. Large functional urban regions such as London, Tokyo, Paris and the San Francisco Bay Area have been obvious centers of global science production with decades and sometimes centuries of increasing science output. However, developments after 2000 have disrupted the global pecking order of science production, as Table 13.4 illustrates.

Europe's spatial distribution of research is skewed toward large metropolitan areas and a handful of college towns. The spatial concentration of research output in some of the smaller European countries such as Denmark, Finland, Sweden and Switzerland is especially pronounced. Table 13.5 gives the total number of publications registered in the Science Citation Index for the 2008–10 period with regions delimited according to the spatial extent of a time distance of 45 minutes from the regional center by the fastest mode of transportation.

Historical data (Matthiessen et al., 2011) show that there is considerable stability in the geographic distribution of European science production,

Table 13.4   Annual growth rate of science output in percent; major
metropolitan centers of science production, 1996–2010 or
2002–2010

Functional urban region	Growth rate (%)	Total output of SCI-indexed articles (2008–2010)
2002–2010		
Beijing	+16.7	101,000
Seoul	+16.4	67,000
1996–2010		
Randstad (Amsterdam)	+2.3	66,000
New York	+2.3	70,000
Boston	+2.2	69,000
Paris	+2.1	77,000
Los Angeles	+2.1	58,000
San Francisco Bay Area	+1.9	76,000
London	+1.5	97,000
Tokyo-Yokohama	+1.5	94,000
Kansai (Osaka)	+1.1	61,000

Source: Andersson et al. (2013).

with centers of gravity—both in terms of mass and network connectivity—
in the three leading and globally important regions of London, Paris and
Randstad.

Sweden, along with Denmark and Finland, is the country with the
world's greatest expenditures on scientific research relative to GDP and
the world's third greatest number of per capita SCI output in 2008–10 after
Switzerland and Denmark (Andersson et al., 2013). As Table 13.5 shows,
the Øresund region (encompassing Copenhagen as well as the Swedish
cities of Malmö and Lund) is Europe's seventh largest agglomeration
of science production, while Stockholm-Uppsala is the eleventh largest
agglomeration. But what *mechanisms* cause scientists to spatially cluster?

ACCESSIBILITY AND CLUSTERING OF SCIENTISTS—A THEORETICAL APPROACH

Assume that space is subdivided into N regions. The scientist must select
one location (i) from these N regions. One location preference argument
is the accessibility to other scientists from i to all N. It is reasonable to
assume that scientists prefer other scientists to have proximate rather than

Table 13.5   Science output in Europe's 25 leading functional urban regions, 2008–2010

Rank	Functional urban region	SCI-indexed articles
1	London	96,856
2	Paris	77,007
3	Randstad (Amsterdam-Rotterdam-Utrecht)	65,527
4	Moskva (Moscow)	45,857
5	Madrid	41,926
6	Berlin	41,923
7	Øresund (København-Lund-Malmö)	38,970
8	Milano (Milan)	37,917
9	Roma (Rome)	37,681
10	Barcelona	36,657
11	Stockholm-Uppsala	35,257
12	München (Munich)	32,132
13	Oxford-Reading	30,374
14	Manchester-Liverpool	30,144
15	Dortmund-Düsseldorf-Köln (Cologne)	29,351
16	Edinburgh-Glasgow	29,151
17	Cambridge	26,927
18	Frankfurt am Main	26,221
19	Genève-Lausanne	25,996
20	Zürich	25,720
21	Wien (Vienna)	24,084
22	Mannheim-Heidelberg	23,324
23	Sheffield-Leeds	22,306
24	Basel-Mulhouse-Freiburg	22,295
25	Bruxelles-Antwerpen (Brussels-Antwerp)	21,957

Source: Andersson et al. (2013).

distant locations. Similarly, we may expect scientists to aim for communication with the greatest possible number of other scientists at a given distance. The definition of accessibility to scientists from area i is:

$$a_i^x = \Sigma_{j=1}^{N} f(d_{ij}) x_j; \qquad (13.3)$$

where:
a_i^x = accessibility to scientists, x, from area i;
$f(d_{ij})$ = a positive and strictly decreasing function of the distance between two areas i and j;
x_j = the number of scientists in area j.

Time, space and capital

The positive convex distance function $f(d_{ij})$ implies that the accessibility to a given number of scientists decreases with increases in the distance between regions i and j. A reasonable and commonly used measure of $f(d_{ij})$ is:

$$e^{-\beta d_{ij}} \text{ with } \beta \geq 0 \text{ and } d \geq 0. \tag{13.4}$$

Here d is defined as the time distance by the transport mode that scientists normally use. This functional form implies that accessibility is a spatial analogue to the discounted total value of revenues in capital theory. An advantage of this functional form is the property that $e^{-\beta d}$ has the limits $+1$ if $d \to 0$ and 0 if $d \to \infty$.

The second important factor in scientists' location choice is the scientific material infrastructure such as laboratories, libraries, supercomputers and other large-scale facilities and equipment in universities and R&D-intensive firms. Noted examples of such infrastructure include CERN near Geneva, the new ESS unit in the Øresund region and the IBM research facility in Connecticut. This can be denoted as the accessibility measure $a_i^s = \sum_j^N e^{-cd_{ij}} S_j$, where S_j = scientific infrastructure in region j. The value of good accessibility to scientific infrastructure will of course decrease with an increase in the number of users, leading to bottlenecks and other congestion phenomena.

A third potentially important factor in the choice of location is the relative real rate of subsidies for scientific research in region i, W_i. We further assume that the level of algorithmic complexity, c_A, remains constant in the short run and acts as a vector of level parameters in the Q-mapping.

It has been shown that a non-linear Eigen-value equation determining the endogenous clustering has an equilibrium solution with a positive equalized rate of return ρ at the associated positive human capital vector $\mathbf{x}$ in:

$$\rho \mathbf{x} = \mathbf{Q}(\mathbf{x}, a^S, \mathbf{W}, c_A); \tag{13.5}$$

where $\mathbf{Q}(\mathbf{x})$ is a continuous, quasi-concave mapping from R^+ to R^+ (Nikaido, 1968).

In the vicinity of equilibrium, $\rho(\mathbf{Q})$ can be locally linearized as $\mathbf{Q}(x) = \mathbf{Q}(x^*)$, where x^* is x in equilibrium. We then have the Eigen-equation:

$$\rho \mathbf{z} = \mathbf{Q}(x^*)\mathbf{z}; \tag{13.6}$$

with the equilibrium growth rate $\rho(\mathbf{Q}(x^*))$. Applying the Perron–Frobenius theorem allows us to conclude that the rate of return to scientific knowledge capital ρ will increase with:

1. an increase in the scientific infrastructure of any region;
2. a decrease in any (transport, transaction or cognitive) distance, d_{ij};
3. a decrease in the general distance friction, β.

Changes of type 1., 2. and 3. influence the rate of return to science capital in all nodes to the same extent—but only in the very long run after full attainment of general equilibrium.

CONCLUSIONS

Inventions and other forms of creativity depend on external financial support. In recent decades, this has become a priority of governments and industries seeking dynamic comparative advantages. However, the share of R&D spending that is devoted to the type of basic scientific research that is usually carried out in universities only accounts for 10 to 30 percent in most countries. This share is especially low in East Asian countries such as Japan and South Korea. One cause of the low share allocated to the scientific infrastructure of society could be the myopic nature of political decision making, especially compared with the typical time horizon of more than a decade in high-tech and other industries that are preoccupied with the development of increasingly complex products and production systems.

In this chapter we represent the complexity of goods and production systems with the help of definitions first proposed by Solomonoff, Kolmogorov and Chaitin. The basic idea is that the slow and steady processes of scientific research generates increasingly complex theories and models, all of which are potentially useful for the more rapidly evolving system of industrial product and process development. In our model, firms perceive scientific theories and results as a more or less fixed knowledge infrastructure that they can make use of in their efforts to innovate products and technologies.

Hollingsworth has shown that the organization of complex research and development projects must be carried out by teams that are much more interdisciplinary and open-minded than is normally the case in industrial R&D. From this we conclude that the development of science and R&D toward increasingly complex theories, models, production systems and goods will generate an increasing demand for more complex cognitive capacity among individual scientists as well as within laboratories and other research organizations at the micro level. Moreover, the increase in expected (but uncertain) individual creativity that accompanies good access to new and diversified knowledge provides strong arguments for locating such micro research organizations in large, open and diverse city regions.

We would thus expect scientific activities to be clustered in space. In line with this hypothesis, we introduce a spatial general equilibrium model of scientific clustering. This model is a non-linear Eigen-equation, in which scientific collaboration gains, R&D support systems and the level of complexity of products and production systems act as determinants of the pattern of clustering of scientists.

The statistics on scientific output in European city regions show that the distribution is strongly clustered in favor of 25 leading regions, most of which are located near the economic core of Western Europe. These regions are centers of future dynamic comparative advantages in the production of complex products. Similar urban clustering phenomena exist on the east and west coasts of North America and along the Tokyo-Hong Kong corridor in East Asia.

APPENDIX 13.1

We have $\rho x = \mathbf{Q}(\mathbf{x}, a^s, \mathbf{W}, c_A)$; where $\mathbf{Q}(\mathbf{x})$ is a continuous, quasi-concave mapping from R^+ to R^+. For such a system a theorem by Nikaido (1968) can be applied.

Assumptions:

1. $\mathbf{Q}(x) = (Q_i(x))$ is defined for all $x \geq 0$.
2. $\mathbf{Q}(x)$ is continuous as a mapping $\mathbf{Q}: R^n_+ \to R^n_+$ except possibly at $x = 0$.
3. $\mathbf{Q}(x)$ is positively homogeneous of order m, $0 \leq m \leq 1$ in the sense that $\mathbf{Q}(x) \geq 0$ and $x \geq 0$. For such a system a theorem by Nikaido (1968) can be applied.

Theorem: Let $\Lambda = \{\mathbf{Q}(x) = \rho x\}$ *for* $x \epsilon p_n$; where:

$$p_n = \left\{ x \mid x \geq 0, \sum_{i=1}^{n} x_i = 1 \right\}$$

is the standard simplex. Then $\mathbf{Q}(x)$ contains a maximum characteristic value which is denoted $\rho(\mathbf{Q})$. Furthermore, if $\mathbf{Q}(x)$ is homogeneous of degree 1, that is, if $m = 1$ as a special case of assumption (c), then $\rho(\mathbf{Q})$ is the largest of all the Eigen-values of $\mathbf{Q}(x)$.

Proof: Nikaido (1968).

14. Looking ahead

The theory of competitive equilibrium is a natural starting point for most economists—whether they approach a partial, general, applied or theoretical market problem. The basic ideas were formulated in the eighteenth century by Adam Smith, and refined and mathematically reformulated by Léon Walras and Gustav Cassel. Mathematicians Abraham Wald and Gérard Debreu brought the theory in contact with modern mathematics and could show that a general equilibrium of non-negative prices and quantities could exist under seemingly reasonable axiomatic assumptions of convexity of preferences and production techniques.

General equilibrium theory is based on an analysis of the differential equations $dz/dt = g(z)$, with z = a vector of excess demands, and $dp/dt = f(p)$ having an equilibrium if ($g(z)$, $f(p) = 0$ or ≤ 0) and ($z, p \geq 0$). The derivation of $f(p)$ and $g(z)$ from preferences and production possibilities of all the numerous agents was an impressive effort by twentieth-century economists and mathematicians.

There are three key issues in general competitive equilibrium theory:

1. *Existence*: Is there any guarantee that an equilibrium is to be found, given sufficient search time? Several existence proofs are available based on fixed-point theorems by Brouwer, Kakutani and others or on Newton algorithm theorems.
2. *Uniqueness*: Will there be a unique general equilibrium or will there be multiple equilibria? Uniqueness is not generally guaranteed. It can for instance be shown that wealth effects can generate multiple equilibria.
3. *Stability*: Is the general equilibrium of a competitive economy globally or at least locally stable? Walras had assumed (in accordance with Adam Smith) that an *invisible hand* guided each market towards an equilibrium state. The invisible hand of the (invisible) decision maker examines each good in the market and increases the price of the good if its demand is more than its supply, and analogously decreases its price if an excess supply is present. Léon Walras had proposed the first such process in 1874. Arrow and Hurwicz (1958) and Arrow et al. (1959) show that the dynamic price adjustment process always converges to an equilibrium if the goods are *gross substitutes*—corresponding to a

situation with omnipresent negative feedback. It was then speculated that the same process would work for any number of "reasonable" markets for divisible goods. However, Scarf (1960) contends that instability is to be expected as demonstrated with the help of a series of counterexamples. Among these is a simple example with a unique equilibrium involving three consumers and three complementary commodities. Scarf (ibid.) demonstrates that if the initial price vector differs from the equilibrium price vector, a process ensues which generates a cycle of non-equilibrium price vectors that never converges to the equilibrium state.

4. *Efficiency*: Edgeworth (1872/1925) shows that states of competitive general equilibrium are Pareto efficient in the sense that an improvement in the welfare of an agent can only occur at the expense of the welfare of others. Edgeworth's argument assumes an exogenously determined distribution of wealth. Much of the attractiveness of general equilibrium theory is associated with its Pareto efficiency property; this has often been used as a benchmark when comparing market equilibria to economic systems run with the aid of politically centralized planning and control of trading and production activities.

Much of the elegance of general equilibrium theory (GET) was achieved at considerable expense in terms of axiomatic simplifications. Indivisibilities and other causes of increasing returns are not compatible with the theory, and interdependencies between producers or consumers can generate positive feedback loops that destroy the stability of the equilibrium states.

These problems are to a great extent the result of the formulation of GET as a static and space-free construct. Debreu's "trick"—which was to use indices to date and locate variables—cannot remedy this general problem of GET. Reformulating GET as a variational inequality model or as a two-dimensional spatial theory has been shown to address many if not all of the problems of neoclassical a-spatial theory (cf. Beckmann and Puu, 1985; Dafermos and Nagurney, 1987).

INSTITUTIONS, NETWORKS, KNOWLEDGE

There are even deeper problems with GET than the ones mentioned earlier in terms of implicit assumptions or disregarded external conditions. The most important of such external conditions are institutions, networks and knowledge.

As pointed out by Adam Smith and later repeated by Leonid Hurwicz, Don Saari, Jean-Pierre Aubin, Arrigo Cellina, Stephen Smale and Hal

Varian, there is a need for economic laws and other *institutions* that act to ensure the consistency of the dynamic working of markets. In fact, competitive equilibrium relies on the *constancy* of a multitude of institutions, as argued by Ronald Coase and Oliver Williamson. Public information as well as private and public knowledge among the agents are also predetermined in GET; these factors are—with an unusually high degree of unrealism—represented as constant techniques of production and unchanging consumer preferences. As already mentioned, most of general equilibrium theory is formulated for an a-spatial economy, with no need for networks that connect agents and their marketable goods to one another.

Thus, a generalization of general competitive equilibrium theory requires putting the games of GET on an arena of institutions, knowledge and networks. This makes it possible to analyze the topological stability and phase transitions that involve structures of production, consumption and market prices.

THE GENERALITY OF CAPITAL IN REPRESENTING GOODS AND FACTORS OF PRODUCTION

In the neoclassical construct the resources of production are conventionally subdivided into labor, capital and land (or natural resources). With the introduction of time and space, resources must be defined in terms of their physical or economic *durability*. Any good will then provide a chain of utility (or returns) over the projected and necessarily uncertain future.

A firm will only offer a labor contract to a potential employee if its owners (or their representatives) expect the net present value of her contribution to be positive. The decision to invest in a new employee is rarely a question of just evaluating the physical strength and stamina of an individual. Instead the prospective employee is evaluated as "human capital" with different productive attributes such as education-induced knowledge, social capital such as connectivity within interpersonal networks and creativity in problem solving. The potential employee must then be evaluated as a capital investment with uncertain returns.

Similarly, a good is only attractive to a consumer if the expected net present value is positive. This value is easy to estimate for a common perishable good such as a banana, but it becomes a much more multifaceted and time-consuming problem for buyers of automobiles, apartments or degree programs.

Ordinary goods, which differ in their durability of returns and complementarity to other inputs in market or household production, should thus be redefined as capital; such capital may contribute to either productive or consumptive purposes. Even the services that people sell are capital. The duration of one of Bob Dylan's performances is an example of the durability of one type of service-derived capital. A musical performance yields an immediate short-term utility flow, and possibly also a longer-term impact flow such as reconfigured social relations or even a new world view. Consultancy services will likewise have a short-term and a long-term flow of returns to the firm buying such services.

Even land should be seen as capital, with returns that are affected by accessibility in social and geographical space, as Frank Knight pointed out. Accessibility is not a free public good; it is the consequence of investments in nodes and links that create networks. Inaccessible land such as most parts of Antarctica would thus have no net present value and is on par with useless buildings and machines.

A general equilibrium theory can be formulated, if based on different forms of capital with differences in durability (and rates of depreciation). Von Neumann (1938/1970) proves that a dynamic deterministic economy model with n capital goods (including labor and land as capital) will have a dynamic saddle point equilibrium with semi-positive economic activities and a positive rate of growth at the equilibrium corresponding to the real rate of interest.

A reformulation of economic theory to take time and space into proper consideration requires that:

1. All goods and services are classified as different forms of capital in terms of the durability of their returns.
2. All goods and services are also classified according to the collectivity of their returns.
3. Goods must be positioned in space according to their accessibility, which influences their returns.
4. Extremely durable goods with collective returns are defined as the infrastructure of an economic system.

Under these conditions, it is possible that a short-term general (neoclassical) competitive equilibrium will exist. It is also possible that a general medium-term growth equilibrium will exist, but only if agents perceive the systemic infrastructure as a stable arena for economic interactions. Agents will however only perceive infrastructural subsets such as institutions, scientific knowledge and transport networks as constant in short-run and perhaps medium-run equilibrating market processes. Even within short periods of time there will be small and sometimes persistent changes to the connectivity of networks, to the level of shared knowledge and to the formal or informal institutional conditions. At some critical level, such changes will cause bifurcations, leading to a phase transition of the economic structure. These transitions invariably cause fundamental changes to the relative prices of goods and to excess demand for various types of capital, as is implied by the application of synergetic theory to economic phenomena.

During these phase transitions, structural (i.e. Knightian) uncertainty will even affect seemingly routine short-term decisions; creativity and innovativeness will thus play an even greater role than in less turbulent periods. The resulting (temporally and spatially bounded) logistical revolutions create unusually widespread opportunities for reaping entrepreneurial profits, but also unusually unsettling experiences for those who are trapped in obsolescent economic roles. They provide a land of opportunity for state-of-the-art innovators, but destruction for those who are set in their ways.

References

Acemoglu, D. and J.A. Robinson (2012). *Why Nations Fail: The Origins of Power, Prosperity and Poverty.* London, UK: Profile Books.

Aldrich, H.E. and M.A. Martinez (2001). "Many are called but few are chosen: an evolutionary perspective for the study of entrepreneurship." *Entrepreneurship: Theory and Practice*, 25(4): 41–56.

Alonso, W. (1964). *Location and Land Use.* Cambridge, MA, USA: Harvard University Press.

Anderson, L.G. and J.C. Seijo (2010). *Bioeconomics of Fisheries Management.* New York, NY: Wiley-Blackwell.

Andersson, Å.E. (1985a). *Kreativitet: storstadens framtid.* Stockholm: Prisma.

Andersson, Å.E. (1985b). "Creativity and economic dynamic modelling." In: D.F. Batten, J. Casti and B. Johansson (eds.), *Economic Evolution and Structural Adjustment.* Berlin: Springer, pp. 27–45.

Andersson, Å.E. and D.E. Andersson (2006). *The Economics of Experiences, the Arts and Entertainment.* Cheltenham, UK and Northampton, MA, USA: Edward Elgar.

Andersson, Å.E., D.E. Andersson and C.W. Matthiessen (2013). *Öresundsregionen: den dynamiska metropolen.* Stockholm: Dialogos.

Andersson, Å.E. and D.E. Andersson (2014). *Byggmarknadens regleringar: ett hinder för Sveriges ekonomiska utveckling.* Stockholm: Entreprenörskapsforum.

Andersson, Å.E. and D.E. Andersson (2015). "Creative cities and the new global hierarchy." *Applied Spatial Analysis and Policy*, 8(3): 181–98.

Andersson, Å.E. and M.J. Beckmann (2009). *Economics and Knowledge.* Cheltenham, UK and Northampton, MA, USA: Edward Elgar.

Andersson, Å.E. and G.V.G. Ferraro (1983). "Accessibility and density distributions in metropolitan areas: theory and empirical studies." *Papers in Regional Science,* 52(1): 141–58.

Andersson, Å.E., T. Fürth and I. Holmberg (1997). *70-talister.* Stockholm: Natur och kultur.

Andersson, Å.E. and B. Johansson (1984). "Knowledge intensity and product cycles in metropolitan regions." IIASA Working Paper WP-84-01, Laxenburg, Austria.

Andersson, Å.E. and A. Karlqvist (1976). "Population and capital in geographical space: the problem of general equilibrium allocation." In: J. Loz and M. Loz (eds.), *Computing Equilibria: How and Why?* Amsterdam: North Holland.

Andersson, Å.E. and J. Mantsinen (1980). "Mobility of resources, accessibility of knowledge and economic growth." *Behavioral Science*, 25: 353–66.

Andersson, D.E. (1997). *Hedonic Prices and Center Accessibility: Conceptual Foundations and an Empirical Hedonic Study of the Market for Condominium Housing in Singapore.* Stockholm: KTH Högskoletryckeriet.

Andersson, D.E. (2005). "The spatial nature of entrepreneurship." *Quarterly Journal of Austrian Economics*, 8(2): 21–34.

Andersson, D.E. (2008). *Property Rights, Consumption and the Market Process.* Cheltenham, UK and Northampton, MA, USA: Edward Elgar.

Andersson, D.E. (2011). "Creative cities need less government." In: D.E. Andersson, Å.E. Andersson and C. Mellander (eds.), *Handbook of Creative Cities*, pp. 327–42.

Andersson, D.E. (2014). "Cities and planning: the role of system constraints." In: D.E. Andersson and S. Moroni (eds.), *Cities and Private Planning: Property Rights, Entrepreneurship and Transaction Costs.* Cheltenham, UK and Northampton, MA, USA: Edward Elgar, pp. 19–37.

Andersson, D.E. and Å.E. Andersson (2013). "The economic value of experience goods." In: J. Sundbo and F. Sørensen (eds.), *Handbook on the Experience Economy.* Cheltenham, UK and Northampton, MA, USA: Edward Elgar.

Andersson, D.E., Å.E. Andersson, B. Hårsman and Z. Daghbashyan (2015). "Unemployment in European regions: structural problems vs. the Eurozone hypothesis." *Journal of Economic Geography*, 15(5): 883–905.

Andersson, D.E., Å.E. Andersson and C. Mellander (eds.) (2011). *Handbook of Creative Cities.* Cheltenham, UK and Northampton, MA, USA: Edward Elgar, pp. 72–84.

Andersson, D.E. and M. Jia (2016). "Official and subjective hotel attributes compared: online hotel rates in Shanghai." Conference paper, 2016 Conference on Regional, Urban and Spatial Economics, Southwestern University of Finance and Economics, Chengdu, Sichuan, China.

Andersson, D.E. and S. Moroni (eds.) (2014). *Cities and Private Planning: Property Rights, Entrepreneurship and Transaction Costs.* Cheltenham, UK and Northampton, MA, USA: Edward Elgar.

Andersson, D.E., O.F. Shyr and J. Fu (2010). "Does high-speed rail accessibility influence residential property prices? Hedonic estimates from southern Taiwan." *Journal of Transport Geography*, 18(1): 166–74.

Andersson, D.E. and J.A. Taylor (2012). "Institutions, agglomeration economies, and interstate migration." In: D.E. Andersson (ed.), *The Spatial Market Process*. Bingley, UK: Emerald, pp. 233–63.

Andersson, H. and P. Lundborg (2007). "Perception of own death risk: An analysis of road-traffic and overall mortality risks." *Journal of Risk and Uncertainty*, 34(1): 67–84.

Anderstig, C. and B. Hårsman (1986). "On occupation structure and location pattern in the Stockholm region." *Regional Science and Urban Economics*, 16(1): 97–122.

Anundsen, A.K., R. Nymoen, T.S. Krogh and J. Vislie (2012). "The macroeconomics of Trygve Haavelmo." *Nordic Journal of Political Economy*, 37(2).

Arrow, K.J. (1986). "Rationality of self and others in an economic system." *Journal of Business*, 59: S385–S399.

Arrow, K.J., H.D. Block and L. Hurwicz (1959). "On the stability of the competitive equilibrium, II." *Econometrica*, 27(1): 82–109.

Arrow, K.J. and L. Hurwicz (1958). "On the stability of the competitive equilibrium, I." *Econometrica*, 26(4): 522–52.

Arthur, W.B. (1983). "On competing technologies and historical small events: the dynamics of choice under increasing returns." IIASA Working Paper No. 83-090, International Institute for Applied Systems Analysis, Laxenburg, Austria.

Arthur, W.B. (1994). "Inductive reasoning and bounded rationality." *American Economic Review* (Papers and Proceedings), 84: 406–11.

Arthur, W.B., J.H. Holland, B.D. LeBaron, R.G. Palmer and P. Tayler (1996). "Asset pricing under endogenous expectations in an artificial stock market." SSRN eLibrary.

Barzel, Y. (1989). *Economic Analysis of Property Rights*. New York, NY: Cambridge University Press.

Baumol, W.J. (2004). *The Free-Market Innovation Machine: Analyzing the Growth Miracle of Capitalism*. Princeton, NJ: Princeton University Press.

Becker, G.S. (1976). *The Economic Approach to Human Behavior*. Chicago, IL: University of Chicago Press.

Beckmann, M.J. (1952). "A continuous model of transportation." *Econometrica*, 20: 643–60.

Beckmann, M.J. (1953). "The partial equilibrium of a continuous space market." *Weltwirtschaftliches Archiv*, 71: 73–89.

Beckmann, M.J. (1972). "Von Thünen revisited: a neoclassical land use model." *Swedish Journal of Economics*, 74: 1–7.

Beckmann, M.J. (1976). "Spatial price policies revisited." *Bell Journal of Economics*, 7(2): 619–30.

Beckmann, M.J. (2000). "Wilhelm Launhardt: location theorist." In: P.W.J. Batey and P. Friedrich (eds.), *Regional Competition*. Heidelberg: Springer.

Beckmann, M.J. and T. Puu (1985). *Spatial Economics: Density, Potential, and Flow.* Amsterdam: North Holland.

Bellman, R. (1958). "On a routing problem." *Quarterly of Applied Mathematics*, 16: 87–90.

Bertaud, A. (2001). "Metropolis: a measure of the spatial organization of 7 large cities." http://alain-bertaud.com.

Bertaud, A. and S. Malpezzi (2003). "The spatial distribution of population in 48 world cities: implications for economies in transition." University of Wisconsin.

Black, F. (1972). "Capital market equilibrium with restricted borrowing." *Journal of Business*, 45(3): 444–54.

Blanchard, O. (2008). *Macroeconomics*. New York, NY: Prentice Hall.

Böhm-Bawerk, E. von (1891). *The Positive Theory of Capital*. London, UK: Macmillan.

Box, G. and D. Cox (1964). "An analysis of transformations." *Journal of the Royal Statistical Society, Series B*, 26: 211–52.

Bracha, A. and D. Brown (2010). "Affective decision-making: a theory of optimism bias." Cowles Foundation Discussion Paper No. 1759.

Braithwaite, R.B. (1955/1968). *Scientific Explanation; A Study of the Function of Theory, Probability and Law in Science.* Cambridge, UK: Cambridge University Press.

Braudel, F. (1979). *Civilisation matérielle, économie et capitalisme, XVe – XVIIIe siècle* (3 volumes). Paris: Armand Colin.

Brems, H. (1968). *Quantitative Economic Theory: A Synthetic Approach.* New York, NY: John Wiley.

Bröcker, J. (2014). "German roots of regional science." In: P. Nijkamp, A. Rose and K. Kourtit (eds.), *Regional Science Matters: Studies Dedicated to Walter Isard*. Berlin: Springer, pp. 87–103.

Bródy, A. (1970). *Proportions, Prices and Planning: A Mathematical Restatement of the Labour Theory of Value.* Amsterdam: North Holland.

Burkard, R.E. and E. Çela (1999). "Linear assignment problems and extensions." In: D.-Z. Du and P.M. Pardalos (eds.), *Handbook of Combinatorial Optimization: Supplement Volume A*. Berlin: Springer, pp. 75–149.

Butos, W. and R. Koppl (1997). "The varieties of subjectivism: Keynes and Hayek on expectations." *History of Political Economy*, 29(2): 327–59.

Cairns, G.A. and R.D. Davis (2005). "Optimal timing of resource development: a comparison of stopping rules under certainty and uncertainty." Working paper, Department of Economics, McGill University, Montreal, QC, Canada.

Cassel, G. (1903). *The Nature and Necessity of Interest*. London, UK: Macmillan.

Cassel, G. (1918/1932). *Theoretische sozialökonomie*. Leipzig: C.F. Winter.

Casti, J.L. and DePauli, W. (2000). *Gödel. A Life of Logic.* Cambridge, MA, USA: Perseus.

Chaitin, G.J. (1966). "On the length of programs for computing finite binary sequences." *Journal of the ACM*, 13(4): 547–69.

Cheshire, P.C. (2011). "Some unintended productivity consequences of good intentions: the British land use planning system." Working Paper, Spatial Economics Research Centre, London School of Economics and Political Science, London.

Cheshire, P.C. and C.A.L. Hilber (2008). "Office space supply restrictions in Britain: the political economy of market revenge." *Economic Journal*, 118(529): F185–F221.

Cheshire, P.C., C.A.L. Hilber and I. Kaplanis (2015). "Land use regulation and productivity—land matters: evidence from a UK supermarket chain." *Journal of Economic Geography*, 15(1): 43–73.

Cheshire, P.C., M. Nathan and H.G. Overman (2014). *Urban Economics and Urban Policy: Challenging Conventional Policy Wisdom*. Cheltenham, UK and Northampton, MA, USA: Edward Elgar.

Cheshire, P.C. and S. Sheppard (1995). "On the price of land and the value of amenities." *Economica*, 62: 247–67.

Clark, A. (1997). "Economic reason: the interplay of individual learning and external structure." In: J.N. Drobak and J.V.C. Nye (eds.), *The Frontiers of the New Institutional Economics*. San Diego, CA: Academic Press.

Clark, C. (2010). *Mathematical Bioeconomics: The Mathematics of Conservation*. New York, NY: Wiley.

Coase, R.H. (1937). "The nature of the firm." *Economica*, 4: 386–406.

Coleman, J.S. (1988). "Social capital in the creation of human capital." *American Journal of Sociology*, 94: S95–S120.

Conlisk, J. (1988). "Optimization cost." *Journal of Economic Behavior and Organization*, 9(3): 213–22.

Cox, W. and H. Pavletich (2016). *12th Annual Demographia International Housing Affordability Survey*. St. Louis, MO: Demographia Institute.

Dafermos, S. and A. Nagurney (1987). "Oligopolistic and competitive behavior of spatially separated markets." *Regional Science and Urban Economics*, 17: 245–54.

De Long, J.B. and A. Shleifer (1993). "Princes and merchants: European city growth before the Industrial Revolution." *Journal of Law and Economics*, 36(2): 671–702.

De Soto, H. (2000). *The Mystery of Capital: Why Capitalism Triumphs in the West and Fails Everywhere Else*. New York, NY: Basic Books.

Deaton, A. (2006). "The great escape: A review of Robert Fogel's 'The Escape from Hunger and Premature Death, 1700–2100.'" *Journal of Economic Literature*, 44(1): 106–14.

Debreu, G. (1959). *Theory of Value: An Axiomatic Analysis of Economic Equilibrium*. New Haven, CT: Yale University Press (Cowles Foundation Monographs Series).

Deneubourg, J.-L., S. Aron, S. Goss and J. Pasteels (1990). "The self-organizing exploratory pattern of the Argentine ant." *Journal of Insect Behavior*, 3(2): 159–68.

Diamond Aircraft (2015). www.diamondaircraft.com. Accessed 27 February 2017.

Dijkstra, E.W. (1959). "A note on two problems in connexion with graphs." *Numerische Mathematik*, 1: 269–71.

Dillenberger, D., A. Postlewaite and K. Rozen (2015). "Optimism and pessimism with expected utility." PIER Working Paper No. 15-009 (5th version).

Dixit, A.K. and R.S. Pindyck (1995). "The new option view of investment." Massachusetts Institute of Technology Working Paper No. 3794-95-EFA.

diZerega, G. (1989). "Democracy as a spontaneous order." *Critical Review*, 3(2): 206–40.

Domar, E. (1946). "Capital expansion, rate of growth, and employment." *Econometrica*, 14(2): 137–47.

Duesenberry, J.S. (1948). "Income—consumption relations and their implications." In: L. Metzler et al. (eds.), *Income, Employment, and Public Policy*. New York, NY: W.W. Norton.

Duesenberry, J.S. (1949). *Income, Saving and the Theory of Consumer Behavior*. Cambridge, MA, USA: Harvard University Press.

Düppe, T. and E.R. Weintraub (2014). *Finding Equilibrium: Arrow, Debreu, McKenzie and the Problem of Scientific Credit*. Princeton, NJ: Princeton University Press.

Dupuit, A.J.É.J. (1844). "De la mesure de l'utilité des travaux publics." *Annales des ponts et chaussées,* Second series, No. 8.

Edgeworth, F.Y. (1872/1925). *Papers Relating to Political Economy* (3 volumes). Paris: Gallica website of the Bibliothèque nationale de France (http://gallica.bnf.fr/), accessed 27 February 2017.

Epstein, R. (1995). *Simple Rules for a Complex World*. Cambridge, MA, USA: Harvard University Press.

Euler, L. (1741a). "Solutio problematis ad geometriam situs pertinentis." *Commentarii academiae scientiarum Petropolitanae*, 8: 128–40.

Euler, L. (1741b). *Scientia navalis sev tractatus – theoriam universam*. St. Petersburg: Typographia Academiae Scientiarum.

Evans, A.W. (1991). "'Rabbit hutches on postage stamps': planning, development and political economy." *Urban Studies*, 28(6): 853–70.

Faustmann, M. (1849/1968). "Calculation of the value which forest land and immature stands possess for forestry." Translated by W. Linnard (1968) from *Allgemeine Forst- und Jagdzeitung* (1849), pp. 27–55.

Fisher, I. (1906). *The Nature of Capital and Income.* New York, NY: The Macmillan Company.

Fisher, I. (1907). *The Rate of Interest: Its Nature, Determination, and Relation to Economic Phenomena.* New York, NY: The Macmillan Company.

Fisher, I. (1930). *The Theory of Interest as Determined by Impatience to Spend Income and Opportunity to Invest It.* Clifton, NJ: Augustus M. Kelley.

Florance, A.C., N.G. Miller, J. Spivey and R. Peng (2010). "Slicing, dicing, and scoping the size of the U.S. commercial real estate market." *Journal of Real Estate Portfolio Management*, 16(2): 111–28.

Florida, R. (2002). *The Rise of the Creative Class.* New York, NY: Basic Books.

Foldvary, F. (1994). *Public Goods and Private Communities: The Market Provision of Social Services.* Aldershot, UK and Brookfield, VT, USA: Edward Elgar.

Fonseca, J.W. (1988). "Urban rank-size hierarchy: a mathematical interpretation." Monograph #8, Institute of Mathematical Geography, University of Michigan, Ann Arbor, MI.

Foss, K., N.J. Foss, P.G. Klein and S.K. Klein (2007). "The entrepreneurial organization of heterogeneous capital." *Journal of Management Studies*, 44(7): 1165–86.

Foss, N.J. and P.G. Klein (2012). *Organizing Entrepreneurial Judgment: A New Approach to the Firm.* Cambridge, UK: Cambridge University Press.

Friedman, M. (1953). *Essays in Positive Economics.* Chicago, IL: University of Chicago Press.

Friedman, M. (1957). *A Theory of the Consumption Function.* Princeton NJ: Princeton University Press.

Friedmann, J. (1987). *Planning in the Public Domain.* Princeton, NJ: Princeton University Press.

Fujita, M. (1989). *Urban Economic Theory: Land Use and City Size.* Cambridge, UK: Cambridge University Press.

Fujita, M. and J.-F. Thisse (2002). *Economics of Agglomeration: Cities, Industrial Location and Regional Growth.* Cambridge, UK: Cambridge University Press.

Gintis, H. (2007). "The dynamics of general equilibrium." *Economic Journal*, 117: 1280–309.

Glaeser, E.L., J. Gyourko and R.E. Saks (2005). "Why is Manhattan so expensive? Regulation and the rise in housing prices." *Journal of Law and Economics*, 48(2): 331–69.

Glaeser, E.L. and D. Mare (2001). "Cities and skills." *Journal of Labor Economics*, 19: 316–42.

Glaeser, E.L., A. Saiz, G. Burtless and W.C. Strange (2004). "The rise of the skilled city." Brookings-Wharton Papers on Urban Affairs, Brookings Institution Press, Washington, DC.

Gode, D. and S. Sunder (1992). "Allocative efficiency of markets with zero intelligence (ZI) traders: markets as a partial substitute for individual rationality." Working Paper 1992:16, Carnegie Mellon Graduate School of Industrial Administration, Pittsburgh, PA.

Gordon, P. and W. Cox (2014). "Modern cities: their role and their private planning roots." In: D.E. Andersson and S. Moroni (eds.), *Cities and Private Planning: Property Rights, Entrepreneurship and Transaction Costs*. Cheltenham, UK and Northampton, MA, USA: Edward Elgar, pp. 155–73.

Granger, C.W.J. (1969). "Investigating causal relations by econometric models and cross-spectral methods." *Econometrica*, 37(3): 424–38.

Granger, C.W.J. (1980). "Testing for causality: a personal viewpoint." *Journal of Economic Dynamics and Control*, 2: 329–52.

Granovetter, M.S. (1973). "The strength of weak ties." *American Journal of Sociology*, 78(6): 1360–80.

Granovetter, M.S. (1978). 'Threshold models of collective behavior." *American Journal of Sociology*, 83: 1420–43.

Grübler, A. (1990). *The Rise and Fall of Infrastructures: Dynamics of Evolution and Technological Change in Transport*. Berlin: Physica-Verlag.

Haken, H. (1978). *Synergetics: An Introduction* (1st edition). Berlin: Springer.

Haken, H. (1983). *Synergetics, an Introduction: Nonequilibrium Phase Transitions and Self-organization in Physics, Chemistry, and Biology* (3rd revised and enlarged edition). New York, NY: Springer.

Haken, H. (1993). *Advanced Synergetics: Instability Hierarchies of Self-organizing Systems and Devices*. New York, NY: Springer.

Hanau, A. (1928). Die Prognose der Schweinepreise (Vierteljahreshefte zur Konjunkturforschung). Berlin: Verlag Reimar Hobbing.

Hardy, G.H., J.E. Littlewood and G. Pólya (1934/1988). *Inequalities*. Cambridge, UK: Cambridge University Press.

Harrod, R.F. (1948). *Towards a Dynamic Economics*. London, UK: Macmillan.

Harvey, D. (1973). *Social Justice and the City*. Baltimore, MD: Johns Hopkins University Press.

Haskel, J. and R. Sadun (2009). "Regulation and UK retailing productivity: evidence from micro data." Discussion Paper No. 7140, Centre for Economic Policy Research, London, United Kingdom.

Hawkins, D. (1948). "Some conditions of macroeconomic stability." *Econometrica*, 16(4), pp. 309–22.

Hayek, F.A. (1931/1967). *Prices and Production* (2nd revised edition). New York, NY: Augustus M. Kelley.

Hayek, F.A. (1941/2014). *The Pure Theory of Capital.* London, UK: Routledge.

Hayek, F.A. (1952). *The Sensory Order.* Chicago, IL: University of Chicago Press.

Hayek, F.A. (1964/1967). "The theory of complex phenomena." In: F.A. Hayek, *Studies in Philosophy, Politics and Economics.* New York, NY: Simon and Schuster, pp. 55–70.

Hayek, F.A. (1973). *Rules and Order* (Volume 1 of *Law, Legislation and Liberty*). Chicago, IL: University of Chicago Press.

Hayek, F.A. (1988). *The Fatal Conceit: The Errors of Socialism* (edited by W.W. Bartley). London, UK: Routledge.

Heckscher, E.F. (1935). *Mercantilism* (2 volumes). London, UK: Allen & Unwin.

Heckscher, E.F. (1941). *Svenskt arbete och liv: från medeltiden till nutiden.* Stockholm: Albert Bonniers förlag.

Hirshleifer, J. (1958). "On the theory of optimal investment decision." *Journal of Political Economy*, 66(4): 329–52.

Hofstadter, D.R. (1979/1999). *Gödel, Escher, Bach: An Eternal Golden Braid.* New York, NY: Basic Books.

Holcombe, R.G. (2011). "Cultivating creativity: market creation of agglomeration economies." In: D.E. Andersson, Å.E. Andersson and C. Mellander (eds.), *Handbook of Creative Cities.* Cheltenham, UK and Northampton, MA, USA: Edward Elgar, pp. 387–404.

Hollingsworth, J.R. (2007). "High cognitive complexity and the making of major scientific discoveries." In: A. Sales and M. Fournier (eds.), *Knowledge, Communication, and Creativity.* London, UK and Thousand Oaks, CA, USA: Sage, pp. 129–55.

Hollingsworth, J.R. (2009). "The role of institutions and organizations in shaping radical scientific innovations." In: L. Magnusson and J. Ottosson (eds.), *The Evolution of Path Dependence.* Cheltenham, UK and Northampton, MA, USA: Edward Elgar, pp. 139–65.

Hotelling, H. (1921). "A mathematical theory of migration." M.S. Thesis, University of Washington, Seattle, WA, United States.

Hurwicz, L. (1960). "Optimality and informational efficiency in resource allocation processes." In: K.J. Arrow, S. Karlin and P. Suppes (eds.),

Mathematical Models in the Social Sciences. Palo Alto, CA: Stanford University Press, pp. 27–47.

Hurwicz, L. (1973). "The design of mechanisms for resource allocation." *American Economic Review*, 63(2): 1–30.

Hurwicz, L. and K.J. Arrow (1972). "Decision making under ignorance." In: C.F. Carter and J.L. Ford (eds.), *Uncertainty and Expectations in Economics: Essays in Honour of G.L.S. Shackle*. Oxford, UK: Basil Blackwell.

ING Economic and Financial Capital (2016). www.ingwb.com/insights/research/2016, accessed 27 February 2017.

Inglehart, R. (1977). *The Silent Revolution: Changing Values and Political Styles among Western Publics*. Princeton, NJ: Princeton University Press.

Inglehart, R. (1997). *Modernization and Postmodernization: Cultural, Economic, and Political Change in 43 Societies*. Princeton, NJ: Princeton University Press.

Inglehart, R. and C. Welzel (2005). *Modernization, Cultural Change and Democracy: The Human Development Sequence*. New York, NY: Cambridge University Press.

Jacobs, J. (1961/1992). *The Death and Life of Great American Cities*. New York: Vintage.

Jevons, W.S. (1875). "Commercial crises and sun-spots." *Nature*, XIX: 33–7.

Johansson, B. and Å.E. Andersson (1998). "A Schloss Laxenburg model of product cycle dynamics." In: M.J. Beckmann, B. Johansson, F. Snickars and R. Thord (eds.), *Knowledge and Networks in a Dynamic Economy* (Festschrift in Honor of Åke E. Andersson). New York, NY and Berlin: Springer.

Johansson, B. and U. Strömquist (2005). *Västsverige och den nya ekonomiska geografin*. Göteborg: Västra Götalandsregionen.

Kaldor, N. (1934). "A classificatory note on the determination of equilibrium." *Review of Economic Studies*, 1: 122–36.

Kaldor, N. (1940). "A model of the trade cycle." *Economic Journal*, 50: 78–92.

Kasper, W., M.E. Streit and P.J. Boettke (2012). *Institutional Economics: Property, Competition, Policies* (2nd ed.). Cheltenham, UK and Northampton, MA, USA: Edward Elgar.

Kauffman, S.A. (1995). *At Home in the Universe: The Search for Laws of Self-Organization and Complexity*. New York, NY: Oxford University Press.

Kemeny, J., O. Morgenstern and G. Thompson (1956). "A generalization of the von Neumann model of an expanding economy." *Econometrica*, 24: 115–35.

Keynes, J.M. (1921). *Treatise on Probability.* London, UK: Macmillan.

Keynes, J.M. (1936). *The General Theory of Employment, Interest and Money.* London, UK: Palgrave Macmillan.

Kirman, A. (2006). "Demand theory and general equilibrium: from explanation to introspection, a journey down the wrong road." *History of Political Economy*, 38(Supplement 1): 246–80.

Kirzner, I.M. (1973). *Competition and Entrepreneurship.* Chicago, IL: University of Chicago Press.

Kirzner, I.M. (1985). *Discovery and the Capitalist Process.* Chicago, IL: University of Chicago Press.

Knight, F.H. (1921). *Risk, Uncertainty, and Profit.* Boston, MA: Hart, Schaffner & Marx.

Knight, F.H. (1924). "Some fallacies in the interpretation of social cost." *Quarterly Journal of Economics*, 38(4): 582–606.

Knight, F.H. (1934). "Capital, time, and the interest rate." *Economica*, 1: 257–86.

Knight, F.H. (1947/1982). *Freedom and Reform: Essays in Economics and Social Philosophy.* Indianapolis, IN: Liberty Press.

Koch, H. von (1904). "Sur une courbe continue sans tangente, obtenue par une construction géométrique élémentaire." *Arkiv för matematik*, 1: 681–704.

Köllinger, P., M. Minniti and C. Schade (2007). "'I think I can, I think I can': overconfidence and entrepreneurial behavior." *Journal of Economic Psychology*, 28: 502–27.

Kolmogorov, A.N. (1965). "Three approaches to the quantitative definition of information." *Problems of Information Transmission*, 1(1), 1–7.

Koopmans, T.C. and M. Beckmann (1957). "Assignment problems and the location of economic activities." *Econometrica*, 25(1): 53–76.

Koppl, R. (2002). *Big Players and the Economic Theory of Expectations.* London, UK: Palgrave Macmillan.

Koppl, R. and D.G. Whitman (2004). "Rational-choice hermeneutics." *Journal of Economic Behavior and Organization*, 55(3): 295–317.

Krugman, P. (1997). *Development, Geography, and Economic Theory.* Cambridge, MA, USA: MIT Press.

Kullback, S. (1959). *Information Theory and Statistics.* New York, NY: John Wiley.

Lakshmanan, T.R., W.P. Anderson and Y. Song (2015). *Knowledge Economy in the Megalopolis: Interactions of Innovations in Transport, Information, Production and Organizations.* London, UK: Routledge.

Lancaster, K.J. (1966). "A new approach to consumer theory." *Journal of Political Economy*, 74: 132–57.

Lange, O. (1957). "Some observations on input-output analysis." *Sankhya: The Indian Journal of Statistics*, 17(4): 305–36.

Langlois, R.N. (2007). "The entrepreneurial theory of the firm and the theory of the entrepreneurial firm." *Journal of Management Studies*, 44(7): 1107–24.

Langlois, R.N. and M.M. Cosgel (1993). "Frank Knight on risk, uncertainty, and the firm: a new interpretation." *Economic Inquiry*, 31: 456–65.

Langlois, R.N. and R. Koppl (1991). "Fritz Machlup and marginalism: a reevaluation." *Methodus*, 3(2): 86–102.

Launhardt, W. (1872). *Die Kommerzielle Trassierung der Verkehrswege.* Hannover.

Launhardt, W. (1882). "Die Bestimmung der zweckmässigsten Standorts einer Gewerblichen Anlage." *Zeitschrift des Vereins Dutscher Ingenieure*, 26: 105–15.

Launhardt, W. (1885). *Mathematische Begründung der Volkswirtschaftslehre.*

Leakey, R.E. (1981). *The Making of Mankind.* New York, NY: Dutton.

Leontief, W. (1953). "Domestic production and foreign trade; the American capital position re-examined." *Proceedings of the American Philosophical Society*, 97(4): 332–49.

Leontief, W. (1956). "Factor proportions and the structure of American trade: further theoretical and empirical analysis." *Review of Economics and Statistics*, 38(4): 386–407.

Lev, B. and H. Theil (1978). "A maximum entropy approach to choice of asset depreciation." *Journal of Accounting Research*, 16: 286–93.

Lintner, J. (1965). "The valuation of risk assets and the selection of risky investments in stock portfolios and capital budgets." *Review of Economics and Statistics*, 73: 13–37.

Löfgren, K.G. (1983). "The Faustmann-Ohlin theorem: a historical note." *History of Political Economy*, 15(2): 261–64.

Lööf, H. and P. Nabavi (2013). "Increasing returns to smart cities." *Regional Science Policy & Practice*, 5(2): 255–62.

Lösch, A. (1955). *The Economics of Location.* New Haven, CT: Yale University Press.

Lucas, R. (1976). "Econometric policy evaluation: a critique." In: K. Brunner and A. Meltzer (eds.), *The Phillips Curve and Labor Markets.* New York, NY: Elsevier, pp. 19–46.

Machlup, F. (1980). *Knowledge: Its Creation, Distribution, and Economic Significance* (Volume 1). Princeton, NJ: Princeton University Press.

Maddison, A. (1982). *Phases of Capitalist Development.* New York, NY: Oxford University Press.

Mandelbrot, B. (1977). *Fractals: Form, Chance, and Dimension.* New York, NY: W.H. Freeman & Co.

Mandelbrot, B. (1999/2008). "How fractals can explain what's wrong with Wall Street." *Scientific American* (September 15; link: https://www.scien tificamerican.com/article/multifractals-explain-wall-street/), accessed 27 February 2017.

Mankiw, N.G., D. Romer and D.N. Weil (1992). "A contribution to the empirics of economic growth." *Quarterly Journal of Economics*, 107(2): 407–37.

Markowitz, H. (1952). "Portfolio selection." *Journal of Finance*, 12: 71–91.

Markowitz, H. (1959). *Portfolio Selection: Efficient Diversification of Investments.* New York, NY: John Wiley & Sons.

Marx, K. (1867). *Das Kapital: Kritik der politischen Oekonomie* (1st volume). Hamburg: Verlag von Otto Meissner.

Masucci, A.P., K. Stanilov and M. Batty (2013). "Limited urban growth: London's street network dynamics since the 18th Century." *PLoS ONE* 8(8): e69469. doi:10.1371/journal.pone.0069469.

Matthiessen, C.W., A.W. Schwarz and S. Find (2011). "Research nodes and networks." In: D.E. Andersson, Å.E. Andersson and C. Mellander (eds.), *Handbook of Creative Cities.* Cheltenham, UK and Northampton, MA, USA: Edward Elgar, pp. 211–28.

Mees, A. (1975). "The revival of cities in medieval Europe: an application of catastrophe theory." *Regional Science and Urban Economics*, 5(4): 403–25.

Menger, C. (1871/1981). *Principles of Economics.* New York, NY: New York University Press.

Mikhailov, A.S. and V. Calenbuhr (2002). *From Cells to Societies: Models of Complex Coherent Action.* Berlin: Springer.

Millward, H. and T. Bunting (2008). "Patterning in urban population densities: a spatiotemporal model compared with Toronto 1971–2001." *Environment and Planning A*, 40(2): 283–302.

Modigliani, F. (1986). "Life cycle, individual thrift and the wealth of nations." Nobel Lecture, Stockholm, Sweden.

Modigliani, F. and R. Brumberg (1954). "Utility analysis and the consumption function: an interpretation of cross-section data." In: K. Kurihara (ed.), *Post Keynesian Economics.* New Brunswick, NJ: Rutgers University Press.

Modigliani, F. and R. Brumberg (1979). "Utility analysis and aggregate consumption functions: an attempt at integration." In: A. Abel (ed.), *Collected Papers of Franco Modigliani* (Volume 2). Cambridge, MA, USA: MIT Press.

Modigliani, F. and M. Miller (1958). "The cost of capital, corporation finance, and the theory of investment." *American Economic Review*, 48(3): 261–97.

Mokyr, J. (1995). "Urbanization, technological progress, and economic history." In: H. Giersch (ed.), *Urban Agglomeration and Economic Growth*. Heidelberg: Springer.

Morishima, M. (1982). *Western Technology and the Japanese Ethos*. New York, NY: Cambridge University Press.

Morishima, M. (1984). "The good and bad uses of mathematics." In: P. Wiles and G. Routh (eds.), *Economics in Disarray*. Oxford: Basil Blackwell, pp. 51–73.

Mossin, J. (1966). "Equilibrium in a capital asset market." *Econometrica*, 34(4): 768–83.

Muth, J.F. (1961). "Rational expectations and the theory of price movements." *Econometrica*, 29(3): 315–35.

Muth, R. (1968). *Cities and Housing*. Chicago, IL: University of Chicago Press.

Myrdal, G. (1927). *Prisbildningsproblemet och föränderligheten*. Uppsala & Stockholm: Almqvist & Wicksell.

Myrdal, G. (1944). *An American Dilemma: The Negro Problem and Modern Democracy*. New York, NY: Harper and Brothers.

Myrdal, G. (1957). *Economic Theory and Underdeveloped Regions*. London, UK: Methuen.

Nachbar, J.H. (2002). "General equilibrium comparative statics." *Econometrica*, 79: 2065–74.

Nachbar, J.H. (2004). "General equilibrium comparative statics: the discrete case with production." *Journal of Mathematical Economics*, 40: 153–63.

Nagurney, A. (1999/2013). *Network Economics: A Variational Inequality Approach*. Berlin: Springer.

Neumann, J. von (1938/1970). "A model of general economic equilibrium." In: F.H. Hahn (ed.), *Readings in the Theory of Growth*. London, UK: Palgrave Macmillan, pp. 1–9.

Neumann, J. von and O. Morgenstern (1944). *Theory of Games and Economic Behavior*. Princeton, NJ: Princeton University Press.

Newman, P.G. and J.R. Kenworthy (1989). *Cities and Automobile Dependence: An International Sourcebook*. Brookfield, VT: Gower Publishing.

Nikaido, H. (1968). *Convex Structures and Economic Theory*. New York, NY: Academic Press.

North, D.C. (1990). *Institutions, Institutional Change, and Economic Performance*. New York, NY: Cambridge University Press.

North, D.C. (1994). "Economic performance through time." *American Economic Review*, 84: 359–68.

North, D.C. (2005). *Understanding the Process of Economic Change*. Princeton, NJ: Princeton University Press.

Obrist, H.U. (2008/2010). "The father of long tails." *Edge* (no pagination).

Oeppen, J. and J.W. Vaupel (2002). "Broken limits to life expectancy." *Science*, 296(5570): 1029–31.

Ohlin, B. (1921/1995). "Concerning the question of the rotation period in forestry." *Journal of Forest Economics*, 1: 89–114.

Ohlin, B. (1933/1967). *Interregional and International Trade.* Cambridge, MA, USA: Harvard University Press.

Olson, M. (1982). *The Rise and Decline of Nations: Economic Growth, Stagflation, and Social Rigidities.* New Haven, CT: Yale University Press.

O'Toole, R. (2014). "Houston's land-use regime: a model for the nation." In: D.E. Andersson and S. Moroni (eds.), *Cities and Private Planning: Property Rights, Entrepreneurship and Transaction Costs.* Cheltenham, UK and Northampton, MA, USA: Edward Elgar: 174–98.

Palander, T. (1935). *Beiträge zur Standorttheorie.* Uppsala: Almqvist & Wicksell.

Pasinetti, L. (1969). "Switches of techniques and the 'rate of return' in capital theory." *Economic Journal*, 79: 508–31.

Peitgen, H.-O., H. Jürgens and D. Saupe (1982/2004). *Chaos and Fractals: New Frontiers of Science* (2nd edition). Berlin: Springer.

Pennington, M. (2002). *Liberating the Land: The Case for Private Land-use Planning.* London, UK: Institute of Economic Affairs.

Piketty, T. (2014). *Capital in the Twenty-First Century.* Cambridge, MA, USA: Harvard University Press.

Pirenne, H. (1936). *Economic and Social History of Medieval Europe.* London, UK: K. Paul, Trench, Trubner & Company.

Polanyi, M. (1958). *Personal Knowledge.* Chicago, IL: University of Chicago Press.

Polanyi, M. (1962). "The republic of science: its political and economic theory." *Minerva*, 1: 54–73.

Polanyi, M. (1967). *The Tacit Dimension.* London, UK: Routledge and Kegan Paul.

Preston, S.H. (1975). "The changing relation between mortality and level of economic development." *Population Studies*, 29(2): 231–48.

Putnam, R.D. (1993). *Making Democracy Work: Civic Traditions in Modern Italy.* Princeton, NJ: Princeton University Press.

Putnam, R.D. (2000). *Bowling Alone: The Collapse and Revival of American Community.* New York, NY: Simon and Schuster.

Puu, T. (1989). *Nonlinear Economic Dynamics.* Berlin: Springer.

Puu, T. (1997). *Mathematical Location and Land Use Theory.* Berlin: Springer.

Puu, T. (2000). *Attractors, Bifurcations, & Chaos: Nonlinear Phenomena in Economics.* Berlin: Springer.

Puu, T. (2005). "On the genesis of hexagonal shapes." *Networks and Spatial Economics*, 5(1): 5–20.

Ramsey, F.P. (1926/1931). "Truth and probability." In: R.B. Braithwaite (ed.), *The Foundations of Mathematics and other Logical Essays*, London, UK: Kegan, Paul, Trench, Trubner & Co., pp. 156–98.

Ramsey, F.P. (1927). "Facts and propositions." *Aristotelian Society Supplementary Volume 7.*

Rebelo, S. (1991). "Long-run policy analysis and long-run growth." *Journal of Political Economy,* 99 (3): 500.

Rentfrow, P.J. (2011). "The open city." In: D.E. Andersson, Å.E. Andersson and C. Mellander (eds.), *Handbook of Creative Cities*, Cheltenham, UK and Northampton, MA, USA: Edward Elgar pp. 117–27.

Rescher, N. (1995). *Luck: The Brilliant Randomness of Everyday Life*. New York, NY: Farrar Straus Giroux.

Ricardo, D. (1817/1996). *Principles of Political Economy and Taxation.* Amherst, NY: Prometheus Books.

Rizvi, S.A.T. (2006). "The Sonnenschein-Mantel-Debreu results after thirty years." *History of Political Economy*, 38(1): 228–45.

Robinson, J. (1963). *Essays in the Theory of Economic Growth*. London, UK: Macmillan.

Robinson, J. (1975). "The unimportance of reswitching." *Quarterly Journal of Economics*, 89(1): 32–39.

Romer, P.M. (1994). "The origins of endogenous growth." *Journal of Economic Perspectives*, 8(1): 3–22.

Rosenberg, N. and L.E. Birdzell (1986). *How the West Grew Rich: The Economic Transformation of the Industrial World*. New York, NY: Basic Books.

Ross, S. (1976). "The arbitrage theory of capital asset pricing." *Journal of Economic Theory,* 13(3): 341–60.

Rosser Jr., J.B. (1999). "On the complexities of complex economic dynamics." *Journal of Economic Perspectives*, 13(4): 169–92.

Rosser Jr., J.B. (2007). "The rise and fall of catastrophe theory applications in economics: Was the baby thrown out with the bathwater?" *Journal of Economic Dynamics and Control*, 31(10): 3255–80.

Ruger, W.P. and J. Sorens (2013). *Freedom of the 50 States, 2013 Edition: An Index of Personal and Economic Freedom*. Fairfax, VA: Mercatus Institute.

Russell, B. (1912). *The Problems of Philosophy.* Oxford, UK: Oxford University Press.

Russell, B. (1912/1992). "On the notion of cause." In: J. Slater (ed.), *The Collected Papers of Bertrand Russell (Vol. 6): Logical and Philosophical Papers 1909–1913*. London: Routledge, pp. 193–210.

Saari, D.G. (1996). "The ease of generating chaotic behavior in economics." *Chaos, Solitons & Fractals*, 7(12): 2267–78.

Saari, D.G. and C.P. Simon (1978). "Effective price mechanisms." *Econometrica*, 46(5): 1097–125.

Sahlin, N.-E. (1990). *The Philosophy of F.P. Ramsey.* Cambridge, UK: Cambridge University Press.

Savage, L.J. (1954). *The Foundations of Statistics.* New York, NY: Dover.

Saxenian, A. (1996). *Regional Advantage: Culture and Competition in Silicon Valley and Route 128.* Cambridge, MA, USA: Harvard University Press.

Scarf, H. (1960). "Some examples of global instability of the competitive equilibrium." *International Economic Review*, 1(3): 157–72.

Schelling, T.C. (1969). "Neighborhood tipping." Working paper, Harvard University Institute of Economic Research, Cambridge, MA, USA.

Schelling, T.C. (1978). *Micromotives and Macrobehavior.* New York, NY: Norton.

Schumpeter, J.A. (1934). *The Theory of Economic Development.* Cambridge, MA, USA: Harvard University Press.

Schumpeter, J.A. (1942). *Capitalism, Socialism and Democracy.* New York, NY: Harper and Brothers.

Schumpeter, J.A. (1954). *History of Economic Analysis.* London, UK: Allen & Unwin.

Sen, A. (1976). *On Economic Inequality.* Oxford, UK: Oxford University Press.

Sen, A. (1982). *Poverty and Famines: An Essay on Entitlement and Deprivation.* Oxford, UK: Oxford University Press.

Sen, A. (2010). "Adam Smith's 'The Theory of Moral Sentiments' (1759): Adam Smith and the Contemporary World." *Erasmus Journal for Philosophy and Economics*, 3(1): 50–67.

Sharpe, W.F. (1964). "Capital asset prices: A theory of market equilibrium under conditions of risk." *Journal of Finance*, 19(3): 425–42.

Shell, K. (1966). "Toward a theory of inventive activity and capital accumulation." *American Economic Review*, 56(2): 62–8.

Siegel, D. and R.J. Hansman (2011). "Development of an auto-land system for general aviation aircraft." Working paper, Department of Aeronautics and Astronautics, Massachusetts Institute of Technology, Cambridge, MA, USA.

Simon, H.A. (1955). "On a class of skew distribution functions." *Biometrika*, 42(3/4): 425–40.

Simon, H.A. (1982). *Models of Bounded Rationality and Other Topics in Economic Theory* (2 volumes). Cambridge, MA, USA: MIT Press.

Simonton, D.K. (2011). "Big-C creativity in the big city." In: D.E.

Andersson, Å.E. Andersson and C. Mellander (eds.), *Handbook of Creative Cities*, pp. 72–84.

Smith, A. (1776/2012). *An Inquiry into the Nature and Causes of the Wealth of Nations*. London, UK and Ware, UK: Wordsworth.

Snickars, F. and J.W. Weibull (1977). "A minimum information principle." *Regional Science and Urban Economics*, 7: 137–68.

Solomonoff, R. (1964a). "A formal theory of inductive inference, part I." *Information and Control*, 7(1): 1–22.

Solomonoff, R. (1964b). "A formal theory of inductive inference, part II." *Information and Control*, 7(2): 224–54.

Solow, R.M. (1956). "A contribution to the theory of economic growth." *Quarterly Journal of Economics*, 70(1): 65–94.

Solow, R.M. (1957). "Technical change and the aggregate production function." *Review of Economics and Statistics*, 39(3): 312–20.

Sonnenschein, H. (1973). "Do Walras' identity and continuity characterize the class of community excess-demand functions?" *Journal of Economic Theory*, 6: 345–54.

Sørensen, F. and J.F. Jensen (2015). "Value creation and knowledge development in tourism experience encounters." *Tourism Management*, 46: 336–46.

Stark, R. and R. Finke (2000). *Acts of Faith: Explaining the Human Side of Religion*. Berkeley, CA: University of California Press.

Sugakov, V.I. (1998). *Lectures in Synergetics*. New York, NY: World Scientific.

Svennilson, I. (1938). *Ekonomisk planering*. Uppsala: Almqvist & Wicksell.

Swan, T.W. (1956). "Economic growth and capital accumulation." *Economic Record*, 32(2): 334–61.

Terborgh, G.W. (1954). *Realistic Depreciation Policy*. Chicago, IL: R.R. Donnelley & Sons.

Theil, H. (1964). *Optimal Decision Rules for Government and Industry*. Amsterdam: North Holland.

Thünen, J.H. von (1826/1930). *Der isolierte Staat in Beziehung auf Landwirthschaft und Nationalökonomie* (3 volumes). Jena: Fischer.

Thurston, R.H. (1878). *A History of the Growth of the Steam-Engine*. New York, NY: D. Appleton.

Tinbergen, J. (1942). "Critical remarks on some business-cycle theories." *Econometrica*, 10(2): 129–46.

Tinbergen, J. (1954). *Centralization and Decentralization in Economic Policy*. Amsterdam: North Holland.

Treynor, J.L. (1961). "Market value, time, and risk." Unpublished manuscript dated 8 August 1961.

Treynor, J.L. (1962/1999). "Toward a theory of market value of risky assets."

In: R.A. Korajczyk (ed.), *Asset Pricing and Portfolio Performance: Models, Strategy and Performance Metrics.* London, UK: Risk Books.

Tukey, J.W. (1957). "On the comparative anatomy of transformations." *Annals of Mathematical Statistics*, 28: 602–32.

Tullock, G. (1993). *Rent Seeking.* Aldershot, UK: Edward Elgar.

Turing, A. (1936). "On computable numbers, with an application to the Entscheidungs problem." *Proceedings of the London Mathematical Society*, 42: 230–65.

Tychonoff, A.N. (1930). "Über die topologische Erweiterung von Räumen." *Mathematische Annalen*, 102(1): 544–61.

Uzawa, H. (1961). "Neutral inventions and the stability of growth equilibrium." *Review of Economic Studies*, 28(2): 117–24.

Varaiya, P. and M. Wiseman (1984). "Bifurcation models of urban development." In: Å.E. Andersson, W. Isard and T. Puu (eds.), *Regional and Industrial Development.* Amsterdam: Elsevier North Holland, pp. 61–88.

Varian, H.R. (1979). "Catastrophe theory and the business cycle." *Economic Inquiry*, 17(1): 14–28.

Veblen, T. (1899). *The Theory of the Leisure Class.* New York, NY: Macmillan.

Viscusi, W.K. and J.E. Aldy (2003). "The value of a statistical life: a critical review of market estimates throughout the world." NBER Working Paper No. w9487.

Wald, A. (1936). "Über einige Gleichungssysteme der mathematischen Ökonomie." *Zeitschrift für Nationalökonomie*, 7: 637–70.

Walras, L. (1874/1896). *Éléments d'économie pure; ou, Théorie de la richesse sociale.* Lausanne: F. Rouge.

Watts, D.J. and P. Dodds (2009). "Threshold models of social influence." In: Peter Hedström and Peter Bearman (eds.), *The Oxford Handbook of Analytical Sociology.* Oxford, UK: Oxford University Press, pp. 475–97.

Weber, A. (1909/1922). *Über den Standort der Industrien* (2nd edition). Tübingen.

Weber, M. (1920/1958). *The Protestant Ethic and the Spirit of Capitalism.* New York, NY: Scribner's Press.

Wicksell, K. (1893/1970). *Value, Capital and Rent.* New York, NY: Augustus M. Kelley.

Wicksell, K. (1898/1936). *Geldzins und Güterpreise: eine Studie über die den Tauschwert des Geldes bestimmenden Ursachen* (English translation from 1936). Jena: Fischer.

Wicksell, K. (1901/1934). *Lectures on Political Economy* (Volume 1). London, UK: Routledge and Kegan Paul.

Wicksell, K. (1914). "Lexis och Böhm-Bawerk." *Ekonomisk tidskrift*, 16(11): 322–34.

Williamson, O.E. (1985). *The Economic Institutions of Capitalism.* New York, NY: Free Press.

Woeginger, G.J. (2003). "Exact algorithms for NP-hard problems: a survey." In: M. Jünger, G. Reinelt and G. Rinaldi (eds.), *Combinatorial Optimization—Eureka, You Shrink!* Berlin: Springer, pp. 185–207.

Wold, H. (1954). "Causality and econometrics." *Econometrica,* 22(2): 162–77.

Zhou, M., H. Wang, J. Zhu, W. Chen, L. Wang, S. Liu, Y. Li, L. Wang, Y. Liu, P. Yin, J. Liu, S. Yu, F. Tan, R.M. Barber, M.M. Coates, D. Dicker, M. Fraser, D. Gonzalez-Medina, H. Hamavid, Y. Hao, G. Hu, G. Jiang, H. Kan, A.D. Lopez, M.R. Phillips, J. She, T. Vos, X. Wan, G. Xu, L.L. Yan, C. Yu, Y. Zhao, Y. Zheng, X. Zou, M. Naghavi, Y. Wang, C.J.L. Murray, G. Yang and X. Liang (2016). "Cause-specific mortality for 240 causes in China during 1990–2013: a systematic subnational analysis for the Global Burden of Disease Study 2013." *The Lancet,* 387(10015): 251–72.

Zipf, G.K. (1949). *Human Behavior and the Principle of Least Effort: An Introduction to Human Ecology.* Cambridge, MA, USA: Addison-Wesley.

Name index

Subject index